# In Search of Legitimacy

## How Outsiders Become Part of an Afro-Brazilian Tradition

Lauren Miller Griffith

berghahn
NEW YORK · OXFORD
www.berghahnbooks.com

First published in 2016 by
Berghahn Books
www.berghahnbooks.com

**Library of Congress Cataloging-in-Publication Data**
Names: Griffith, Lauren Miller.
Title: In search of legitimacy : how outsiders become part of an Afro-
  Brazilian tradition / Lauren Miller Griffith.
Description: New York ; Oxford : Berghahn Books, [2016] | Series:
  Dance and performance studies ; volume 7
Identifiers: LCCN 2015026949 | ISBN 9781785330636 (hardback : alk.
  paper) | ISBN 9781785330643 (ebook)
Subjects: LCSH: Capoeira (Dance)--Social aspects--Brazil. | Capoeira
  (Dance)--Study and teaching--Brazil. | Visitors, Foreign--Brazil--Social
  conditions. | Culture and tourism--Brazil. | Blacks--Brazil--Social life
  and customs.
Classification: LCC GV1796.C145 .G75 2016 | DDC 793.3/1981--dc23
LC record available at http://lccn.loc.gov/2015026949

**British Library Cataloguing in Publication Data**
A catalogue record for this book is available from the British Library

*Cover image:* Capoeira *by Rodrigo Denúbila.*
*Reproduced under a CC BY-SA 2.0 license.*
*https://www.flickr.com/photos/rdenubila/4246964130*

ISBN 978-1-78533-063-6 hardback
ISBN 978-1-80073-181-3 paperback
ISBN 978-1-78533-064-3 ebook

# In Search of Legitimacy

D
A
N
C
E

A
N
D

P
E
R
F
O
R
M
A
N
C
E

S
T
U
D
I
E
S

# DANCE AND PERFORMANCE STUDIES

General Editors:

**Helen Wulff**, *Stockholm University* and **Jonathan Skinner**, *Queen's University, Belfast*

Advisory Board:

**Alexandra Carter, Marion Kant, Tim Scholl**

In all cultures, and across time, people have danced. Mesmerizing performers and spectators alike, dance creates spaces for meaningful expressions that are held back in daily life. Grounded in ethnography, this series explores dance and bodily movement in cultural contexts at the juncture of history, ritual and performance, including musical, in an interconnected world.

# Table of Contents

# Acknowledgements

I am truly humbled by the extensive amount of support and encouragement I received during various stages of researching and writing this book. First, I would like to thank Mestre Iuri Santos and the members of Estrela do Norte in Bloomington, Indiana for being so welcoming of my research agenda. My mind and body both bear the marks of your instruction. I am also indebted to Mestre Valmir, Mestre Cobra Mansa, Aloan, and all of the members of FICA Bahia for allowing me to conduct research at their academy. So too do I owe a debt to the capoeira pilgrims who are at the heart of this study.

I owe a great intellectual debt to Tom Green at Texas A&M University, who was willing to take on an enthusiastic albeit somewhat naïve undergraduate who wanted to study anthropology and dance. Anya Royce provided invaluable guidance through all my years at Indiana University, striking the ideal balance between structured support and freedom so that I was able to grow as an independent scholar. I would also like to thank Marvin Sterling, Paula Girshick, Eduardo Brondizio, Steven Selka, and Richard Bauman, who all provided key insight and support at the early stages of this project. I have also benefited greatly from the support of colleagues at the various institutions where I have taught since 2010, primarily Jonathan Marion at the University of Arkansas, whose interest in the topic of apprenticeship pilgrimage has pushed me to think about this concept in new and productive ways. I would also like to thank Helena Wulff and Jonathan Skinner for their support of this project.

I have been fortunate to receive the support of two outstanding writing groups during different phases of this project. The ongoing support from Tershia Pinder-Grover, Jennifer Ellis, Meera Algaraja, and Marie Brown, during our weekly virtual writing group sustained me during some very difficult years. Without you, I am not certain I would have had the stamina to complete this manuscript. At Hanover College, I would like to thank Susanne McDowell and Syndee Knight for helping me to stay on schedule with the final stages of revising this manuscript. I would also like to thank my students at Northern Arizona University, Central Michigan University, the University of Arkansas, and Hanover College, especially those in my World Ethnographies course whose candid critiques of other authors' work were in the forefront of my mind as I made final revisions to my own manuscript. Flavia Barbosa was also of great assistance in the final preparation of this manuscript.

Finally, none of this would have been possible without the ongoing support of my family. I would especially like to honor my late grandfather, JL Stiener without whom my 2008 field trip would have been impossible. I will never be able to repay the debts I owe to my parents, Debbie Miller and Don Miller, first for believing that becoming an anthropologist was a reasonable career path, and second for stepping outside of their own comfort zones and visiting me in the field. Last but not least, I would like to thank my husband Cameron Griffith, who is also my dearest colleague and coauthor, for his unwavering support of my research interests and career goals.

# Introduction

## A Professional Pilgrimage and the Origins of This Book

I was a little nervous as I packed my bag on the first day that I would officially start my work studying capoeira in Brazil. Camera? Check. Notebook? Check. Uniform? I had that too, though I hoped not to need it. I was hoping to do more observing than participating at this first encounter. I was told to meet Mestre Iuri Santos[1] and two members from the Estrela do Norte group, the group I trained with back in the United States, outside of the FICA academy at 9:30 am. I arrived on time, but no one from my home group was there. I was on my own, negotiating my first interactions with the students of FICA Bahia. Was there a single Brazilian among this group? I really was not sure. Everyone was chatting in Portuguese, but most of them looked like foreigners. Was that Japanese guy from São Paulo or Tokyo? I talked to the highest ranking person I could find, hoping to explain my predicament and find a quiet corner to hide in until my group arrived and I could be properly introduced. No such luck.

"Do you have clothes?"
"I do, yes."
"You can change clothes over there. Make yourself at home."[2]

Well that settled it, I had clothes and I was expected to get dressed and join the group. Okay, this might be all right I thought. Sure the uniforms are different, the people are sure different, but it is the same martial art. Right? Same instruments, same songs, same movements. Well, maybe not exactly. This was unlike anything I had ever experienced. I knew they would be good but had no idea how different their style of capoeira would be from mine. What am I doing here? I thought about trying to slip out unnoticed, but by this point my group from Indiana had arrived. The fact that our teacher, Mestre Iuri, joined the circle while his two other students, Camille and Jerome, remained outside observing in their street clothes did little to calm my nerves, but I saw no way out. I was going to have to go through with it.

I sighed inwardly with relief when I saw who my partner would be. It was one of Mestre Iuri's friends who I had met a few nights earlier. He had already seen me play and knew what to expect. In the back of my mind, I wondered if it was just luck that had us lined up so that we would play, or if he had purposely put himself in the right spot to help me save face. I was nervous. After all, just a few minutes beforehand, I had been yelled at by the *mestre* (master) in charge of the event because I was not singing. How, I wondered, do I sing when I cannot understand a word you are saying? I moved my mouth like a fish, hoping he would not notice that I was not actually making a sound. When I began to play, I was shaking from head to toe. I fell a few times and got caught in every trap that my partner set, but we laughed our way through it and he gave me a great big hug at the end.

Afterward, I thought, that was not really so bad. Sure, I was horribly out-matched, but I survived my first FICA *roda*, escaping without a mark. Wait, what is this? Why is everyone looking at me? Why is the *mestre* headed this way? A kiss on the hand, and I am being led back into the *roda. Que droga* (damn), I thought, this is not going to be good. A short song praising my *mestre*; was this sincere or sarcastic, the art of *malícia*? No time to analyze, time to focus on the kick coming at my head. Judging from the smirk on his face, that was not the right defense. Why am I lying on the floor? How did this happen? Every time he knocks me down, he looms over me and holds up his fingers, counting how many times I have fallen. This lump in my throat is a familiar feeling; I know what comes next. Please take mercy on me before the tears come spilling out. Martial artists do not cry. He runs out of fingers and finally the game is over, and I exit as gracefully as possible thinking, "You have got to be kidding me. This is the group I am going to be working with? The study I am hoping will launch my career?" At the moment, I was nearly paralyzed with fear, and the thought of abandoning my research agenda crossed my mind more times than I would like to admit. However, when the first sting of humiliation wore off, I realized I had at least made a memorable entrance into this community. It was time to get to work.

As Bira Almeida, author and capoeira *mestre* says:

> To live the Capoeira philosophy requires sweat, mental discipline, some-times pain, and always the magical experience of kneeling under the berimbau ... One must feel the philosophy from inside out because only his or her personal participation will make it real. (Almeida 1986: 7)

I can speak of this phenomenon because I have experienced it personally "from the inside out." I can offer a robust view of capoeira because of my own engagement as an observing participant. I have used this phrasing, rather than the more commonly used "participant-observation," to indicate that my *primary* role as a participant in this community and the majority of my time in class was spent training alongside the other students, but I also recorded my observations of these sessions as soon as possible after leaving the academy each day. Increasingly, reflexive ethnographers teach us that "learning through practice involves not simply mimicking other's but creating one's own emplaced skill and knowing in ways that are acceptable to others" (Pink 2009: 36). An important component of learning, either as a student or as an ethnographer, is coming to embody practice in a culturally sanctioned way.

Merleau-Ponty (1989) laid the groundwork for much of this work through his focus on the body in the act of perception. This perspective encourages us to *see* beyond the visual, pun intended. The notion that people perceive the world through five distinct senses is not a universal truth, but one "folk model" among others (Pink 2009: 51). Nearly five years of being an observing participant in both Brazil and the United States afforded me an entrance into this community that might otherwise have been difficult to access and inducted me into a bodily understanding of *capoeiristas'* practice. Embodied dimensions of behavior are often obscured in conversations but displayed and experienced in practice (Pink 2009: 84), which is why interviews or mere observations would not have sufficed to give me an insider's view of this performance art.

Because participant-observation fieldwork has become the hallmark of anthropology, it would be easy for me to gloss over the messiness of this technique with disciplinary jargon. However, my engagement as a participating observer was not as simple as taking classes and writing notes. I was actually engaged in apprenticeship, becoming more like my study subjects with each subsequent class as the *mestre* attempted to break my body of its old habits. I had to bring a level of self-consciousness to this learning process (Pink 2009: 72), not just learning the movements, but thinking in a very abstract way about *how* my fellow students and I were learning the movements. Doing this while gasping for air or suspended upside down in a headstand was not an easy task. At times, I wondered why I could not have been one of those anthropologists that sits on the sidelines quietly taking notes, but in the end, this study would have been largely impossible without such vividly lived experiences.

In a project such as mine that involves direct and intensive participation in the very activity that I study, the necessity of using the body as a research tool gives tangible reality to theory. Throughout the long process of learning capoeira, my physical and theoretical orientations to the world have changed. In fact, my body taught me things about capoeira that my mind was not ready to grasp. Maintaining a superficial Cartesian division between mind and body impoverishes our overall learning experience; "embodiment is what makes the knowledge experientially real" (Strathern 1996: 164). As Nick Crossley (2006) points out, all body work is undertaken within the context of a network of social relations. One neither passively replicates societal norms nor acts with complete free will, but negotiates an embodied identity in the space between these two extremes. Therefore, one of my goals in writing this book is to convey the sensuality of experience that is central to learning a practice like capoeira.

For a performance anthropologist, capoeira is like a dream come true. It combines music, dance, sparring, and acrobatics into one ritual that can be used for resistance or celebration, for politics or play. Capoeira is a metagenre (see MacAloon 1984; see also Marion 2008), meaning that while composed of these individual performance elements, taken together they constitute something greater than the sum of the individual parts. What intrigued me the most, however, about my initial introduction to capoeira was the intense dedication of its non-Brazilian practitioners. Capoeira was much more than a pastime to them; it was a way of life. I have seen practitioners uproot their lives, quit their jobs, and leave their partners all in service of becoming better *capoeiristas*. This is particularly striking when I consider that capoeira originated with Afro-Brazilian slaves, and authentic capoeira continues to be associated with being black and Brazilian. Most of the individuals in my study do not fit these parameters.

I first encountered capoeira as an undergraduate student with the Austin, Texas branch of the Fundação Internacional de Capoeira Angola (FICA). FICA is one of the largest and most well-known *Capoeira Angola* franchises. The term "franchise" is not widely used in the capoeira community but is one I find useful when referring to capoeira organizations with one flagship group, normally located in Brazil, and several satellite groups located throughout Brazil or the rest of the world. Both discourse and dress in the satellite groups celebrate their relationship to the franchise. By wearing the group's logo and frequently invoking the standards and expectations of the primary *mestre,* students are inducted into the franchise's imagined community (see de Campos Rosario, Stephens, and Delamont 2010: 109). These satellite groups sometimes, but not always, pay dues or royalties to the flagship group, periodically visit the flagship group, or fundraise on behalf of the flagship group, which is often economically disadvantaged relative to the satellite groups in the case of international franchises. Sometimes, social dramas (Turner 1987) erupt between the satellite groups and the flagship group, which will lead to either attempts at repairing the relationship or to the splintering of the satellite group into its own organization. Both of the groups with which I have trained originated out of a schism between their founder and subordinate teachers.

The FICA franchise was established by Mestre Cobra Mansa and his two close colleagues Mestre Valmir, who oversees the FICA Bahia chapter, and Mestre Jurandir, who oversees FICA Seattle. All three of these gentlemen emerged from the tutelage of Mestre Moraes of the Grupo Capoeira Angola de Pelourinho

(GCAP). Mestre Cobra Mansa is Brazilian and also holds American citizenship because of his status as an international cultural figure. He is officially based out of Washington, D.C., but spends a large percentage of his time traveling around the world teaching workshops. He also spends several months of the year in Brazil overseeing his charitable institution, Kilombo Tenonde, through which he teaches urban youth (and international volunteers) about native ecology and permaculture. The official headquarters of FICA may be in Washington, D.C., but the symbolic heart of FICA is located in Salvador da Bahia under the direction of Mestre Valmir. There are also satellite groups located throughout South America, North America, Europe, Asia, and Africa.

The international chapters of FICA generally defer to Cobra Mansa's authority, yet he encourages each group to develop according to their own spirit, respecting cultural differences that are deeply rooted among his diverse body of students. Capoeira historian Gerard Taylor said that FICA "provides a model for a democratically run group, and manages to maintain a balance between being open (that is, listening to what participants think is important), and at the same time being traditional in the sense of holding to *Capoeira Angola* rituals and that Cobra Mansa is clearly the mestre of the group" (2007: 213). Mestre Cobra Mansa gives each branch of the organization considerable latitude to determine their own direction, but no one questions his position at the helm of the organization. Throughout this work, I indicate which branch of the FICA organization I am discussing by following the FICA abbreviation with a city name (i.e., FICA Stockholm). However, because FICA Bahia is my primary referent for this work, it is often simply referred to as FICA.

In 2002, after initially approaching my undergraduate mentor at Texas A&M University with a half-baked plan to study anthropology and dance, I was "gently" redirected toward the study of capoeira. My research methods were rather loosely constructed and essentially involved visiting FICA Austin for several training sessions. I was eager to try the "deep hanging out" that I had read about in my anthropology classes, but was not entirely sure of what that meant. Coming from a rather sheltered, middle-class suburban upbringing, I was not prepared for what I would encounter. My first session was prosaic enough. The training session took place at a local recreation center not terribly different from the dance studios I had known as an adolescent. The second observation, however, took place in a commune where people of roughly my age, sometimes with children, grew their own food and practiced a variety of arts including capoeira. This was the first indication I had that I would be studying a subculture with an alternative value system rather than just a fitness club.

The timing of my involvement with this group was less than ideal, but ultimately quite fitting given the line of inquiry I would follow in my later work. After a single introductory session, I was encouraged to attend a series of workshops being taught by a visiting capoeira instructor from Rio de Janeiro. At the time, I did not realize the significance of this event. Right out of the gate, I was encountering evidence of an international network of teachers and students, which confers legitimacy upon both parties as international invitations add to a teacher's prestige and training with a Brazilian ensures that foreigners understand how things really work. The workshop had been designed for people who had been practicing capoeira for at least a year. As a complete novice, I was barred from the partner exercises everyone else was doing and forced to practice my attack moves with a chair. My attacks were evidently less intimidating than I would like to think; a stray kitten eventually jumped in the chair and lazily swatted at my legs while I poured sweat and wondered if I was really cut out for this kind of work.

When I moved to pursue my graduate studies in Bloomington, Indiana, I was pleased to learn that there was a local capoeira group where I could continue both my physical training and my academic study of capoeira. This group, however, had a different affiliation than the first chapter with which I had trained. This group was originally established as a satellite chapter of Grupo Acupe. The latter is based in Salvador da Bahia, Brazil, and is headed by Mestre Marrom who is a former student of Mestre João Pequeno. In October of 2006, this group became independent of Mestre Marrom and adopted its new name Estrela do Norte.

The leader of Estrela do Norte is Mestre Iuri Santos, who moved from Brazil to Bloomington in 1998. While the present work deals only tangentially with Estrela do Norte, my entrance into the capoeira community was profoundly shaped by members of this group, Mestre Iuri in particular. My performance style bears the mark of his instruction. From January of 2005 through July of 2008, when I officially began my research in Brazil, I trained with this group two or three times per week and participated in many performances with them in Bloomington and around the greater Indianapolis area. The members of this group are hungry for information about capoeira and eagerly engaged me in academic discourse about my research. My ideas have been profoundly colored by my experiences with them, and I am continually grateful for their support.

Like both Jensen (1998) and Grazian (2004), my domestic research site was a welcome respite from the demands of academic life. Jensen took refuge at the Rose Bowl, a honky-tonk in Urbana-Champaign, Illinois, and Grazian felt himself drawn to the local jazz clubs surrounding the University of Chicago. They were both seeking genuine intimacy that seemed lacking in the ivory tower. Capoeira groups across the United States attract university students and other intellectuals, so I cannot say I felt the same break between town and gown as I moved to and from our rehearsal space. However, because practices took place at a local charter school, our group attracted students of all ages, and it was refreshing to encounter more demographic diversity than was the norm on campus.

Clearly, the domestic portion of my field research was meaningful both personally and professionally, but knowing how important traveling to Brazil was for members of the capoeira community, I was committed to undertaking fieldwork abroad as well. That I would be working in Brazil was a given, and narrowing this down to a particular city was not much harder. Salvador da Bahia, Brazil, commonly referred to as either Salvador or just Bahia, is popularly regarded as the cradle of capoeira. In reality, there is evidence that historical developments took place in Rio de Janeiro and Recife among other places, but Bahia nonetheless remains the center of most *capoeiristas'* fantasies. The city stars in the dreams of foreign *capoeiristas* who desire immersion in the world of capoeira. These individuals romanticize the city, imagining that capoeira permeates every aspect of social life. One foreign *capoeirista* told me he thought it would be like Hollywood with capoeira celebrities on every corner. In reality, however, this city of nearly three million inhabitants is much like any other city in which most of the residents have jobs, families, and social lives that do not revolve around capoeira.

This realization can be hard for some *capoeiristas* who prefer the staged authenticity (MacCannell 1976) of the Pelourinho district, where UNESCO has restored the quaint pastel-colored colonial buildings. Here the forlorn twang of the *berimbau* (a percussive, single-stringed instrument) really does ring out from every corner and every trinket shop. In an area that comprises just a few city blocks, there are numerous capoeira academies and at least two well-regarded instrument fabrication shops. Pelourinho, however, is also populated by the poor, hungry, and criminal elements of society, throwing the haves and have-nots into stark contrast with one another. Thus, Bahia, and particularly Pelourinho, is an ideal site for investigating the negotiations between foreigners and Brazilians who together comprise the imagined community of capoeira.

On a preliminary research visit to Bahia in July of 2005, I attended training sessions with Grupo Acupe under the leadership of Mestre Marrom. This academy is well off the beaten path, and most tourists would only visit this academy if they had a personal connection to the group. My taxi driver even had trouble finding the street and eventually dropped me off and told me to walk the rest of the way. As I was a student of his own protégé, Mestre Marrom welcomed me graciously into his group for my brief visit, even refusing payment because I was already a paying member of the Indiana branch. I was to find that this graciousness was actually quite remarkable, and most *mestres* expect foreigners to pay a fee for attending class regardless of their affiliation.

Despite being able to train for no cost, I was not free from other obligations that come with being a relatively wealthy visitor. For example, he asked me to take photos of the academy highlighting the deterioration of the building: fallen rafters, exposed wiring, and out-of-date plumbing. He hoped I would use them in grant applications to help him create an office space and a library for his students. Unfortunately, the aforementioned schism between Mestre Maroom and Mestre Iuri prevented us from collaborating on any such applications. What this experience did lend to my research, however, was the dual sense of camaraderie and obligation extended by members of the local group to visiting members from abroad. It also instilled in me a sense of respect for what these *mestres* are trying to do for their students. Whereas many of the foreign *capoeiristas* who I write about here tend to see learning capoeira as an end in and of itself, many *mestres* see capoeira as a tool for mentoring at-risk youth in their communities.

During the following summer, 2006, I returned to Salvador da Bahia for a two-month long feasibility study. During the time that I was in Bahia, Mestre Iuri and his family were also in town. Mestre Iuri and I attended a class at Mestre Curio's academy in the Pelourinho district. Mestre Iuri was charged a lower rate than was I because he was from Salvador, but I was barely left with enough cash to pay for my taxi home that evening. In contrast to my experience with Mestre Marrom during the previous summer, I was treated as an outsider and was charged an exorbitant amount for taking class with the well-known teacher. I also took classes with lesser-known instructors in town and found that teaching such classes for foreign tourists is a mainstay of their economic stability. In comparing these two field trips, I concluded that there is a great difference between visiting Bahia as a member of a satellite group and as a free agent that lacks the proper credentials of group membership, a topic that I explore more fully in chapter 4.

In 2008, I undertook a more extended period of fieldwork. My arrival coincided with another of Mestre Iuri's visits to Bahia; this time he brought two students from our group with him. Mestre Iuri has led a number of such trips for his students since his arrival in Indiana. Past trips have involved training with Mestre Marrom, visiting other academies, and going on various touristic excursions.

The trip in 2008 was the first official trip under the group's new title, which gave students the freedom to train at a number of different locations. We spent several evenings training and attending events at the Pierre Verger Foundation, an organization that introduces local children to a variety of Afro-Brazilian cultural practices, including capoeira. The building also houses a fairly extensive library on Afro-Brazilian culture. However, the bulk of the Indiana students' two-week trip was spent touring the city and taking a weekend excursion to the countryside. Mestre Iuri had been planning this group trip for a year, but it was a surprisingly small group that ultimately decided to go. Financial concerns as the U.S. dollar hit an all-time low, combined with tightened visa requirements, may be to blame more than a lack of interest among the Indiana students. Though steeped in the history and lore of capoeira, the two students who did accompany Mestre Iuri did not know what to expect from their visit to Brazil.

## Methods

After two weeks of touring and training with members of the Bloomington group, I began my official affiliation with FICA Bahia. I chose to conduct my research at this particular academy because it attracts a large number of foreign students, and during my time in Bahia, there were students from more than twenty-five different countries who participated in classes and *rodas* (weekly performance events). The

FICA Bahia academy is located on the fifth floor of a commercial building on Rua Carlos Gomez, a main street connecting the historic Pelourinho area to the more affluent neighborhoods of Campo Grande, Vitoria, and Barra. This is the area known as the *centro,* which has unfortunately been described by some Salvador residents as "a crack den," and this street in particular is known for muggings and petty theft. It is adjacent to the area known as Dois de Julio, which boasts one other capoeira academy, the Associação de Capoeira Angola Navio Negreiro (ACANNE), as well as fruit and flower stands, butcher shops, and kiosks selling traditional herbs and religious paraphernalia. On most days, *capoeiristas* can take an elevator up to the academy; however, a bit too frequently, the broken elevator sign means a hefty climb and a good cardiovascular warm-up before class.

The personality of this group is instantly evident upon stepping out of the elevator. The bright yellow columns and colorful murals scream for attention. The four yellow columns have been painted with black patterns: serpents on one, perhaps a nod to Mestre Cobra Mansa's namesake, and zebra stripes on another, the zebra being a legendary animal in the origin myths of capoeira and a nod to the group's Africanist orientation. This color combination signifies that the group belongs to the lineage of Mestre Pastinha, whose favorite soccer team wore black and yellow.

At the far end of the room, a wall of glass windows provides a wonderful vista onto the high-rises and palm trees of the city but also creates a greenhouse effect making spring and summertime workouts at noon a particular test of stoicism. At the front of the room is a storage area for benches and instruments. Beside the door, both on the floor and on a shelf more than six feet off the ground, are altars containing candles and other offerings associated with *Candomblé,* the local Afro-Brazilian religion whose deities have long standing ties to capoeira. To the right and the left of the entryway are dressing rooms, segregated by sex. By the women's dressing room is a small business area with a desk, computer, telephone, a few chairs, and a bookcase with many texts on Afro-Brazilian culture. There is also a kitchenette with a water filtration unit and sink for washing dishes. The left wall has been nearly covered in a giant mural of the *orixás, Candomblé* deities, surrounding a waterfall. In the far right corner of the room is a large framed chart that traces the lineage of selected capoeira *mestres.* All other open spaces have been covered with framed photographs of current capoeira *mestres* and players, as well as historical photographs and documents.

The bulk of my fieldwork took place at this academy, though conversations with *capoeiristas* at other academies and observations at *rodas* throughout the city convince me that the general patterns I found at FICA apply to many other academies as well. However, it bears mentioning at the outset of this work that FICA is steered by a capoeira scholar, which may explain why they were so welcoming of my research agenda. Mestre Cobra Mansa has been actively involved in researching both the historical aspects of capoeira and the contemporary manifestations of similar traditions in Western Africa, and he has given several presentations and coauthored articles on his research. Also, because FICA is an international organization, members of FICA Bahia are accustomed to the presence of foreigners and are perhaps more able to see both the benefits and drawbacks to this type of tourism than are individuals at groups that receive fewer guests.

According to Mestre Valmir, the leader of the FICA Bahia group, it is "on the account of this globalization of capoeira thing, and on account of our group's profile that we receive many foreigners." Therefore, interacting with foreigners is a daily affair for him. Almost everyday, he says, he is in contact with someone from abroad that has come in search of capoeira. In addition to having a scholarly orientation and emphasizing its status as an international organization, the group is located in a business district rather than a *favela* (slum) and counts many students and professionals among its members. One member was even running for political office during my time there. This too may help explain why international students felt more comfortable training at FICA than with some of the other groups in the city.

It should not be assumed that FICA Bahia is representative of all capoeira academies. One female *capoeirista* from London said that training at FICA was a great experience, especially in comparison to a group in Fortaleza where "they made [her] feel stupid." Like any organization, FICA is multifaceted and complex, but generally speaking, people who trained there were content with the workings of the group. Many *capoeiristas* admitted that there was racism and marginalization of foreigners at some academies, but not at FICA. This is likely one of the reasons that FICA is so popular among foreign *capoeiristas*. FICA also has a larger international network than do most capoeira academies. With many satellite groups located worldwide, the three *mestres* and the assistant instructors within the organization are in near-constant circulation, leading workshops abroad and often encouraging attendees to come and train with the group in Bahia. So while the general phenomenon I discuss in this book, apprenticeship pilgrimage, *is* applicable to other academies, the relative ease with which non-Brazilians were accepted at FICA is not necessarily the norm in all academies.

FICA Bahia maintains an intense training schedule relative to other groups in the area. Movement classes are offered from 12 pm–2 pm *and* from 7 pm–9 pm on Mondays, Wednesdays, and Fridays. Although the majority of local students choose to attend either the midday or the evening sessions, many foreign students attend both sessions. In addition, on Tuesdays and Thursdays, there is a one-hour music class from 7 pm–8 pm immediately followed by a two-hour movement class from 8 pm–10 pm. The academy hosts weekly *rodas* on Saturdays from 9:30 am until roughly 1 pm, which is attended by FICA students as well as individuals from other academies and the very occasional spectator (either Brazilian or foreign).

I spent approximately fourteen hours per week at the academy between the beginning of August and the end of December 2008 as a full participant in the academy's activities. My preparation with Estrela do Norte had given me a solid foundation for participating in these classes, neither as an expert nor as a novice, but somewhere in between. Because I wanted to develop a kinesthetic understanding of what the students were experiencing, and because I preferred to be seen primarily as a fellow *capoeirista* and not as a researcher, I did not take any notes during these sessions. I completed my field notes as soon as possible after returning to my apartment after training sessions while my memories were still fresh in my mind. The one exception was when I had stopped by the academy one evening just to interview someone. When he did not show up for our interview, I stayed in my street clothes and observed the lesson.

At the end of class, it was not uncommon for a group of students to go to a nearby café and have a meal or just fruit juices together. While one American female who had made previous trips to Brazil assured me that in the past these outings tended to be integrated, during 2008 most of the outings I attended were comprised almost exclusively of non-Brazilians. Because of the size of the city in which I was working and the nature of our community, which comes together for brief periods of training and then disperses, it was difficult to keep tabs on members of the capoeira group outside of class. But as the months progressed, the foreigners, especially those who were in Brazil for more than just a few weeks, began to spend more and more of their leisure time together. Most of these outings revolved around going to the beach or visiting other capoeira academies. The conversations at these informal events almost always revolved around capoeira and thus became part of my data as well. I also complimented my participation at the academy with archival research at the local library and interviews.

The Biblioteca Central maintains a collection of news articles that have been written on capoeira, which their staff was gracious enough to share with me. The bulk of these articles were written in the mid-to-late 1990s and the early 2000s. Although there were some articles that provided general information about capoeira, including coloring pages and activities for children, the majority of these articles focused on the growing international interest in capoeira. Articles written before this date typically present capoeira as a form of folklore rather than a living tradition, discussing the quaint performances that take place at local folk festivals or lamenting that the older *mestres* who once enjoyed such esteem as fighters are now living in poverty. I treated this archival material as supplementary to my primary methods, providing context for how capoeira was viewed within Brazilian society at large.

I conducted formal interviews with ten local *capoeiristas* and fourteen foreign *capoeiristas*. The roughly hour-long interviews followed a standardized format; I asked for general demographic information, then inquired about their attitudes toward the globalization of capoeira, and finally asked them to rank the importance of eleven different characteristics for a *capoeirista* using a five-point Likert scale. This sample was very diverse in terms of how much time they had spent training capoeira. Whereas some had trained for many years (one of the *mestres* has more than three decades of experience to his credit), others had only been training for a year or less. While seven individuals identified as black and seven identified as white, four claimed mixed heritage (using either the term *pardo* or *mestizo*), and the remaining six either cited other ethnicities or declined to answer this question. However, the surface level diversity of the interviewees' ethnicity can be deceiving as only one individual in the foreign sample was of African descent. The gender distribution was likewise skewed. Although I interviewed a total of eight females, only one of them was Brazilian. The issue of gender equity within capoeira is taken up in chapter 5.

The four years of fieldwork I had conducted with Estrela do Norte in Bloomington, Indiana, prior to my engagement with FICA had allowed me to build a grounded theory about how one goes about claiming legitimacy within capoeira. The eleven most important themes that emerged during this inductive phase became the eleven qualities I explored in my international fieldwork. These themes became the primary codes I used in analyzing my field notes and interview data from 2008, paying particular attention to the relationships between these codes and markers of an individual's legitimacy within the academy and within the capoeira community at large.

## Autoethnography and Reflexivity

While acknowledging that her remarks will be controversial, Sara Delamont (2007), anthropologist and capoeira scholar, characterizes autoethnography as "lazy" and fraught with ethical dilemmas. She also claims that it puts us on the wrong side of power—aligning with our own interests (class, nationality, etc.) rather than those of the marginalized individuals who many if not most anthropologists have come to champion since the latter part of the twentieth century (Delamont 2007). This text is not meant to be an autoethnography; however, I cannot escape the fact that as an observing participant, my actions influenced those of the other students and teachers with whom I interacted and are therefore frequently used as illustrative examples. I also unapologetically use the first-person throughout the book. Making use of my standpoint as an observing participant without losing sight of my core research objectives, however, requires a healthy dose of reflexivity.

Anthropologist Jennifer Robertson defines reflexivity as "the capacity of any system of signification, including a human being—an anthropologist—to turn back upon or mirror itself" (2002: 785). Anthropologist Philip Salzman adds that it is "the constant awareness, assessment and reassessment by the researcher of the researcher's own contribution/influence/shaping of intersubjective research and the consequent research findings" (2002: 806). The reflexive turn in ethnography was originally intended as a critical corrective to the omniscient tone taken in early ethnographies, in which authors failed to consider how their presence and methods of data collected influenced the behaviors of those around them and shaped their findings (Robertson 2002). Unfortunately, as Delamont (2007) points out, in many cases it devolves into an obsessive concern with the self. At its best, reflexively examining our own reactions to various scenarios in the field provides researchers with new avenues of inquiry that we can explore with our consultants; at its worst, it implies that we can never understand another human being if his or her identities are different from our own.

My own embodied experiences in the field prompted me to ask many questions about learning capoeira that I might not have been attuned to had I sat on the sidelines. On the other hand, had I been a more detached observer, I might have seen other things that were invisible to me as a participant. Either way it is largely a moot point because from the very beginning of my engagement with capoeira, no teacher ever allowed me to just observe the lesson without participating. Similarly, in her study of the transnational practice of yoga, Sarah Strauss found that "participation in yoga classes was absolutely essential, not only to gaining credibility in the eyes of the community, but also to the personal bodily understanding of the transformations these practices make possible" (2005: 60). She found that practitioners were reluctant to discuss their experiences with individuals who could not empathize as fellow yogis (Strauss 2005). Although *capoeiristas* have certainly shared their experiences with nonpractitioners, my membership in this community gave us a shared basis of understanding that was integral to my study.

While any individual's engagement with her community will be more complex than a simple accounting of her social identities can explain, I nonetheless feel compelled to disclose how my various positionalities as a white, Western woman influenced my ability to record the data that is of central importance to this study. I consider myself a pseudonative ethnographer because while demographically I was very similar to many of the foreign *capoeiristas* I was studying (mid-twenties, well-educated, and middle class), I began practicing capoeira in order to undertake academic research, rather than the other way around. At times, I found it challenging to study individuals whose social identities were so similar to my own, and it was often difficult for me to define myself in relation to them. I am not alone in this confusion. E Patrick Johnson found that his multiple identities influenced his performance as a fieldworker to the point where he could hardly separate himself from the activities occurring around him. He writes:

> The multiple identities I performed—black, middle class, southern, gay, male, professor—influenced my ethnographic experience as/of the Other. Therefore, I construe my ethnographic practice as an "impure" process—as a performance. Moreover, rather than fix my informants as static objects, naively claim ideological innocence, or engage in the false positivist "me/them" binary, I foreground my "coauthorship," as

it were, of the ethnographic texts produced in this volume, for I was as integral to the performance/text-making process as were my informants. (Johnson 2003: 10)

As a white North American anthropologist and *capoeirista,* I was constantly slipping between insider and outsider status. Playing the part of a detached observer would have been nearly impossible given the fact that most local Brazilians saw me as no different from the other foreigners that came to train at their academy.

Perhaps, as Charles Lindholm has suggested, the conflicting identities of an anthropologist predisposes us to ask questions about authenticity (2008: 141). Never was this more relevant to me than when one of the *mestres* I was interviewing told me it was good for *capoeiristas* to be involved in this kind of academic research because otherwise the academy would not be interested in capoeira. Although I was generally upfront that my academic interest in capoeira predated my actual participation, many people seemed to forget this. Given these circumstances, I embraced my role in the coconstruction of discourse about the capoeira experience.

Although discourse within the capoeira community focuses on equality and inclusivity, the reality often falls short of this stated goal. Women in particular represent a class of individuals who have struggled for recognition within the field. As such, I would be remiss in not discussing my own positionality as a woman and how this affected my fieldwork. As Sprague and Zimmerman write, "the standpoints of those who have historically been intellectual outsiders are particularly valuable in revealing the distortions of mainstream white upper-class male frameworks" (2004: 42). This logic can be extended to any social field in which one group has maintained control. In this case, being a woman allows me to understand the gendered dynamics of capoeira in a way that is slightly different from that of a man, an important contribution given that this is the first book-length scholarly monograph on the embodied experience of studying capoeira from an American woman's perspective. At the same time, however, I would not go so far as to suggest that a female perspective is superior to a male one; rather, the more diversity of perspectives available on a topic, the more complete our collective understanding of that phenomenon will be.

There were both benefits and drawbacks to my identity as a woman in the capoeira academy. On the one hand, I was not seen as a threat to the other students at the academy. Rather, given the predominant attitude of machismo, I was part of a group that needed to be protected. Though impossible to quantify, I felt that the majority of the men at the academy were gentler with me in the *roda* than they might have been with another male. On the other hand, however, I was subjected to the same predatory advances, both within the academy and outside of it, that all of the foreign females I talked to had experienced. Most of this romantic attention was assumed to be harmless, and I cannot recall a single woman who explicitly discussed this as part of a larger pattern of female oppression, but it nonetheless indexed a significant difference in terms of how males and females were perceived within capoeira.

My gender also had implications for my mobility. As a relatively young woman, I did not feel that I could walk through certain parts of town by myself or at certain times of day. This fear for my own safety grew over time, as I not only became the victim of a crime, but was repeatedly warned (by men) that I should not be out by myself. On more than one occasion, this advice was given to me by passing motorists who slowed down to offer me a ride home, which in and of itself can be a threatening proposition. Other women did not feel this same inhibition, and one of my consultants regularly rode her bicycle at night to travel between the academy and her apartment, passing unharmed through an area known for muggings. I return to these gendered dynamics in chapter 5, but mention them here so the reader can understand how my various identities influenced my data collection.

## Plan for the Book

This book contributes significantly to scholarly discussions of pilgrimage and acquisition of embodied knowledge. Since at least the 1970s, social scientists have found a high degree of overlap between tourism and pilgrimage (see Turner and Turner 1978; see also Cohen 1979). Believing that humans have a deep need for sacred, or at least significant, experiences that stand apart from their quotidian lives, recent scholars suggest that in today's more sacred society, tourism fills a similar role as does religious pilgrimage (see Badone and Roseman 2004; see also Digance and Cusack 2001). However, much of the research that follows this line of reasoning focuses on the significance of journeys to places that have a unique meaning for individuals rather than groups. The phenomenon I explore here, however, focuses on the sense of obligation an individual feels to visit Brazil because of the norms in the capoeira community.

This sense of obligation is ultimately related to globalization, a topic that I address in chapter 2. Prior to capoeira being taken abroad, there was little reason to ask whether or not non-Brazilians would be seen as legitimate tradition bearers. However, now that capoeira is practiced worldwide, Brazilians and others have begun to question who has the credentials to be called a *capoeirista*. This is not a trivial matter. The *capoeiristas* I am writing about do not just practice capoeira as a form of athletic conditioning or as a way to make friends. It has become a core part of their identity. Their extreme commitment and their need to be seen as legitimate in the eyes of practitioners from the art's homeland is what motivates their travel to Brazil, making it qualitatively different than an individual's idiosyncratic pilgrimage to a pop star's final resting place or a particularly notable baseball stadium. Chapter 2 addresses the questions of legitimacy that have arisen as Brazilian teachers have traveled abroad and begun teaching students who vary dramatically in terms of demographics from the original tradition bearers.

A desire for transformation is a core component of all pilgrimage, whether religious or secular, but the form of pilgrimage I am describing here focuses on a particular type of transformation. Apprenticeship pilgrimage, which I explore more fully in chapter 3 can be understood as travel to the birthplace or other communally ratified hub of practice with the explicit goal of studying that art or sport under the tutelage of a local master. Some foreign *capoeiristas* will go to Brazil just to see the sights and, perhaps, watch a few capoeira games. These are not pilgrims. Others will make a more concerted effort to join a local capoeira group and become an apprentice to local *mestres*. But just as one would not go and knock on the door of the Shaolin temple and expect immediate entrance, these individuals must prepare themselves by taking stock of their identities and adopting the right attitude. Upon entering the local capoeira scene in Brazil, they must negotiate their own legitimacy as members of this tradition vis-à-vis the standards established by the local capoeira community. In chapter 4 I discuss the preparations one makes before going to Brazil, as well as how one's lineage will influence his or her reception upon arrival in Brazil. In chapter 5 I discuss the body's role in authenticity and how having traditional markers of authenticity can facilitate one's acceptance into the local community. However, it is not impossible for those without these markers to gain legitimacy, which is an issue I address in chapter 6.

A *capoeirista* will be judged according to different criteria at different levels of the community. At the level of the academy, where individuals spend hours training together and getting to know one another, personal characteristics like one's dedication and attitude will be important. Beyond the academy, however, a *capoeirista* will have to prove his or her worth by executing the form properly. The form of capoeira is difficult to learn, largely because it demands a balance of adhering to tradition and cultivating an individual style within the context of improvisational play. Chapter 7 addresses the importance of form in capoeira as well as how one learns to balance tradition and innovation in the *roda*. In chapter 8, I distinguish form from skill and ask whether or not being skilled is an important aspect of being seen as legitimate. In chapter 9, I argue that having gained both skills and credibility during their pilgrimage, the *capoeirista* ideally returns home even more committed to his or her identity as a *capoeirista*.

Throughout the book, I have chosen to retain the actual names of the *mestres* and other teachers with whom I worked. They all granted their consent to be named during our interviews, and furthermore, I believe they should get public recognition for the wonderful mentors and artists that they are. However, the names of my fellow students have been masked to protect their privacy. As an observing participant, it is hard to draw a clear line between when I was acting as "researcher" and when I was just being myself. I think it would be unfair to hold people accountable, years after the fact, for offhand comments they may have made to a fellow capoeira student rather than an academic researcher. In developing pseudonyms, I thought of the characteristics I admired the most in each individual and found a name that reflected that meaning. Wherever possible, I tried to choose a name that had the same ethnic connotations as an individual's actual name. I hope my esteemed capoeira colleagues will see these new names as a sincere attempt to respect their privacy and honor their contributions to this book.

## Notes

1. Throughout this book, I follow the convention adopted by de Campos Rosario, Stephens, and Delamont (2010) in using the names of recognized capoeira teachers, whose identities would be hard to conceal, and use pseudonyms for students.
2. Tem roupa? Tenho, sim. Pode trocar a roupa lá. Fica á vontage.

## Works Cited

Almeida, Bira. 1986. *Capoeira, a Brazilian Art Form: History, Philosophy and Practice*. Berkeley, CA: North Atlantic Books.

Badone, Ellen, and Sharon R Roseman. 2004. "Approaches to the Anthropology of Pilgrimage and Tourism." In *Intersecting Journeys: The Anthropology of Pilgrimage and Tourism*, edited by Ellen Badone and Sharon R Roseman, 1–23. Urbana: University of Illinois Press.

Cohen, Erik. 1979. "A Phenomenology of Tourist Experiences." *Sociology* 13 (2): 179–201.

Crossley, Nick. 2006. "The Networked Body and the Question of Reflexivity." In *Body/ Embodiment: Symbolic Interaction and the Sociology of the Body*, edited by Dennis Waskul and Phillip Vannani, 21–34. Hampshire, UK: Ashgate Publishing.

De Campos Rosario, Claudio, Neil Stephens, and Sara Delamont. 2010. "'I'm Your Teacher, I'm Brazilian!' Authenticity and Authority in European Capoeira." *Sport, Education and Society* 15 (1): 103–20.

Delamont, Sara. 2007. *Arguments against Auto-Ethnography*. The British Educational Research Association Annual Conference, University of London.

Digance, Justine, and Carole M Cusack. 2001. "Secular Pilgrimage Events: Druid Gorsedd and Stargate Alignments." In *The End of Religions?: Religion in an Age of Globalisation*, edited by Carole M Cusack and Peter Oldmeadow, 216–29. Sydney: Department of Studies in Religion, University of Sydney.

Grazian, David. 2004. "The Symbolic Economy of Authenticity in the Chicago Blues Scene." In *Music Scenes: Local, Translocal, and Virtual*, edited by Andy Bennett and Richard A Peterson, 31-47. Nashville, TN: Vanderbilt University Press.

Jensen, Joli. 1998. *Nashville Sound: Authenticity, Commercialization, and Country Music*. Nashville, TN: Vanderbilt University Press.

Johnson, E Patrick. 2003. *Appropriating Blackness: Performance and the Politics of Authenticity*. Durham, NC: Duke University Press.

Lindholm, Charles. 2008. *Culture and Authenticity*. Malden, MA: Blackwell Publishing.

MacAloon, John J. 1984. "Olympic Games and the Theory of Spectacle in Modern Societies." In *Rite, Drama, Festival, Spectacle: Rehearsals toward a Theory of Cultural Performance*, edited by John J MacAloon, 241–80. Philadelphia, PA: Institute for the Study of Human Issues.

MacCannell, Dean. 1976. *The Tourist: A New Theory of the Leisure Class*. Berkeley: University of California Press.

Marion, Jonathan S. 2008. *Ballroom: Culture and Costume in Competitive Dance.* Oxford: Berg.

Merleau-Ponty, Maurice. 1989. *Phenomenology of Perception.* Translated by C Smith. London: Routledge.

Pink, Sarah. 2009. *Doing Sensory Ethnography.* Los Angeles: Sage.

Robertson, Jennifer. 2002. "Reflexivity Redux: A Pithy Polemic on 'Positionality.'" *Anthropological Quarterly* 75 (4): 785–92.

Salzman, Philip Carl. 2002. "On Reflexivity." *American Anthropologist* 104 (3): 805–13.

Sprague, Joey, and Mary Zimmerman. 2004. "Overcoming Dualism: A Feminist Agenda for Sociological Methodology." In *Approaches to Qualitative Research: A Reader on Theory and Practice,* edited by Sharlene Nagy Hesse-Biber and Patricia Leavy, 39–61. New York: Oxford University Press.

Strathern, Andrew J. 1996. *Body Thoughts.* Ann Arbor: The University of Michigan Press.

Strauss, Sarah. 2005. *Positioning Yoga: Balancing Acts across Cultures.* Oxford: Berg.

Taylor, Gerard. 2007. *Capoeira: The Jogo de Angola from Luanda to Cyberspace.* Vol. 2. Berkeley, CA: North Atlantic Books.

Turner, Victor. 1987. *The Anthropology of Performance.* New York: Paj Publications.

Turner, Victor, and Edith Turner. 1978. *Image and Pilgrimage in Christian Culture.* New York: Columbia University Press.

# Chapter 1

# A Brief History of Capoeira

| | |
|---|---|
| Iê! | Iê! |
| Bahia minha Bahia | Bahia, my Bahia |
| Capital é Salvador | Capital is Salvador |
| Quem não conhece a Capoeira | He who doesn't know Capoeira |
| Não pode dar seu valor | Cannot give it its value |
| Capoeira vem da África | Capoeira came from Africa |
| Foi Africano que inventou | It was an African that invented it |
| Todos podem aprender | Everyone can learn |
| General e também doutor | General and doctor too |
| Quem desejar aprender | He who wants to learn |
| Vem aqui em Salvador | Come here to Salvador |
| Procure o Mestre Pastinha | Find Mestre Pastinha |
| Ele é o professor | He is the professor |
| Camaradinha … | My dear friend … |

This traditional song, a *ladainha,* is often sung at the start of a capoeira event. It was the first *ladainha* I ever learned, and I loved its words so much that I recited it as poetry before I learned its proper rhythm. For me, this song exemplifies what it means to be a *capoeirista,* particularly in this era of globalization. No longer is this martial art restricted to poor, Afro-Brazilian men as it was during Brazil's colonial period and the early days of the New Republic; today it can theoretically be practiced by generals and doctors too. Initially, I found this song to be comforting because it gave me confidence that I, as a white woman from the United States, could also become a *capoeirista.* But over time, I began to question its idealism. I wondered if generals and doctors really *could* become *capoeiristas,* and even if they could, I wondered if they *should,* especially if their adoption of the art might detract from the liberatory potential of the practice. For now, let me put this question on hold by pointing out that the lyrics indicate that these new populations will be welcomed into the fold only if they are willing to put in the time and effort needed to learn from the masters.

As suggested in this song, many practitioners believe that the best way to learn capoeira is by training in Salvador da Bahia, Brazil. The city of Salvador, sometimes referred to simply as Bahia, is known domestically and internationally as a bastion of traditional African culture. For the non-Brazilian *capoeirista,* traveling to Bahia has become an almost essential part of their advancement within the social field. Yet the question exists whether or not this kind of travel is enough to grant a general, a doctor, or a white female anthropologist full membership in the capoeira community. This book provides some answers.

## Introduction

To begin this chapter, I offer a vignette of a typical capoeira event in the hopes that it will allow my readers to picture this metagenre (MacAloon 1984; Marion 2008), which is often referred to as a "dance-fight-game." I also describe the two primary styles of capoeira. While this book is primarily focused on the *Capoeira Angola* style, understanding the difference between the two has important implications for some of the ideological debates that affect students. The primary debate introduced in this chapter is whether capoeira is an African or a Brazilian invention.

It is my position that the actual origins of capoeira are less important than the discourse about its origins. As I argue, the idea of capoeira being a local invention fit handily into the early twentieth-century movement to identify certain arts as being quintessentially Brazilian. On the other hand, the idea of capoeira being an African invention that endured despite repression during the colonial period aligns more closely with the black consciousness movement.

Many of the non-Brazilians who encounter capoeira through television and film will not be exposed to these issues. However, for those who want to become *capoeiristas* themselves, they will be increasingly involved in these ideological debates. Those individuals may ultimately have to grapple with a conflict between their own social identities and those most valued in capoeira. They, like myself, may come to question whether or not the song quoted above accurately describes the ease of nontraditional *capoeiristas* entering the social field.

## The Dance-Fight-Game Known as Capoeira

As the designated hour approaches, a student lays out the instruments in their proper order on a long wooden bench. This is not just any student, this is someone who has been trusted to handle the most sacred objects involved in the capoeira event. The three *berimbaus* occupy a privileged place in the center of the bench.

Students are scattered about the room, stretching, practicing their handstands, and talking in small clusters. Gradually, some of the players move to the bench and pick up an instrument. The most advanced ones take the *berimbaus,* and the novices pick up the cowbell and the scraper.

Once every instrument has been claimed, and the remaining *capoeiristas* sit in a ring around the orchestra. Two *capoeiristas* squat in front of the *berimbaus,* waiting for the appropriate moment to enter the circle and begin their game. *Ding, ding, ding, ding, ding,* the *gunga berimbau* calls the room to order. *Ching, ching, dong, ding* [rest], *ching, ching, dong, ding* [rest], the *gunga* starts the rhythm. The *medio* chimes in next: *ching, ching, ding, dong* [rest], *ching, ching, ding, dong.* Now the *viola*: *ching, ching, ding, dong, dong, ching, ching, ding, dong, dong.* Now that the three *berimbaus* are in harmony, the *pandeiros* (tambourines) begin.

The *mestre* belts out a loud "*Iê,*" stretching the second syllable out over two or three seconds. His voice jars the assembly into attention, signaling a break between the profane and the sacred. The students sitting in a circle create a physical barrier between the ritual space and the rest of their environment; the music activates this space. The *mestre* sings a *ladainha,* a litany that evokes the ancestors and tells a story about the city of Bahia. A foreign *capoeirista* visiting Bahia closes her eyes and lets the memories of these recently visited places wash over her. As the *mestre* finishes this song, he starts a call and response song. As this song begins, the other percussive instruments begin to play. "Long live God," the *capoeiristas* sing, and the two players at the foot of the *berimbau* open their arms toward the sky. "Long live my *mestre,*" they continue, "the one who taught me." The two players gesture toward their teacher. The *mestre* starts to lead a new song and lowers the *gunga* to the ground, signaling to the two players that they may begin.

One player touches his fingertips to the ground and then to his forehead; the other makes the sign of the cross on her chest. The players tentatively edge away from the orchestra, trying to sense what the other will do. The brief stalemate is broken when one player presses her weight into her hands, balancing on one leg while the other sweeps in a circular motion. Her opponent dodges, extending his body as close to the ground as possible, dreadlocks puddled on the floor. From this position, he propels his body into a headstand, completes a 360-degree spin, and ends the movement by lowering his legs into an outstretched V on the floor. To avoid this trap, his opponent does a cartwheel over his legs. She pauses in midair, holding a handstand position for a fraction of a second before crashing to the ground. The onlookers erupt into laughter, and the *mestre* immediately switches to a different song: *O facão bateu em baixo, A bananeira caiu* (the machete struck low, the banana tree fell). For those in the know, the *mestre's* song choice underscores the girl's folly, comparing her to a banana tree that has just been chopped down.

Dusting herself off, the girl gets up, and the two players resume their game. The spinning, leaping, kicking, and dodging continues under the watchful eye of the *mestre* who is always ready to enhance the spectacle with an appropriate song. He is also responsible for calming the players down if their game becomes too heated. Gasping and sweating, the players eventually hear the *gunga* calling them back to their starting positions. With a brief embrace, the two players exit the ring, and two more take their place.

*Capoeiristas* do not spar, fight, or dance capoeira; they "play." Portuguese has three words that translate into English as play. *Tocar* is used for playing an instrument, *jogar* is used for playing a sport, and *brincar* connotes the carefree play of childhood. *Capoeiristas* most often use the second word, though *brincar* is used on occasion to celebrate the most joyous, friendly, and fun performances. Practitioners are called *capoeiristas,* and their masters are called *mestres.* Both the circle in which they play capoeira and the performance event itself are referred to as a *roda.* At the front of the *roda* is an orchestra that is typically composed of three *berimbaus,* one or two *pandeiros,* an *atabaque* (drum), an *agôgô* (double cowbell), and a *reco-reco* (scraping instrument).[1] These terms are West African in derivation; the same terms are used for musical instruments in *Candomblé,* the African-derived spirit possession religion that thrives in Bahia.

The *berimbau* is the most revered instrument in the capoeira orchestra. It consists of a wooden bow with a wire stretched across it. Today, this wire is taken from the inside of a tire, and capoeira academies often have a stack of discarded tires in a corner, waiting for more experienced students to don gloves and carefully strip out the wire with a knife. Affixed to the bow is a hollow gourd, which acts as a resonating chamber. Striking the wire with a stick called a *baqueta* while holding a smooth stone or old coin in one of three positions determines the pitch. A basket rattle looped over the middle and ring fingers accompanies this percussive sound. These instruments are often embellished with decoration. Sometimes geometric patterns will be burned into the wood. Other times, the bow and/or gourd might be painted with colors that signify an affiliation with the state of Bahia, the nation of Brazil, or even the Rastafarian's green, yellow, and red. Oftentimes the colorful *lembrança* (remembrance) ribbons that have come to symbolize the city of Salvador are tied to the top of the instrument.

The *roda* begins before anyone picks up an instrument. Players typically dress better for these events than they do for their regular training sessions. Khaki pants replace the sweatpants worn during training, and some of the older *mestres* may even arrive wearing dress shoes instead of their typical soccer shoes. In some academies, a special offering may be made to the *mestre's* primary *orixa* (deity), or incense may be burned to cleanse and sanctify the space. When it is time to begin, two players kneel in front of the *berimbau,* sometimes using their hands to draw invisible religious signs such as crosses on their bodies or on the ground, while someone sings a solo to commemorate people and places dear to capoeira. The players' gestures sometimes signal a religious affiliation, normally either *Candomblé* or Christianity, though the participation of nonreligious *capoeiristas* means that just as often these gestures are hollow facsimiles of an embodied tradition.[2]

After a short call and response song praising God, old *mestres,* the slaves who brought this tradition to Brazil, or the city of Salvador, the players cartwheel into the center and begin a playful, embellished physical dialogue in which they plan their moves with the foresight of champion chess players. Players trade "questions" and "answers" in these improvised bodily conversations.[3] The *mestre* or an advanced student will lead a call and response song, which the other participants echo, that comments on the action in the *roda.* Lewis (1992) identifies the physical game of capoeira as the primary channel of communication and songs as metacommunicative devices that add nuance to the participants' and spectators' interpretations of the exchange going on within the *roda.* There are no points awarded, but *capoeiristas* believe that one player has been victorious when the other runs out of responses to her attacks.

There are two primary styles, *Capoeira Angola* and *Capoeira Regional,* though hybrids certainly exist and are growing in popularity. While I have had the opportunity to observe both, my participation was limited to the *Capoeira Angola* style and thus forms the backbone of this book's analysis. Both styles incorporate instruments and singing in their play, though the exact composition of the orchestra is more flexible in the *Capoeira Regional* style. Many of the same songs are used in both styles, but they are sung faster in *Capoeira Regional* than they are in the *Capoeira Angola* style. The basic step in both styles is the *ginga,* a swaying motion in which players' feet essentially trace the shape of a W on the floor while their arms swing from side to side, blocking their face with the arm closest to the midline of the W. This is the moving base from which many movements originate and a neutral stance to which players may return at any moment during the game.

Despite these similarities, visually, the two styles are readily distinguishable from one another. J Lowell Lewis, anthropologist and performance scholar, characterizes *Capoeira Angola* as more of a playful pastime and *Capoeira Regional* as "fundamentally agonistic" (1992: 113). *Capoeiristas* in the *Capoeira Regional* style wear white clothing for their training. *Angoleiros,* on the other hand, often wear black pants and their academy's T-shirt, the color of which often signifies their lineage. *Capoeira Regional* players wear a colored belt to denote their rank; however, there is no standardized color system, and the ranking system varies from one academy to the next. *Angoleiros* wear no such belts. *Capoeira Regional,* in general, is played at a much faster pace than is *Capoeira Angola.* The body is also held more upright in *Capoeira Regional,* and players focus on fast, high kicks, often executed from a spinning base. Arial movements such as back flips or back handsprings are not uncommon in this type of play. *Angoleiros* keep their movements much closer to the ground, and the most common attack movements are kicks, spinning or straight, executed from a crouched position with one or both hands on the ground for support. Evasive movements are kept very close to the floor and require more strength and control than speed. However, *Capoeira*

*Angola* players do occasionally return to a standing position, particularly during the *chamada,* which is an interlude during play that is sometimes incorrectly used as a recovery period, but traditionally has greater significance.

The *chamada* is a particularly sophisticated, ritualistic aspect of the capoeira that is particularly apparent in the *Capoeira Angola* style. One player will "call" the other over to him or her by posing with arms outstretched in one of a handful of prescribed positions. Generally, the caller's feet will be placed hips-width apart with one several inches behind the other. Distributing his or her weight in this manner provides the caller with a more secure base. Standing with one's feet together often results in the other player bringing the caller down with a leg sweep; however, skilled players will sometimes stand in this way to underscore their confidence and superiority. When the other player meets the caller, they move back and forth together for several seconds with their bodies held close together, often touching at the hands or, less often, with one player's head pressed against the other's stomach with the upright player resting his or her hands lightly on the other's head. When both players are standing erect, they can complete this movement face-to-face or with one player standing directly behind the other.

*Capoeristas* sometimes say this tradition descends from slaves' mockery of how Portuguese plantation owners danced. Calling a *chamada* can be used to reestablish a friendly tone if a game has become too heated. However, it is just as often used to underscore a particularly skillful move made by the caller, who is highlighting his or her virtuosity by creating this small "time out" so the opponent and spectators alike can reflect on what just transpired. Regardless of why it is used, the *chamada* is often broken by one player delivering an unexpected attack, much like the slap-hand game (see Downey 2005 for an excellent description of the use of *chamadas*). The kind of deceptiveness often seen at the end of the *chamada* is key to understanding the aesthetics of *Capoeira Angola,* and the sneaky survival strategies necessitated by slavery persist in today's practice of the art (see Brough 2006).

Many *capoeiristas* are acutely sensitive to the reputation of their style, lineage, and academy. To the chagrin of practitioners in other camps, *Capoeira Angola* is often labeled the more "authentic" or "African" of the two major styles. I have found this attitude to be more prevalent among the younger generations of *capoeiristas,* particularly non-Brazilians who are already anxious about their position in the legitimacy hierarchy. Capoeira historian Gerard Taylor explains that older *mestres* are often more tolerant of different capoeira groups because of their greater experience, whereas the younger students are more prone to misunderstanding and quick to assume that groups that are different are inherently inferior:

> This has created an exclusivist attitude among some Capoeira Angola students, as if they are in some way VIP inheritors of the authentic capoeira,

and that anyone wearing a cordao or doing acrobatic techniques in the roda is in some way not quite as "real" and true to the original as they are. The "more Angola than thou" way of thinking of a small percentage of Capoeira Angola's new generation of international students is surely an unfortunate characteristic. (Taylor 2007: 147)

His assumption about this generational behavior may be true, but he does not provide evidence for this position to his readers. His comments on the exclusivist attitude indicates the younger generation's desire to be perceived as authentic performers of capoeira, but may also speak to his group's position outside this taken-for-granted dichotomy of *Capoeira Regional* versus *Capoeira Angola,* which raises insecurities in many *capoeiristas* who play a budding style labeled *Capoeira Contemporânea.*[4]

*Capoeira Contemporânea* is generally considered to be a hybrid of the *Capoeira Regional* and *Capoeira Angola* styles. While some *Capoeira Contemporânea* groups play the slower and craftier *Capoeira Angola*-style games at the beginning of their *rodas* and then transition to the faster and more acrobatic *Capoeira Regional* games toward the end of their *rodas,* others see it as a true agglutination of the two styles (Mwewa, de Oliveira, and Vaz 2010). Many *Capoeira Angola* and *Capoeira Regional* players alike disparage *Capoeira Contemporânea* for its deviations from tradition, though a growing number of practitioners in Brazil and abroad identify with it.

One female *capoeirista* who practices the *Capoeira Contemporânea* style in the United States told me that she thought *Capoeira Angola* was reactionary and overly defensive about the popularity of *Capoeira Regional,* saying, "*Regional* is fighting so *Angola* must be ludic; *Regional* allows no shirt so *Angoleiros* have to tuck in their shirts; *Regional* wears their pants low and sexy so *Angola* wears their pants up high." As she said this, I was surprised by the intensity and mockery in her voice. Insiders will often describe *Capoeira Angola's* prohibition against bare feet, shoulders, and midriffs as a way of paying respect, but it is equally possible, as my consultant suggested, that these distinctions have been exaggerated as a way of maintaining clear boundaries between the two styles.

With the proliferation of idiosyncratic styles growing exponentially in the United States and Europe, a new generation of *capoeiristas* is starting to refute this dichotomy, but many groups' insecurities are evident in their hypersensitive adherence to traditional practices and it is not surprising to find that capoeira's traditions are sometimes preserved more assiduously in many non-Brazilian groups than they are in Brazil. It is also quite possible that the intensity of each party's belief in their style's superiority may be connected to the ideological associations between *Capoeira Angola* as a marker of racial identity and *Capoeira Regional* as a marker of national identity. These associations are firmly rooted in the history of capoeira's development.

## Slavery and the Persecution of Capoeira

Capoeira can be thought of as a "secular ritual" and "narrative drama" that encapsulates the history of struggle against and triumph over oppression (D'Aquino 1983: 6). According to the legend most fervently defended by practitioners of the *Capoeira Angola* style, African slaves brought capoeira to Brazil along with other elements of their language, religion, and culture. Indeed, it shares a great number of commonalities with arts from the African diaspora, and instruments that resemble the *berimbau* are still in use in parts of Western Africa. But it is unlikely that capoeira was brought over in its current form, as no one yet has been able to find a perfect antecedent still in practice (see Assunção 2005). It is more likely that slaves from different parts of Africa each contributed to the development of capoeira, and a hybrid form emerged out of their pastimes. Dancer and literary theorist Barbara Browning notes that the individual moves in capoeira were most likely an African invention, "but the strategic blending of fight and dance occurred in Brazil, under specific pressures" (1995: 91). Lewis (1992) suggests that capoeira did not emerge in its present form until the late eighteenth century.

Some scholars have sought the origins of this art by tracing the etymology of the word *capoeira*. One popular hypothesis is that the word *capoeira* is derived from the word *capão,* chicken coop, because capoeira resembles a cockfight. It has also been suggested that the association with capons (castrated cocks) came from the habit of slaves playing capoeira near an old poultry market in Rio de Janeiro (see Lewis 1992: 43). The other common hypothesis is that capoeira was often played in the grassy areas where jungle vegetation had been cleared and that the word for capoeira is therefore derived from the indigenous Tupi terms for extinct (*puêra*) and forest (*caá*). Both of these seem plausible on the surface, but supporting evidence for these hypotheses is scant (see Lewis 1992).

Browning (1995) has expressed some of the same concerns I have had about relying too heavily on linguistic evidence to find the source of capoeira. Because *capoeiristas* delight in "saying one thing and meaning another" (Browning 1995: 93), students today should be wary of overly literal interpretations of the various etymological hypotheses. From an anthropological perspective, the particular form of a folk history defended by the culture bearers of a tradition is often more important than historical veracity (Green 2003a: 1). It is far more useful to examine how such narratives are employed and why they have continued salience in the modern world. For example, capoeira discourse repeatedly ties the art to the physical resistance of maroon societies such as the Quilombo dos Palmares, even though there is little concrete evidence to support such a connection (Lewis 1992).

Both *Capoeira Angola* and *Capoeira Regional* bear the stamp of colonial policies that encouraged secrecy and social marginalization that encouraged a Machiavellian approach to survival. Like other African-derived defensive systems in the New World (Green 2003b: 130), early *capoeiristas* had to conceal the true nature of their art because of whites' fear and mistrust of their African slaves. Slave revolts and disturbances throughout the Caribbean, like the St Dominique rebellion, contributed to the anxieties of whites living in Brazil during the colonial period (Taylor 2005: 277). During the colonial era, there was at least one enslaved black *and* one freed black or mulatto for every white member of society (Marquese 2006). In this context, slaves' drumming was interpreted by whites not as harmless fun, one of the few diversions they have to distract them from the horrors of slavery, but as a threat, sending secret messages about rebellion from one plantation to the next. To repress this perceived threat, colonial officials created laws that regulated the leisure-time activities of the slaves.

Once the Portuguese royal court, fleeing Napoleon's army, relocated to Rio de Janeiro in 1808, the vices of capoeira became a matter of public debate (Assunção 2005: 9). The court's arrival intensified fears about capoeira, which was accompanied by concerns about foreign spies and court conspiracies. As a result, Magistrate Paulo Fernandez Viana and the police force he directed aggressively persecuted *vadiagem* (Taylor 2005: 306–7). *Vadiagem* refers to the art of loafing and is a term that is sometimes used synonymously with capoeira because it has traditionally been a favored pastime of the lower-class black males who are popularly viewed as being vagrants. As the political climate of Brazil changed, first becoming an independent nation still ruled by a monarch and then becoming a republic, the public's mistrust of capoeira was less about the possibility of a slave revolt and more about the *capoeiristas'* growing reputation as thugs that could interfere with democratic processes.

An ordinance passed in 1830 forbade drumming and other forms of entertainment for both enslaved and free blacks, but it was only in 1890, after emancipation, that a criminal code was established to specifically outlaw capoeira. The code imposed strict, sometimes deadly, punishments for being caught playing capoeira. The Criminal Code of 1890 (Articles 402–404) threatened *capoeiristas* with a two- to six-month jail sentence. The 1890 sanction was due in large part to *capoeiristas'* employment by politicians as bodyguards and ballot stuffers, which resulted in "render[ing] elections farcical" (Assunção 2005: 93).

Though practiced almost exclusively by the lower classes, some middle-class visionaries were able to see within capoeira the seeds of a martial training program that could be used with the police and armed forces. In the early 1900s, several individuals promoted using capoeira for physical training exercises within the military, which they believed would promote a patriotic attitude toward Brazil's own sporting forms (Downey 2002). In a move that underscores the elites' continued preference for European traditions over Brazilian ones, this request was denied by Parliament on the basis of it being Brazilian (Talmon-Chvaicer 2008: 113). Nonetheless, a few individuals, like Sinhozinho in Rio de Janeiro, began to institutionalize capoeira despite its prohibition (Talmon-Chvaicer 2008: 113).

Unfortunately, Sinhozinho's contributions to capoeira are only just beginning to come to light because of widespread erroneous beliefs that capoeira in Rio de Janeiro was extinguished because of official prohibition. Historians and practitioners alike have preferred to focus on the Bahia as the cradle of capoeira.

It is not coincidental that the most intense persecution of capoeira took place in Rio, the center of Brazil's political universe at that time. It was here that politicians were most likely to employ capoeira gangs to sway the political process in their favor. In Bahia, by way of contrast, practicing capoeira was never explicitly cited as a reason for arrest (Assunção 2005: 120). Many *capoeiristas* in Bahia relied upon the influence of powerful patrons and the blind eye of the police to keep them out of prison (Assunção 2005: 122). Despite this fact, the severe punishments accorded to *capoeiristas* figure prominently in the narratives many Bahian capoeira instructors pass on to their students and audiences in the United States. Even if actual punishment was somewhat unlikely for *capoeiristas* in Bahia, the ever-present threat of persecution during this period led to an emphasis on the more ludic (playful) aspects of capoeira as it was played in conjunction with general sociability, drinking, and gambling (Almeida 1986: 29).

## Regionalist Discourse and the Valorization of Folk Arts

Two contradictory trends emerged at the turn of the twentieth century, which help contextualize the racial politics of capoeira. Following emancipation in 1888, Brazilian elites made a vigorous effort to deny the African heritage of the Brazilian people. This coincided with the scientific heyday of eugenics, which deemed non-European peoples inferior to whites. As a result, Brazil embraced a policy of whitening, ostensibly to improve the genetic stock of its people. But at the same time, by the turn of the twentieth century, Brazilians were also trying to cultivate a unique national identity and turned to "authentic" cultural forms drawn from the *povo* (people), including Afro-Brazilians. Here I am using the term authentic to refer to elite's perceptions of folk traditions as being unique and uncontaminated by outside influences. During this time, both capoeira and samba moved from being marginalized practices sequestered in the black spaces of culture to symbols of national identity (see Vianna 1999: 10 on samba).

Despite the prevalence of racism during the early twentieth century, public intellectuals took a strong role in bringing recognition to Afro-Brazilian culture, ushering in a phase during which the discourse of regionalism became popular. Brazilian writers encouraged the public to look for "a 'national' character" in Afro-Brazilian cultural practices and empathize with Afro-Brazilians' histories, no matter how distant that may have been from their own experience (Taylor 2007: 18). Intellectuals who promoted a discourse of miscegenation were influential in the popularization of samba, as were the artists involved in the modernist movement who advocated the Brazilianization of international trends. Gilberto Freyre in particular called the public's attention to the contributions Afro-Brazilians had made to their country. Although Freyre's writings were often simplistic and romanticized Brazilian slavery, particularly the relationship between master and slave, his work did play a role in the early valorization of Afro-Brazilian culture and should be remembered for that.

By the 1920s, the term *regional* had come into vogue. This is around the time that Gilberto Freyre published his *Regionalist Manifesto* (1955). Freyre takes pride in Brazil's unique cultural history, believing that the history of European/African relations in Portugal prior to their discovery of Brazil set the stage for more congenial race relations than are present elsewhere in the new world. This is an attitude that persists in the myth of racial democracy despite the lived reality of discrimination experienced by many Afro-Brazilians. The *Regionalist Manifesto* also privileged Brazilian traditions over those that were imported from abroad. Regionalist in this context "stood for popular folk culture associated with Brazil's regions, often the Northeast" (Taylor 2007: 20). Capoeira was still illegal at this time, but the prevalence of the discourse on folklore raised its profile and may have encouraged government officials to turn a blind eye. Even while *capoeiristas* were being persecuted by the state, they were being celebrated by folklorists as popular heroes (Downey 2002).

In addition to the intellectuals' pleas for the public to valorize Brazil's unique arts, the popularity of these forms was hastened by the elite's taste for the "national exotic" (Vianna 1999: 24). Here again the historical trajectories of capoeira and samba dovetail nicely. Vianna articulates three elements of samba's rise to fame as a national symbol: (1) it involved different social groups, from poor Afro-Brazilians to domestic and foreign intellectuals and elites; (2) its codification as a form and its rise to prominence happened concurrently; and (3) its specific path was a result of the push and pull of various agendas rather than one coherent movement (Vianna 1999: 112). Capoeira similarly gained national attention as a result of intellectual patronage and federal recognition in the form of Getúlio Vargas's proclamation that it was Brazil's national sport. Its codification, at least in the case of *Capoeira Regional,* was an essential component of its elevation, though the push and pull of different agendas also resulted in the formalization of a second style, *Capoeira Angola.*

By the time of the 1930 revolution, when Getúlio Vargas was installed by the Brazilian military, the 1890 penal code prohibiting capoeira was generally no longer enforced (Taylor 2007: 20). One of Vargas's goals was to reduce class antagonism by integrating lower-class individuals into Brazilian society by elevating their folk traditions to the level of national culture (Talmon-Chvaicer 2008: 114). However, this strategy was more about appeasement than really valorizing African contributions to Brazilian life. It also provided revenue for the state and for the generation of *mestres* born in the 1920s and 1930s; giving performances sponsored by the Bahia Tourism Office conferred upon them a certain measure of prestige (Capoeira 2006: 43). It was also at this time that Bahian capoeira *mestres* first attempted to organize (Cruz 2006: 22), but their attempts did not lead to any long-term coherence of the field.

In 1937 the second Afro-Brazilian Congress, organized in part by folklorist and Afro-Brazilian specialist Edison Carneiro, took place in Salvador. It brought positive attention to the Afro-Brazilian religion *Candomblé* and raised the status of capoeira to that of "an art form and an expression of Afro-Bahian identity" (Assunção 2005: 151). While Carneiro's aim was to valorize African contributions to local culture, this valorization also paved the way for white Brazilians to usurp African bodily practice. The result was that many whites, particularly intellectuals, began to celebrate Afro-Brazilian arts as part of the nation's multiculturalism while simultaneously downplaying the trauma of slavery and persistent economic inequalities (Joseph 2006: 32).

Despite this attempt at organization, capoeira was still governed by an "anything goes" mentality, allowing individual *mestres* to privilege efficacy over fidelity to tradition and take on apprentices if and when they saw fit. All of this was about to change, however, when one particular *mestre* undertook a series of reforms that brought capoeira more in line with the aims of the Estado Novo. The reign of dictator/president Getúlio Vargas from 1937–45 is known as the Estado Novo, a period during which nationalistic propaganda was used extensively in support of Vargas's repressive stranglehold over the Brazilian people. On the surface, Afro-Brazilian arts that had been used as tools, real or symbolic, of resistance against the elites did not fit this model. However, they could be made to fit these aims by "modernizing and emphasizing their 'morally uplifting' tenets" (Taylor 2007: 22). This created the perfect situation for Mestre Bimba (born Manuel dos Reis Machado, 1899–1974) to bring his version of capoeira to the fore.

Mestre Bimba is remembered for both his role in institutionalizing capoeira and the innovations he brought to the art. Although his own style of play, recordings of which have been made available on YouTube, in many ways resembles the *Capoeira Angola* style more than it does the present-day *Capoeira Regional* style, he is responsible for incorporating movements from *batuque* and Asian martial systems into capoeira. *Batuque* was a martial dance/game practiced by African and Afro-Brazilian men, and is considered by many to be a precursor to capoeira. This artistic cannibalism reinforced the African aspects of capoeira and is thus less offensive to capoeira purists, whereas the adoption of throws from judo was more controversial.

Bimba's systematized pedagogy created a clear progression for students, which was marked by their receipt of colored scarves. Not only did these scarves indicate their level, they also served as extrinsic rewards for students' training.[5] Setting standards and rewarding students for progress was one way to instill the virtues of hard work and dedication, which aligned with the Estado Novo philosophy. Mestre Bimba also required that his students either be gainfully employed or enrolled in school. Together, these requirements brought an aura of respectability to capoeira and began the process of elevating it from vagrancy to art (see Reis 2004). Because Bimba's structured hierarchy required long-term enrollment and payment, it excluded poor Afro-Brazilians. This has led many to consider *Capoeira Regional* "whiter" than *Capoeira Angola* (Reis 2004: 195; Assunção 2005; Downey 2005: 176–81), despite the fact that Capoeira Regional groups today are quite racially diverse. That Bimba's students were educated also increases the likelihood that they would have been familiar with Freyre's writings on the value of folk traditional and regional identity, which played a significant role in the public's acceptance of capoeira.

*A Tarde,* Bahia's premier newspaper, had been a vociferous critic of capoeira during the early part of the 1900s. But suddenly, in the mid 1930s, their stance changed. In 1936, they ran an article that actually argued for the development of capoeira as a national fight, much like jujitsu was for Japan or pugilism for the United States ("A Inaguracao do Parque Oden" 1936). By 1948, *A Tarde* was applauding the "traditional" and "picturesque" capoeira that took place at an important religious festival ("A Alegria Fez Praca no largo da Conceicao" 1948). Within a relatively short amount of time, capoeira had gone from something that the public feared to a quaint symbol of a bygone era to be idealized during public festivals. In the 1950s, Mestre Bimba was becoming more widely recognized in Bahia and throughout Brazil. In 1953, Mestre Bimba's fame was augmented when Vargas, now a democratically elected president in spite of his earlier dictatorial rule, proclaimed that capoeira was Brazil's national sport (Talmon-Chvaicer 2008: 123). This, along with the overall discourse of nationalism that pervaded Vargas's regime, led to the perception of capoeira as a distinctly Brazilian invention. But the *Capoeira Angola* style was on the verge of codification as well and would bring with it a commitment to the Afrocentric origins of capoeira.

Mestre Pastinha (born Vicente Ferreira Pastinha, 1889–1981) learned capoeira as a child from an African slave. Mestre Pastinha opposed the mixture of capoeira with other systems and became the figurehead of capoeira purists. Throughout his career he dedicated himself to preserving the African traditions in capoeira and was revered by local intellectuals such as novelist Jorge Amado. To this day, many practitioners of the *Capoeira Angola* style pride themselves on practicing the more "African" of the two major styles. D'Aquino even reported occasionally hearing of *Angoleiros* referring to one another as "Africanos" in the 1980s (1983: 153), which indicates a close ideological association between the *Capoeira Angola* style and Africa, though I have never heard this form of address used. While Pastinha's leadership did not result in as many formal changes as did Bimba's, his contributions were equally important. His ability to convene many masters under the banner of a single school made it possible for the *Capoeira Angola* style to be seen as a coherent school despite the multiplicity of styles it embraced. Had he not done this, it is very likely that *Capoeira Regional* would have become the hegemonic form of capoeira. Indeed, at one point, that future seemed almost assured.

## Institutionalization and Globalization

For many years, *Capoeira Regional* academies were far more prevalent than *Capoeira Angola* academies, and after the mid 1960s, Pastinha's academy may have been the only one dedicated to *Capoeira Angola* (Taylor 2007: 110). The first national Brazilian capoeira meeting was held in 1968 and showed a clear preference for the *Capoeira Regional* style. The 1970s marked a period of retrenchment for *Capoeira Angola,* particularly when Pastinha was forced to vacate his academy in the historical district so that a restaurant could be established in his facility. Mestre Pastinha passed away in 1981, impoverished and alone after being forced to give up this source of livelihood.

The historic district of Salvador known as the Pelourinho has been a contested site in the midst of Bahia's tourism development, especially as local authorities sought recognition as a UNESCO world heritage site. The UNESCO guidelines provide a framework for local communities to articulate what it is that makes their local attractions valuable enough to be considered part of our world heritage (Collier 2006). While on the one hand this can be an excellent way of preserving cultural traditions that might otherwise crumble in the face of modernization and globalization, it also implies that other traditions are not worthy of preservation, an ethnocentric attitude with which many anthropologists, myself included, would be uncomfortable.

Designating a place such as Pelourinho as a world heritage site can also have other unintended consequences. The Bahian Institute of Artistic and Cultural Patrimony (IPAC), which is responsible for the preservation or "regeneration" of the historic district of Pelourinho, "had in the 1990s expelled thousands of residents and transformed their homes into boutiques, museums, and NGO headquarters" (Collier 2006: 280). In other words, they prioritized the commodification of history and culture as a tourist attraction above the well-being of local residents, most of whom were poor Afro-Brazilians. By forcing the poor, Afro-Brazilians from their homes, they further marginalized the very population that had historically been responsible for creating and maintaining the traditions that they wanted to showcase to foreign guests and wealthier domestic tourists. As Collier writes, "the rapid removal to distant slums of thousands of working people from a historical center in which they were able to survive in ways impossible on Salvador's periphery appears catastrophic" (2006: 290). Today, the Pelourinho, which is ironically named for an old pillory where masters sent their slaves to be whipped, features shops, hotels, restaurants, and capoeira academies that are housed in restored, pastel-colored colonial buildings.

After Mestre Pastinha's departure from the capoeira scene, *Capoeira Regional* became more visible and prevalent throughout Brazil. This was in part thanks to the new military government that assumed power in 1964. The military government stressed the importance of sports and physical education, and they took an interest in unifying the diverse capoeira groups that had emerged since the end of its prohibition (Talmon-Chvaicer 2008: 123). The Programa Nacional de Capoeira, organized by the military at the end of the 1960s, and the Departamento Especial de Capoeira, organized in 1972 by the Federaço Brasileira de Pugilismo, were two attempts at unification. These organizations dictated objective standards such as the levels of advancement within capoeira and a belt system to indicate rank based upon the colors of the Brazilian flag (Talmon-Chvaicer 2008: 123). Their efforts were largely unsuccessful, and today great variation exists between different academies.

Attempts at codifying capoeira so that individuals can compete in formal tournaments have also had unimpressive results. Attempting to turn capoeira into a sport with a standardized system for awarding points, as was done in the 1960s and 1970s, ignores much of the inherent complexity within the art, such as its theatricality and cunning (Downey 2002). Changing the scoring rubric to focus more on the aesthetic qualities of capoeira has just led to new problems within the realm of competition-capoeira. This newer model has resulted in competitors emphasizing acrobatic flourishes at the expense of interaction between the players, which is just as antithetical to capoeira's true nature as is a purely agonistic variant (Downey 2002).

By the 1970s, issues of legitimacy already plagued the capoeira community. In Rio de Janeiro, a board of examiners made surprise visits to capoeira academies in order to evaluate the teacher and his academy.[6] By 1984, an official capoeira organization, the Cariocan Confederation, began operating in Rio, and within three years, there were rumblings that nonconfederation teachers should be banned from teaching (Taylor 2007: 133). Despite many such attempts at unifying capoeira, this remains a contentious issue today, and few federations have had any success.

Despite going into a short period of quasidormancy, increased activism for black rights in the latter half of the military regime created a moment in which *Capoeira Angola* began to be seen as a tool of social consciousness. It was at this point that Anglophone notions of blackness began to significantly influence Brazilian notions of blackness. During the repressive military regime, it was safer to emulate the cultural artifacts produced by the black movement in the United States, like Motown soul music and "Afro" haircuts, than it was to explicitly protest racial and class issues (Taylor 2007). The civil rights movement in the United States and the decolonization of many African countries created the right climate for Brazil to establish like-minded institutions such as the Centro de Cultura e Arte Negra (Black Culture and Art Center) in São Paulo in 1971, the Grupo Negro (Black Group), and the *bloco afro* Ile Aiye (an all-black performance group) in Salvador in 1974, the Sociedade de Intercambio Brasil-Africa (The Brazil-Africa Exchange Society) in Rio in 1974, and the Instituto de Pesquisa das Culturas

Negras (Research Institute of Black Cultures) in Rio in 1975 (Taylor 2005: 120). It also created a climate in which the revitalization of *Capoeira Angola* would almost inevitably have a black pride agenda. The *Capoeira Angola* renaissance took place in the 1980s and is largely attributed to the work of Mestre Moraes and his Grupo de Capoeira Angola Pelourinho (GCAP).

The 1970s saw the expansion of capoeira beyond the borders of Brazil. *Capoeira Regional* was the first style to take root abroad, but in the intervening years, *Capoeira Angola* too has gained a foothold outside of Brazil. The Brazilian capoeira instructors who traded Brazil's beaches for chillier climates have not been part of a permanent exodus. Rather, they have instituted an international network in which foreign *capoeiristas* visit Brazil, and Brazilian teachers make short sojourns to teach abroad. In 1994, Mestre Moraes and his GCAP organized "The First International Encounter" for *capoeiristas*. This event brought North American and European *capoeiristas* to Salvador, the epicenter of the capoeira community, where they encountered legendary *mestres* and local *capoeiristas* (Assunção 2005: 189). Today, international encounters such as these are extremely common with one being advertised nearly every month in the guidebook that the tourism board in Salvador distributes to visitors. International capoeira encounters also take place throughout the rest of the world. These events create a sense that the very diverse and geographically decentralized capoeira community is, in fact, a closely knit group with similar goals and experiences (Miller 2010).

## Capoeira in Popular Culture

Many individuals outside of Brazil gain their first exposure to capoeira through popular culture. Film is one such avenue. In 1993, a film titled *Only the Strong* featured an ex-military capoeira expert who used his knowledge of this martial art to engage troubled Miami youth in more productive avenues of conflict resolution and community-building (Lettich et al. 1993). To play *Catwoman* with all of the leonine grace that the namesake character deserves, Halle Berry studied capoeira, and many of the movements were incorporated into the 2004 film (Kane 2004). And try as I might, I cannot erase the memory of Dustin Hoffman's intentionally pitiful enactment of capoeira moves in the comedy *Meet the Fockers,* in which Hoffman's use of an "exotic" and esoteric art highlights how different his character is from the more pragmatic, ex-CIA agent played by Robert De Niro (Gilenna 2004). A more serious portrayal can be found in the film *Besouro,* which tells the story of Manuel Henrique Pereira, a Brazilian man whose capoeira prowess in the early 1900s has been mythologized by practitioners (Andrade 2009).

Television programs have also added to the visibility of capoeira outside of Brazil. In the National Geographic program *Deadly Arts,* black-belt Josette D Normandeau travels the world to study six different martial forms: capoeira in Brazil, *muay thai* (Thai boxing) in Thailand, karate in Okinawa, aikido in Japan, *kalaripayattu* in India, and savate in France. While in Brazil, Normandeau not only studies the form of capoeira, but also explores the culture of Salvador, learns how capoeira is linked to the history of Brazilian slavery, and experiences firsthand the deceitful trickery that is the hallmark of capoeira (Kumar). More recently, the National Geographic program *Fight Science,* analyzed the biomechanics of several different martial arts to measure their efficacy (Brenkus and Stern 2010). Though not the fastest or most powerful, capoeira was deemed by the scientists on this program to be the most efficient, generating enough force from a single kick to potentially stop an opponent's heart (Brenkus and Stern 2010). Capoeira has also been featured in video games like *Street Fighter III, Rumble Fighter,* and the *Tekken* series with the memorable character Eddie Gordo.

In addition to these mass media portrayals, there are a number of instructional videos, web sites, and books available for purchase. However, as I discuss in chapter 7, these instructional aids are generally not seen as legitimate sources of knowledge. Although popular culture is expanding the pool of potential capoeira students, only a small percentage of those who encounter capoeira in this way will become true converts to its lifestyle. As I demonstrate in the rest of the book, this demands extreme dedication and fulfillment of one's obligations as a member of a larger community.

## Conclusion

Long gone are the days when everyone in the capoeira community knew one another personally, if, in fact, those days ever existed. Now the capoeira community is fractured geographically and linguistically with monolingual Russians and Japanese being as committed to their practice as Portuguese-speaking Brazilians. This community is so large that most members will never have face-to-face interactions. Nonetheless, the capoeira social field functions as an imagined community (Anderson 1983). Members feel a connection with one another because they share a corpus of stories, songs, and movements.

The prevalence of the Internet throughout the capoeira community intensifies this feeling of shared participation with web sites, chat rooms, and social networking sites like capoeiraespaco.com and Facebook facilitating the flow of information about capoeira across the world. These conversations are certainly eased by the use of a common language like Portuguese, but even this is not entirely necessary. Multilingual imagined communities have been known to transcend speech communities if they have a shared set of symbols. For example, the *berimbau* is a ubiquitous symbol instantly identifiable by members of the capoeira community. However, even this is not entirely necessary for an imagined community to exist on the Internet. Today, *capoeiristas* who speak different languages can achieve at least some degree of exchange by copying and pasting content from Internet sites and chat rooms into a web-based translation program.

Foreign *capoeiristas* take pride in being part of this commitment system, knowing that others care about the same things that they do. Being part of a commitment system means seeing oneself "in terms of a system of symbols that [is shared] with other believers," which enables an individual to feel a connection with others who have similarly appropriated these symbols (Stromberg 1986: 98). Commitment to a cultural system encourages cohesion and solidarity within the group; however, it does not mean that every member of the community will adhere to an identical belief system (Stromberg 1986: 98). As I argue in subsequent chapters, the solidarity of the capoeira commitment system is undercut by individuals' membership in competing identity groups like their race, nationality, and gender.

The present landscape of the capoeira community would most likely be unrecognizable to the African slaves who first brought its seeds to the New World. Today, it is officially recognized as part of Brazil's national patrimony; then it was a dangerous sign portending rebellion. Today it provides income to thousands, most significantly to those who were chastised as vagrants in an earlier era. These turning points have altered the terrain of the social field, and the rules of the game must be shifted in accord with these changes. Now women are tolerated, and sometimes even celebrated, in the *roda*. Foreigners, whether this is good or bad, are starting to write capoeira songs in languages other than Portuguese and are beginning to assume leadership roles within the field. I marvel at the fact that these radical changes have taken place in a mere century; I also bring a healthy dose of cynicism, asking if it is really possible for foreigners to exert such agency in a world that has long been the preserve of Afro-Brazilian men.

## Notes

1. Scholars of capoeira differ in terms of how much importance they attribute to the various instruments in the orchestra. In my experience with both FICA and Estrela do Norte, for example, the *atabaque* is of far more importance than D'Aquino (1983) noted in her work, which may be related to our different samples or the changes that accompanied the resurgence of *Capoeira Angola* after her study was completed. Whereas Lewis reports never having seen the *reco-reco* used outside of Brazil (1992: 135), this instrument was a regular part of our orchestra in the Indiana group with which I trained.

2. Stephens and Delamont (2013) found that while some British students take the initiative to learn about the various religious traditions present in Brazilian culture, diasporic capoeira is largely areligious in that while some terms from *Candomblé* may be used within the capoeira lexicon, its ideology is rarely invoked directly. This contrasts with what I encountered in my own training as a member of an *Capoeira Angola* group in the United States. Members of our group tended to be quite aware of *Candomblé* and its associations with capoeira. These differences are likely attributable to the fact that Stephens and Delamont have primarily worked with *Capoeira Regional* groups in the United Kingdom, whereas my work focuses on what they call "purist Angola groups" (Stephens and Delamont 2013).

3. Though this metaphor is generally taken for granted by most *capoeiristas*, the questions are the attack moves, and the answers are either escape moves or counterattacks.

4. Lewis argues that recent developments in capoeira, primarily the new hybrid style that he calls *capoeira atual* (though my consultants called it *Capoeira Contemporânea*), have been

significantly influenced by foreign *capoeiristas*. He claims that as U.S. *Capoeira Regional* players started traveling to Brazil to experience capoeira in its original context, they encountered the *Capoeira Angola* style and began integrating movements from this style into their repertoires. He argues that "this was especially true of black players, who saw in the *Angola* style a continuity with their own African heritage" (Lewis 1992: 65). While not an implausible hypothesis, and the U.S. black identity movement has had an effect on many people throughout the diaspora, the spread of *Capoeira Angola*, or elements of it, outside of Brazil cannot be solely attributed to this phenomenon. Today there are many groups in the United States and elsewhere throughout the world that are learning *Capoeira Angola*, not the hybrid form, from Brazilian teachers who have never played *Capoeira Regional* and who advocate what they see as the more traditional form of capoeira with evangelical zeal.

5. Today colored belts have replaced these scarves, though *Capoeira Angola* academies have resisted their use.

6. At this time, capoeira classes were almost exclusively taught by males. Throughout this work, the unqualified use of the masculine pronoun is intended to reference the hegemonic dominance of males in capoeira. While some females are attaining *mestre* status, they are still the exception rather than the rule and are far more common in the *Capoeira Regional* style than in the *Capoeira Angola* tradition, which is the focus of this book.

## Works Cited

"A Alegria Fez Praca no Largo da Conceicao." 1948. *A Tarde.*

"A Inaguracao do Parque Oden." 1936. *A Tarde.*

Almeida, Bira. 1986. *Capoeira, a Brazilian Art Form: History, Philosophy and Practice.* Berkeley, CA: North Atlantic Books.

Anderson, Benedict R. 1983. *Imagined Communities: Reflections on the Origin and Spread of Nationalism.* London: Verso.

Andrade, Patrícia and João Daniel Tikhomiroff. *Besouro.* Directed by João Daniel Tikhomiroff. Brazil: Phase 4 Films. 2009.

Assunção, Matthias Röhrig. 2005. *Capoeira: The History of an Afro-Brazilian Martial Art, Sport in the Global Society.* London: Routledge.

Brenkus, John, and Mickey Stern. 2010. *Fight Science: Stealth Fighters.* National Geographic.

Brough, Edward Luna. 2006. "Jogo de Mandinga (Game of Sorcery): A Preliminary Investigation of History, Tradition, and Bodily Practice in Capoeira Angola," MA thesis. Ohio State University.

Browning, Barbara. 1995. *Samba: Resistance in Motion, Arts and Politics of the Everyday.* Bloomington: Indiana University Press.

Capoeira, Nestor. 2006. *A Street-Smart Song: Capoeira Philosophy and Inner Life.* Berkeley: North Atlantic Books.

Collier, John. 2006. "'But What If I Should Need to Defecate in Your Neighborhood, Madame?': Empire, Redemption, and the 'Tradition of the Oppressed' in a Brazilian World Heritage Site." *Cultural Anthropology* 23 (2): 279–328.

Cruz, José Luiz Oliveira. 2006. *Historias e Estorias da Capoeiragem.* Bahia: P555 edições.

D'Aquino, Iria. 1983. "Capoeira: Strategies for Status, Power and Identity," PhD dissertation. University of Illinois.

Downey, Greg. 2002. "Domesticating an Urban Menace: Reforming Capoeira as a Brazilian National Sport." *The International Journal of the History of Sport* 19 (4): 1–32.

Downey, Greg. 2005. *Learning Capoeira: Lessons in Cunning from an Afro-Brazilian Art.* Oxford: Oxford University Press.

Freyre, Gilberto. 1955. *Manifesto Regionalista de 1926.* Rio de Janeiro: Ministério da Educação e Cultura, Serviço de Documentação.

Gilenna, Greg, Mary Ruth Clarke, Jim Herzfeld, Marc Hyman, and John Hamburg. *Meet the Fockers.* Directed by Jay Roach. Los Angeles: Universal Studios. 2004.

Green, Thomas A. 2003a. "Sense in Nonsense: The Role of Folk History in the Martial Arts." In *Martial Arts in the Modern World,* edited by Thomas A Green and Joseph R Svinth, 1-12. Westport, CT: Praeger.

Green, Thomas A. 2003b. "Surviving the Middle Passage: Traditional African Martial Arts in the Americas." In *Martial Arts in the Modern World,* edited by Thomas A Green and Joseph R Svinth, 129-148. Westport, CT: Praeger.

Joseph, Janelle Beatrice. 2006. "Capoeira in Canada: Brazilian Martial Art, Cultural Transformation and the Struggle for Authenticity," MS thesis. University of Toronto.

Lettich, Sheldon, and Luis Esteban. 1993. *Only the Strong.* Directed by Sheldon Lettich. Los Angeles: Twentieth Century Fox.

Kane, Bob, Theresa Rebeck, John D. Brancato, Michael Ferris, John Rogers *Catwoman.* Directed by Jean-Christophe Comar. Los Angeles, CA: Warner Brothers, 2004. DVD.

Kumar, Ashkay, "Capoeira," YouTube video, 47:04, from a documentary televised by National Geographic Channel in 2004, posted by CapoeiraPassion, July 18, 2015, https://www.youtube.com/watch?v=vzEYwQa--i0.

Lewis, J Lowell. 1992. *Ring of Liberation: Deceptive Discourse in Brazilian Capoeira.* Chicago: University of Chicago Press.

MacAloon, John J. 1984. "Olympic Games and the Theory of Spectacle in Modern Societies." In *Rite, Drama, Festival, Spectacle: Rehearsals toward a Theory of Cultural Performance,* edited by John J MacAloon, 241–80. Philadelphia, PA: Institute for the Study of Human Issues.

Marion, Jonathan S. 2008. *Ballroom: Culture and Costume in Competitive Dance.* Oxford: Berg.

Marquese, Rafael de Bivar. 2006. "The Dynamics of Slavery in Brazil: Resistance, the Slave Trade and Manumission in the 17th to 19th Centuries." *Novos Estudos—CEBRAP* 74: 107–23.

Miller, Lauren. 2010. "Capoeira." In *Martial Arts in Global Perspective,* edited by Thomas A Green and Joseph R Svinth, 37-42. Santa Barbara, CA: ABC-CLIO.

Mwewa, Muleka, Marcus Aurélio Taborda de Oliveira, and Alexandre Fernandez Vaz. 2010. "Capoeira: Cultura do Corpo, Esquemas, Exportação Identitária." *Agora para la Educación Física y el Deporte* 12 (2): 151–62.

Reis, Leticia Vidor de Sousa. 2004. "Mestre Bimba e Mestre Pastinha: A Capoeira em Dois Estilos." In *Artes do Corpo,* edited by Vagner Gonçalves da Silva, 189-223. São Paulo: Selo Negro Edicoes.

Stephens, Neil, and Sara Delamont. 2013. "Mora Yemanja? Axe in Diasporic Capoeira Regional," In *The Diaspora of Brazilian Religions,* edited by C Rocha and MA Vasquez, 272-288, Leiden: Brill.

Stromberg, Peter G. 1986. *Symbols of Community: The Cultural System of a Swedish Church*. Tucson: The University of Arizona Press.

Talmon-Chvaicer, Maya. 2008. *The Hidden History of Capoeira: A Collision of Cultures in the Brazilian Battle Dance*. Austin: University of Texas Press.

Taylor, Gerard. 2005. *Capoeira: The Jogo de Angola from Luanda to Cyberspace*. Vol. 1. Berkeley, CA: North Atlantic Books.

Taylor, Gerard. 2007. *Capoeira: The Jogo de Angola from Luanda to Cyberspace*. Vol. 2. Berkeley, CA: North Atlantic Books.

Vianna, Hermano. 1999. *The Mystery of Samba: Popular Music and National Identity in Brazil*. Chapel Hill: The University of North Carolina Press.

# Chapter 2

# The Challenges of Teaching and Learning Capoeira Abroad

One of my consultants, a fairly advanced female *capoeirista* from England named Amity, was having drinks with her teacher one evening in a British pub. He is Afro-Brazilian and has been able to establish his academy in London thanks to his marriage to a British woman. Perhaps it was the alcohol or perhaps it was his way of venting some personal frustrations, but this man told Amity that she could not ever really understand capoeira if she was not black. Having awarded her several belts (markers of graduation), Amity's teacher clearly appreciated her skill and saw her as at least a semi-insider. At the same time, however, he also denied that she would be able to attain the highest levels of understanding because of her race. Most *capoeiristas* take a quite different stance, at least when speaking publically, but it raises the question of whether or not an outsider can ever become a real part of the capoeira community.

## Introduction

There are a number of words in *capoeiristas'* everyday vocabulary that index their interest in authenticity: real, genuine, actual, legit, true, pure, and so on. For example, I was told repeatedly that I would understand how capoeira really is when I got to Brazil. And while some of my interviewees disagreed with the assertion that there was a difference between authentic and inauthentic capoeira, they would also quickly point out that the street shows at tourist attractions like the Mercado Modelo were not real capoeira. This made me wonder why tourist capoeira was not considered real and why foreigners tended to have so much anxiety that they were not getting the "real deal" in their classes abroad. That so many *capoeiristas* would simultaneously deny the authentic/inauthentic dichotomy and then obsess over what was or was not "real" capoeira was puzzling to me. The conclusion to which I arrived was that the concepts of authenticity and legitimacy needed to be separated.

What I propose is approaching capoeira, or any community of practice (Lave and Wenger 1991) with contested standards of authenticity, from the position of legitimacy within an economy of authenticity. This approach involves identifying the different kinds of legitimacy markers that are valued in the community and asking how these categories relate to one another. This chapter first reviews some of the different scholarly approaches that have been taken to study authenticity and then articulates a four-stage process by which *capoeiristas* achieve legitimacy within this social field. I then turn to the issue of teachers' legitimacy, arguing that much of the anxiety non-Brazilian *capoeiristas* feel regarding their own standing is rooted in larger debates over who has the authority to present themselves as a *mestre*.

## The Slippery Slope of Legitimacy and Authenticity

One of the reasons that the concept of authenticity is so problematic is its typical association with stasis. When "authentic" is taken to mean unchanged or uncorrupted, protecting the authenticity of that item or practice often involves artificial preservation. The protectorates of authenticity can thus inadvertently stall the natural development of a cultural practice.

Badone argues that authenticity is "not an absolute value but rather ... a culturally and historically situated ideal that is believed to exist by individuals or groups of individuals in specific social settings" (2004: 182). Different audiences use different criteria for labeling something authentic, which helps to explain why there are so many definitions of authenticity (Armstrong 2004; Grazian 2004; Bruner 2005). Attributing authenticity to a person or practice is laden with emotion, often complicated by a lack of criteria by which to assess authenticity. Many have tried to rectify this scenario by either trying to define authenticity or listing the requisite qualities for someone to claim authenticity. In his book, *Culture and Authenticity*, anthropologist Charles Lindholm (2008) takes a comprehensive look at issues of authenticity and calls attention to the debates surrounding the processes used to verify authenticity. He argues that artistic works like paintings can be verified either scientifically or charismatically. The former technique has a feeling of certainty, yet it "undermines the charismatic aura" of the artwork. Charismatic authentication, based on the "feeling" one gets from a piece, may be more satisfying on an emotional level, but is also more contentious (Lindholm 2008). To apply this to the study of martial arts, having the appropriate lineage or credentials, like a belt, would be markers of scientific authenticity. Convincingly embodying the creative ethos of the martial art would be a marker of charismatic authenticity. But when examining the authenticity of performers, rather than the artifact of a performance, subjectivity and emotion are hard to avoid.

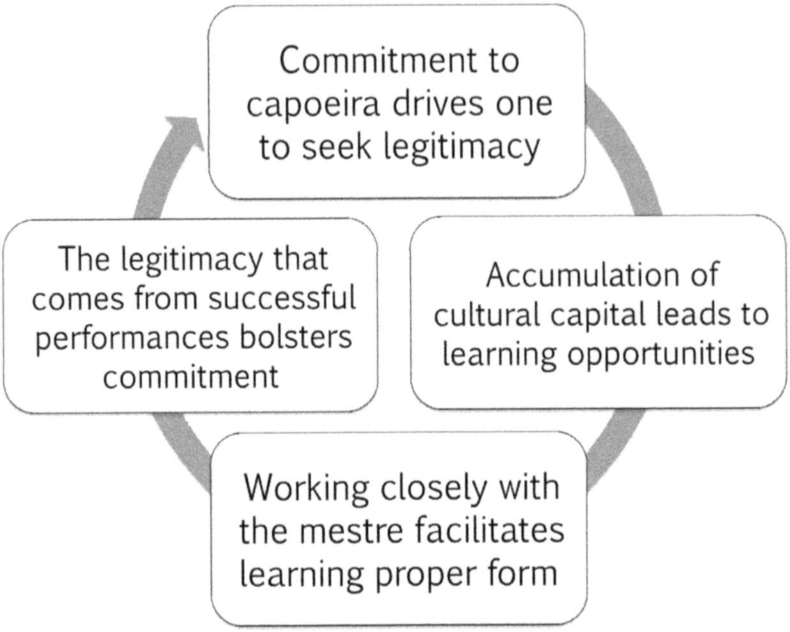

Commitment to capoeira drives one to seek legitimacy

The legitimacy that comes from successful performances bolsters commitment

Accumulation of cultural capital leads to learning opportunities

Working closely with the mestre facilitates learning proper form

*Figure 2.1 Model of Legitimacy Acquisition*

Authenticity is socially situated and contextually dependent (Peterson 2005), which opens the door for one's authenticity to be questioned even if he or she appears to fit the criteria. This necessitates moving beyond merely listing the traits that contribute to authenticity and trying to understand how people acquire and make use of their cultural capital, the nonmonetary assets that help one get ahead within a particular social field. Present typologies are inadequate for understanding the overall discussion of authenticity (Peterson 2005: 1092), which is why I instead propose a more dynamic model with four categories that together help explain how one goes about claiming legitimacy within capoeira.

Within this model, one's deep commitment to capoeira is what initially motivates his or her quest for legitimacy in the eyes of the community. Within capoeira, an individual's ability to claim formal legitimacy is dependent upon his or her relationship with a *mestre*. This relationship will be facilitated if one amasses enough cultural capital to subvert the mass-class style of instruction that has come to dominate in popular capoeira academies. This cultural capital may come from a combination of two sources: traditional cultural capital that is associated with inborn traits like race and nationality or charismatic cultural capital that is dependent upon one's individual characteristics like attitude and humility. Working closely with the *mestre* increases the likelihood that the student will be able to learn the nuance of capoeira's form, an issue to which I return to in chapter

7. Successfully executing this form increases the performer's legitimacy within the eyes of the community at large, which reinforces his or her commitment to capoeira and perpetuates the cycle.

I use the term authenticity in reference to an intangible essence attributed to people, performances, or works of art while reserving the term legitimacy for the strategic jockeying for position within a social field. In this sense, authenticity is a judgment call most often made across social boundaries. For example, lay audiences who do not understand the nuance of capoeira might judge the authenticity of one performer over another based on superficial and stereotypical characteristics. Legitimacy, on the other hand, is a judgment call made within the boundaries of a social field. Because insiders understand the rules of the game, they are in a better position to determine whether or not one is a legitimate participant.

Legitimacy is the result of centripetal movement within a social field. The ultimate marker of authenticity is earning a title like *treinel* (teacher), *contramestre* (assistant *mestre*), or *mestre*, but only if the title is awarded by someone who is seen as having the authority to do so (i.e., a well-respected *mestre*). The legitimacy of an individual, however, is apparent in everyday practices. An individual with a high degree of legitimacy will have his or her innovations accepted as purposeful, effective, and beautiful. Lower level markers of legitimacy include increased duties within the group, like leading class or being allowed to play the most important instruments during a performance, and close association with the teacher both inside and outside the academy.

## Questions of the Teacher's Authenticity and Legitimacy

The global capoeira boom has created many economic opportunities for Brazilian *capoeiristas* wanting to live and teach abroad. However, globalization has intensified debates over who is considered a real *capoeirista* with the authority to teach abroad (see De Campos Rosario, Stephens, and Delamont 2010; see also Wesolowski 2012). This is primarily a judgment of one's authenticity. When novices abroad do not have the context for evaluating legitimacy, they often evaluate a teacher's authenticity based on whether he or she fits their stereotypical notion of a *capoeirista*.

Teachers bolster their authenticity by promoting their real and/or imagined connections with the Brazilian homeland (see Wesolowski 2012). For example, the first capoeira instructors in Canada were not necessarily professional performers or educators, but rather migrants with "overt" markers of Brazilian identity that were sought out by Canadians interested in exotic lifestyles (Joseph 2008: 198). However, these men were then later displaced by more highly trained *capoeiristas* who arrived specifically to teach capoeira, a much different motivation than the first wave of teachers (Joseph 2008: 198). The second wave of teachers were more legitimate in the sense that their training had allowed them to move into a more central position within the capoeira social field than had the original teachers who relied primarily on overt markers of Brazilianness. This does not mean, however, that stereotypical markers of authenticity have ceased to be important. For example, Stephens and Delamont (2006) have found that teachers in Britain who are not of African descent make it a goal to tan their skin, which is an interesting strategy to compensate for their lack of stereotypical markers of authenticity. However, as students outside of Brazil become savvier, a teacher's success abroad is largely dependent upon a combination of having the right lineage, which is a marker of legitimacy, and having stereotypical markers of authenticity (i.e., being an Afro-Brazilian man).

For teachers, lineage refers not only to the *mestre(s)* with which one trained, but also to the manner in which he or she was granted permission to teach abroad. Because there is no licensing requirement for capoeira teachers abroad, theoretically anyone who wants to promote himself or herself as a teacher can do so; however, a teacher is seen as more legitimate if he or she has the backing of a well-respected *mestre* in Brazil. This issue is at the root of concerns over foreign *capoeiristas'* legitimacy. If the community cannot control the quality of the *mestres* going out to teach in other parts of the world, then it is unlikely that their students will be unquestionably accepted when they journey to Brazil. This was made very clear at one of the *rodas* I observed when a well-respected *mestre* asked two of the foreign students who their *mestre* was and then waved his hands dismissively saying he did not know who that was but anyone worth training with would be one of his students.

Although the Brazilian government has encouraged the licensure of domestic capoeira teachers (see Wesolowski 2012), in actual practice, each *mestre* judges for himself when his students have become skilled enough to begin using the title of *mestre*. In general, an individual is not recognized as a *mestre* until he has trained for twenty to twenty-five years (see Stephens and Delamont 2010). However, some *mestres* award their students a *mestre* title of their own much earlier, around the ten-year mark. Still other *capoeiristas* claim the title of *mestre* without the official blessing of their own teacher. Frequently, this reflects a schism between the teacher and the student. For example, the three *mestres* of FICA broke away from Mestre Moraes, the leader of GCAP to form their own organization. When asked who made them *mestres,* they respond that it was through capoeira. In other words, their reputation within the capoeira community is so strong that they were able to claim this title for themselves without having their legitimacy called into question. Others who take this approach, however, may be mocked and dismissed as frauds if they have not achieved the same degree of legitimacy within the community.

Sometimes *mestres* will baptize their protégés with this title just prior to their departure for the United States or Europe. This timing could be related to a number of factors. First, it may not be wise for the *mestre* to graduate his student while the apprentice still lives in Brazil because this could introduce a new competitor if the younger *mestre* opts to open his own academy. On the other hand, the granting of a title just before one leaves Brazil may be given as a gift to bolster the student's credibility when he or she goes abroad to teach (Taylor 2007: 237). In this case, the titling is more about pragmatics than it is about indicating their attainment of the skill set a *mestre* should have. In other cases, the receipt of a title in this manner may reflect a monetary arrangement between *mestre* and apprentice (Taylor 2007: 237). It is not uncommon for a *mestre* to earn remittances from his students even after they have gone abroad and set up their own academies.

Not all teachers abroad have been given approval from a recognized *mestre*. By the early 1980s, the capoeira community already was dealing with the issue of what D'Aquino calls "pseudo-*mestres*," which she defines as "individuals who have adopted the title of *mestre* to themselves but who do not merit it" (1983: 89). She points to the performers at the tourist market known as the Mercado Modelo as an example of these individuals who are widely disparaged within the community. Though many of these performers are quite skilled, their performances do not conform to the ritual expectations of a *roda*. Instead, they focus on performing dramatic acrobatic flourishes and frequently interrupt their "games" to pose with tourists.

Now that capoeira has become a global phenomenon, there is an additional class of self-made *mestres* who clearly lack community support. "VARIG *mestre*" is a disparaging term that my consultants applied to *capoeiristas* who begin calling themselves *mestres* when they leave Brazil (see also Wesolowski 2012). VARIG is the name of the national airline, which is the site of these "*mestres*" autograduation. These individuals assume the title without the official blessing of their teachers because of the cache associated with it. At this point in the globalization of capoeira, migrants know that their potential pool of students is savvy enough to want their teachers to be "real" *mestres*. When I asked them about the authenticity of capoeira outside of Brazil, rather than disparaging non-Brazilians who try but fall short in their performances of capoeira, most of the Brazilian *capoeiristas* focused their critiques on these teachers because they are cheapening the title of *mestre*. These critical attitudes are widely spread throughout the capoeira community (Almeida 1986; Assunção 2005; Downey 2005; Taylor 2007).

Leaving Brazil before one receives the title of *mestre* is a risky endeavor, even if that individual, who is generally at the rank of *contramestre* or *treinel* (one and two steps below *mestre,* respectively), has his or her *mestre*'s permission. If these individuals sever ties with their *mestre* once they establish their own academy abroad, it is questionable whether or not these individuals will be able to continue progressing within the field. Such individuals may get stuck at the *contramestre* level despite their great skill in playing and teaching capoeira. In a scenario such as this, one course of action is to initiate a relationship with a different *mestre* and serve a term of apprenticeship before asking for the title. However, this might involve unwanted obligations or cause tension between the new *mestre* and the one from whom the *contramestre* sought independence. It is also conceivable that the *contramestre* could be elevated to the role of *mestre* by the community, as was the case with the FICA *mestres*. As his students and others in the local community recognize his authority and expertise, they might begin calling him *mestre*. However, with the controversy surrounding self-titled *mestres,* it remains to be seen whether or not the Brazilian capoeira community will recognize the promotions made by the capoeira community abroad in the same way that they recognize the leaders of FICA.

There is little consensus in the capoeira community about how to solve this problem. Nestor Capoeira, who has written several books on capoeira and has taught both in Brazil and abroad, asserts that an authoritative confederation "would be the only way to legitimize *capoeira*" (Capoeira 2006: 98–99). Yet he recognizes that this would run counter to the decentralized nature of capoeira, which is one of the main reasons it was able to survive persecution during the colonial period and early days of Brazil's independence (Capoeira 2006: 98–99). Because authority in capoeira was so dispersed, it was resistant to governmental oppression, operating underground until the social climate was more amenable to its growth.

Many *mestres* in Brazil today are well-respected cultural figures who have been invited to teach in schools and universities and whose events are promoted in official tourism brochures. However, the taint of the *malandro* has not been entirely eradicated from capoeira, with VARIG *mestres* being its latest incarnation. The VARIG *mestre* is the modern-day equivalent of the old *malandro* who bent the rules of society in order to survive. Yet rather than admiring this win-at-all-costs attitude that is prized within the context of the *roda,* the capoeira community remains skeptical of the work they are doing abroad.

The problems that *mestres* face abroad are not always about their lineage. Some *mestres* teaching abroad will also have to contend with non-Brazilians' stereotypes about what a "real" *capoeirista* looks like. Remember my earlier point that judgments about authenticity are often made across social boundaries by relatively uneducated outsiders who operate on stereotypes. This is the case with many foreigners who make snap judgments about a Brazilian teacher based on the color of his skin. As discussed in depth in chapter 5 being Afro-Brazilian often carries a certain cache for outsiders unfamiliar with the complex history of capoeira and the nuance of its form. For example, Mestre Preguiça, who has taught capoeira in the San Francisco area for twenty-five years, found a great deal of acceptance for Brazilian culture. However, his greatest challenge in being accepted as a capoeira instructor was the fact that he is not black (Portela 2008).

Most *capoeiristas* also expect their teachers to be Brazilian. De Campos Rosario, Stephens, and Delamont have stressed that in the United Kingdom, reminding students of their nationality is an important way for Brazilian teachers to underscore their "authenticity" (2010: 104). The teacher with whom they worked in Tolnbridge once declared, "*I'm* your teacher, *I'm* Brazilian" (De Campos Rosario,

Stephens, and Delamont 2010: 105). This was a statement both of his authority and his authenticity, the latter being necessary to repair challenges to the former incurred when several of his students had been taking classes with other teachers. By conjoining these two statements, he implies that anyone who is not Brazilian is not worthy of being considered a capoeira teacher.

Non-Brazilians who presume to have enough legitimacy within the capoeira social field to market themselves as teachers are often subjected to a great deal of criticism, both by Brazilians and by other foreigners. Whereas a novice foreigner might be treated as something of a novelty or praised for at least trying a new art, non-Brazilian teachers are rarely afforded any such indulgences. One possible interpretation of this is that nationality is more entwined with legitimacy for foreigners who want to teach capoeira versus those who simply want to play capoeira. One of my interview subjects told me about a French man who decided to dedicate his life to capoeira. He trained constantly, traveled to Brazil, and quit his job to teach capoeira. The Brazilian *capoeiristas*, however, cruelly teased him and refused to accept him because no matter how hard he tries to act like a Brazilian, he will always be French.

Various interview subjects told me they felt that there existed a level beyond which foreigners would not be permitted to advance. An American man named Cary, for instance, taught capoeira in Ireland for a few years. For him, visiting Brazil was intertwined with his interest in teaching. He said that in his group there is an unspoken rule that non-Brazilians need to visit Brazil before being able to teach. However, he said he had also heard of some *mestres* who will not graduate a foreigner up to the level where he or she would be able to teach on their own. This reluctance makes some wonder why *mestres* would bother teaching foreigners at all if they thought there was a limit on what they could accomplish. Economic incentive provides the most obvious answer to the outsider, but most foreign *capoeiristas* who visit Brazil treat their practice like a calling and the monetary relationship between teacher and student is unlikely to be their primary motivation for teaching.

## Conclusion

When capoeira was first introduced to Europe and the United States, students were not yet savvy enough to evaluate a teacher based on his, or more rarely her, legitimacy. Therefore, they relied on stereotypical markers of the teacher's authenticity, mainly those that indexed the teacher's relationship to Brazil and/or the African diaspora. Some of these teachers were no doubt highly qualified; others were not. Today *mestres* back in Brazil, as well as some of the savvier students abroad, are invested in making sure that teachers are legitimate and can provide evidence that they have moved to a central position within the capoeira social field. However, the tradition of autograduation continues, which leads some Brazilians to dismiss the quality of capoeira instruction taking place abroad.

The legitimacy of self-titled *mestres* is an important issue for the capoeira community in general, but non-Brazilian *capoeiristas'* tend to be more concerned with their own legitimacy. Sometimes, this anxiety is expressed in terms of one's physical ability to practice a black, Brazilian art form. There is also the question of whether or not it is ethical for foreigners, regardless of skin color, to appropriate the art of a structurally disadvantaged group. Yet another issue is whether or not foreigners can ever truly understand the culture that gave rise to capoeira; though given the regional diversity of Brazil, a similar charge could be levied at *capoeiristas* from outside of Bahia. In the next chapter, I explain how travel can be used as a way to overcome some of these doubts, and in chapter 5, I take up the issue of whether or not one can be accepted by the local community if he or she does not fit the traditional characteristics of a *capoeirista*.

## Works Cited

Almeida, Bira. 1986. *Capoeira, a Brazilian Art Form: History, Philosophy and Practice*. Berkeley, CA: North Atlantic Books.

Armstrong, Edward G. 2004. "Eminem's Construction of Authenticity." *Popular Music and Society* 27 (3): 335–55.

Assunção, Matthias Röhrig. 2005. *Capoeira: The History of an Afro-Brazilian Martial Art, Sport in the Global Society*. London: Routledge.

Badone, Ellen. 2004. "Crossing Boundaries: Exploring the Borderlands of Ethnography, Tourism, and Pilgrimage." In *Intersecting Journeys: The Anthropology of Pilgrimage and Tourism*, edited by Ellen Badone and Sharon R Roseman, 180–90. Urbana: University of Illinois Press.

Bruner, Edward M. 2005. *Culture on Tour*. Chicago: The University of Chicago Press.

Capoeira, Nestor. 2006. *A Street-Smart Song: Capoeira Philosophy and Inner Life*. Berkeley, CA: North Atlantic Books.

D'Aquino, Iria. 1983. "Capoeira: Strategies for Status, Power and Identity," PhD dissertation. University of Illinois.

De Campos Rosario, Claudio, Neil Stephens, and Sara Delamont. 2010. "'I'm Your Teacher, I'm Brazilian!'Authenticity and Authority in European Capoeira." *Sport, Education and Society* 15 (1): 103–20.

Downey, Greg. 2005. *Learning Capoeira: Lessons in Cunning from an Afro-Brazilian Art*. Oxford: Oxford University Press.

Grazian, David. 2004. "The Symbolic Economy of Authenticity in the Chicago Blues Scene." In *Music Scenes: Local, Translocal, and Virtual*, edited by Andy Bennett and Richard A Peterson, 31-47. Nashville, TN: Vanderbilt University Press.

Joseph, Janelle Beatrice. 2008. "'Going to Brazil': Transnational and Corporeal Movements of a Canadian-Brazilian Martial Arts Community." *Global Networks* 8 (2): 194–213.

Lave, Jean, and Etienne Wenger. 1991. *Situated Learning: Legitimate Peripheral Participation*. New York: Cambridge University Press.

Lindholm, Charles. 2008. *Culture and Authenticity*. Malden, MA: Blackwell Publishing.

Peterson, Richard A. 2005. "In Search of Authenticity." *Journal of Management Studies* 42 (5): 1083–98.

Portela, Maira. 2008. "Lingua da Capoeira." *Correio da Bahia,* 5 May.

Stephens, Neil, and Sara Delamont. 2006. "Samba no Mar: Bodies, Movement and Idiom in Capoeira," *In Body/Embodiment: Symbolic Interaction and the Sociology of the Body,* edited by Dennis Waskul and Phillip Vannani, 109-122. Hampshire: Ashgate Publishing Limited.

Taylor, Gerard. 2007. *Capoeira: The Jogo de Angola from Luanda to Cyberspace.* Vol. 2. Berkeley, CA: North Atlantic Books.

Wesolowski, Katya. 2012. "Professionalizing Capoeira: The Politics of Play in Twenty-First-Century Brazil." *Latin American Perspectives* 39 (2): 82–92.

# Chapter 3

# Travel as a Way to Overcome Doubts

In the low lighting of the film studio, I could barely see where I was going. Our silhouettes danced across the canvas backdrop with more grace that I actually thought myself to possess. The game became faster and faster with our bodies spinning and twirling in perfect time until the next pair took the floor and displaced us. They played for just a minute or two before our teacher interrupted. Not everyone can play so fast, he admonished, just the advanced students or Lauren, she has been to Brazil. I did not necessarily think that I was advanced enough to play fast, but I did have another marker of distinction. I had been to Brazil. I had firsthand experience in the cradle of capoeira, a point that was regularly remarked upon after I returned from my fieldwork. Travel, I had learned, is an important way for *capoeiristas* to augment their cultural capital.

## Introduction

In this chapter, I describe various types of travel that help an individual claim a more central position within the capoeira social field. I begin by describing domestic travel, primarily short-term trips to train with visiting Brazilian teachers at workshops, though this category also includes trips made by individuals who seek out *mestres* at other academies in their region in order to acquire expertise they cannot achieve at home. The next category of travel I address is the recreational trip to Bahia. This type of travel exposes foreigners to various manifestations of Afro-Brazilian culture like capoeira and *Candomblé*. The majority of travelers in this category are non-*capoeiristas*, though some *capoeiristas* do undertake this type of travel as well, especially if they are novices, feel intimidated by playing with local *capoeiristas*, or are unconcerned with augmenting their own legitimacy by virtue of training with a local academy. Non-Brazilian *capoeiristas*, however, are often critical of these tourists and are much more invested in being seen as legitimate by the local community. They are the ones who I label apprenticeship pilgrims and whose experiences are my primary concern in this text.

## Domestic Travel

When I first started working with the *capoeiristas* in Austin, the thing that struck me most was their intense focus on Brazil as the center of their practice. Despite the fact that so many of them were living in a commune and swapping clothing with one another because they could not afford to buy new, they kept talking about the trips they wanted to make to Brazil. Even before the Great Recession of 2008, this did not seem feasible to me given their current financial situations. In reality, many of the *capoeiristas* who want to visit Brazil will never have the opportunity. For them, the next best thing is to train with a Brazilian teacher who is visiting their region, either by hosting that individual at their own academy or by traveling to a nearby city where that individual is offering a workshop (commonly referred to as *eventos*). Domestic capoeira travel of this nature shows that the individual is invested in developing personal and group networks within the greater capoeira community. It also provides exposure to more players and provides additional opportunities for challenge and growth.

In any given month, there are more than a dozen *eventos* offered worldwide. Most events span the length of a weekend and coincide with a visit from a Brazilian teacher. For example, an online announcement for a workshop taking place in April of 2013 announced that a particular teacher would be coming to the United States "for the first time" and encouraged students to come train with him by announcing his lineage (a student of Mestre Paulinho Sabia) and the amount of time he has trained capoeira (twenty-six years). It is significant that this teacher's credentials were so blatantly foregrounded in the advertisement because, as I explained in the previous chapter, many non-Brazilian students have become skeptical consumers of capoeira instruction. However, I think it is even more significant that this visit is announced as the teacher's first, implying both that this is an expected part of a Brazilian teacher's professional trajectory, and second, that it is the first of several visits he will make to the United States. There is also a sense of urgency; register now and you can be a part of this monumental moment. If and when this *mestre* becomes truly famous, the students in attendance can say, "I knew him when …." Opportunities such as these allow non-Brazilians to demonstrate their commitment to capoeira and begin developing an international network that simultaneously bolsters their legitimacy and lays the groundwork for potential visits to Brazil in the future. And, to avoid overlooking too obvious, attending a workshop provides an opportunity for them to enhance their skill set.

These events generally start with a *roda* on the first evening, which may or may not be open to the public. The subsequent days are packed with classes, most on capoeira, but Afro-Brazilian dance and percussion classes may also be offered. At an event that Estrela do Norte hosted in Indiana in 2008, students worked with a Brazilian choreographer to prepare a routine that included dances of the *orixás* and *maculele*, a martial form that involves sticks and "symbolises slaves dancing on the sugar plantations" (De Campos Rosario, Stephens, and Delamont 2010: 113). Capoeira events also commonly feature lectures, round tables, discussion sessions, or even screenings of documentary films on capoeira. These presentations generally converge upon themes like capoeira history and philosophy, though an area of emerging concern is globalization and the future of capoeira. One FICA-sponsored event that I attended with the members of Estrela do Norte explicitly took up the issue of women's growing role in capoeira (see chapter 5).

Workshops are important because they increase a *capoeirista*'s connection to the larger community. After several members of Estrela do Norte attended a conference with Mestre João Grande in Oberlin, Ohio, Mestre Iuri said, "at workshops you have a lot of fun, but you only remember about ten percent of what you learn." Though it is interesting to be exposed to a different teacher's way of performing capoeira, fixing new movement in a *capoeirista*'s repertoire is not the primary function of these events. Rather, interacting with other *capoeiristas* at an event like this gives shape to an otherwise vague sense belonging to this imagined community. Returning from one of these workshops, a fellow member of Estrela do Norte said, "I always knew I was part of the capoeira family, but until this weekend, I didn't know how I fit in." In the *roda*, players can see how their style differs from that of another group, and though most *Angoleiros* deny that this is important, they can see how their group compares with others in terms of skill. Participants also develop a better sense of the stylistic continuity between teachers in the same lineage. At the same time, however, the general ethos of celebration at these events contributes to a sense of community. Thus, it makes sense that my friend would have walked away with a better sense of how he belonged to the social field.

For *capoeiristas* who cannot travel to Brazil, taking advantage of workshops to make connections with the wider community is particularly important. Attending a capoeira event with a Brazilian *mestre* is the next best thing and can be used as a proxy for international travel. A member of Estrela do Norte said to me one evening, "let's face it, we're a long way from Brazil," but attending workshops with other capoeira groups "makes all of our groups stronger, we've got their support, they'll have our support." Not only does attending an event benefit the individual, but it also reinforces connections between groups. This kind of domestic travel sets up a system of reciprocity with other groups. Groups that host an event often feel a sense of obligation to attend subsequent events that are hosted by groups that attended their event. Because teachers working outside of Brazil will typically have fewer opportunities to work with their own *mestre* after leaving the country, these reciprocal relationships can be quite important to an individual's success abroad and should be the focus of more study.

A member of Estrela do Norte seconded this position saying, "that's definitely the nature of it, that's why it was created … we need to have connections with each other to keep *our* community strong." This student's emphasis on the word "our" is interesting and implies that there are a number of capoeira communities within the larger social field. He was explaining that because our group is so far from Brazil, both literally and figuratively, it takes extra effort to create coherence, and as the first comment suggests, groups on the periphery of the social field cannot take for granted that they will automatically have the support of Brazilian groups.

At these events, capoeira instructors that have not yet earned the title of *mestre* have an opportunity to strengthen their relationship with leaders in the field. A capoeira teacher has two primary sources of evidence to support his bid for becoming a *mestre,* whether officially through a teacher's blessing or informally through community support. The first is his own skill in the *roda.* As I heard time and again from my consultants in Brazil, and as I personally experienced, younger *mestres* and *contramestres* tend to play more vigorously in the *roda,* even with beginners, than do more established *mestres* because they are still trying to prove themselves.

The other way for a teacher to demonstrate his excellence is through his students' abilities. This primarily includes physical and musical skill, but may also include proper demonstrations of respect and knowledge about Brazilian culture. For example, when our group arrived late to a workshop session because we had just arrived in town, I was sent to apologize to the *mestre* in Portuguese because, at that time, I was the only student in the group who could do so. This action indicated our respect of the *mestre's* time and, perhaps more importantly, indicated that our group takes Brazilian culture seriously enough to spend time learning the language. Should the *contramestre* be seeking to establish an apprenticeship relationship with an established *mestre,* these events can be an important site for such relationships to be built.

For those *capoeiristas* who do not have the opportunity to attend a formal event, which can be quite costly when taking into account the registration fees, travel expenses, and opportunity costs of taking time off from work to travel, there is another option. Periodically attending classes at a nearby academy that are taught by a Brazilian instructor is another way for these *capoeiristas to* establish a connection with Brazil. Groups that are entirely composed of non-Brazilians without an established teacher are referred to as "study groups" within the FICA tradition. Participants in a study group may not have weekly access to a Brazilian teacher, but with reputable groups now in nearly every major American metropolis, it is not difficult to visit a Brazilian teacher from time to time. This kind of domestic travel allows *capoeiristas* to establish ties with the wider community and helps them feel like they are part of an extended family.

Occasionally, *capoeiristas* from other parts of the United States would visit our group in Bloomington. In one instance, the woman who visited us was explicit about traveling what she called "the domestic circuit," an extremely informal network of capoeira groups scattered about the country. She arrived unannounced, but members of the group quickly rallied to make her feel at home. Several of us went out to dinner with her after class, eager to talk about our group and to hear about her experiences. She even "couch-surfed" at the home of one of our members that night. A Brazilian teacher working in the United Kingdom identifies such acts of support for visiting *capoeiristas* as evidence of social cohesion and a strong commitment to one's identity as a *capoeirista* (De Campos Rosario, Stephens, and Delamont 2010: 111). A long-term member of Estrela do Norte compared traveling on this circuit with being like a tourist "but being inside the culture when you go," getting to experience "the real thing." For those who are able to do so, visiting other capoeira groups within their own country or region provides *capoeiristas* with "communities of belonging" through which "players are encouraged to network and to look within the group for support and friendship" (Joseph 2006: 4). Taking advantage of this informal network also allows *capoeiristas* to quickly access what Dean MacCannell (1976) calls the backspaces of a culture, where tourists often assume that authenticity resides.

## Recreational Trips to Brazil

While domestic travel is important for gaining expertise that one's group at home cannot provide and for building connections with other groups in the capoeira community, many *capoeiristas* want to visit the actual source of capoeira. Of course, they are not the only tourists who visit Bahia. This section explores the different ways that the "Africanness" of Bahia, which still resonates deeply in quotidian life, is presented to tourists. The individuals who undertake recreational trips to Brazil will have differing degrees of exposure to capoeira. While some will know nothing more about it than what they read in their guidebook, others may indeed be practitioners. However, the *capoeiristas* who are satisfied with recreational trips that do not include serious training tend to either be novices and/or unconcerned with gaining external validation for their legitimacy as *capoeiristas*.

Attending a *Candomblé* ceremony is often high on a tourist's list of desired activities. During 2008, I talked to one foreign couple, who were not *capoeiristas*, about the tour they had taken with an unlicensed tour guide they met in the Pelourinho district. He asked them if they would like to visit a *Candomblé* ceremonial center and then made a big show of interpreting the symbols that identify an otherwise nondescript building as a house of worship. They interpreted this as an indication that they had entered the backstage area of the culture, seeing something they would not have had access to otherwise. I chose not to destroy their fantasy by telling them that several well-established tour operators regularly take tourists to see *Candomblé* ceremonies at this location and others throughout the city.

In 2006, I spoke with a tour operator who organizes trips to visit *Candomblé* ceremonies. He considers himself a guardian of the *Candomblé* traditions, and because he himself practices the religion, he has a vested interest in making sure tourists behave appropriately. He is disgusted by tour guides who only take tourists to these events for the money and disrespect the religion by acting inappropriately. He also expressed disdain for the folklore shows that represent the *orixá* dances. He recognizes that they are putting on a show and may want to choreograph some dances representing *Candomblé* but takes issue with the dancers imitating possession on stage. He is concerned that tourists do not recognize the difference between the show and the ritual, leaving Salvador with a skewed perspective of his religion.

Another tour guide I interviewed in 2006 specializes in Afro-Brazilian cultural tourism and teaches a class that certifies tour guides to take tourists to *Candomblé* ceremonies. He has been involved with the tourism industry since he was nine years old. He had to start working at such an early age because his father was imprisoned during the military coup. He acknowledges that the information he gives his students on *Candomblé* is very basic because the religion is so complicated. Like the other individual I interviewed, he professes a deep respect for the culture and traditions of *Candomblé*. Perhaps the most interesting element of our conversation was his mention of how money is changing the traditions of both capoeira and *Candomblé*. He expressed the sentiment that when groups charge tourists for watching their rituals, they lose their meaning and become mere shows. He advocated instead taking tourists to local capoeira academies to observe weekly *rodas* and attending ceremonies that accept donations but do not charge a formal entrance fee. In other words, he thought that tourists should be steered away from religious rituals and toward more secular ones where their presence would be less polluting.

In Brazil today, capoeira exists simultaneously as a vital activity for many locals, especially poor children who claim it as a central part of their identity, and as a capitalistic venture with academies, tour agencies, and shopkeepers promoting their capoeira-related offerings to visitors. Capoeira has become big business in Brazil, especially in Bahia. This can be partially attributed to non-Brazilian *capoeiristas'* interest in visiting Bahia, but in truth, the trend began much earlier. This commodification of capoeira dates back to the emergence of the regionalism discourse by public intellectuals like Freyre. As soon as the public began to see capoeira as an expression of their cultural patrimony, it was quickly caught up in a tug of war between those who saw it as an uncommodifiable expression of authenticity and those who wanted to make a buck off of it if they could. At the same time that leftist university students in São Paulo were championing the practice of capoeira as the very embodiment of Brazilian authenticity (Assunção 2005: 178), entrepreneurs in Bahia were milking it as a tourist attraction.

Tour guides in Bahia began showcasing capoeira as early as the 1960s. In 1966, Mestre Pastinha took a group of his students to Africa to give a capoeira demonstration at the First World Festival of Black Art. This was a much-publicized event and a victory for those in the Africanist camp who put a high value on the African origins of capoeira. This trip is particularly significant considering that Pastinha learned capoeira from an African slave and was now given the opportunity to bring it back to its homeland. Following this event, visiting his academy became practically obligatory for tourists visiting Salvador (Lyrio 2007).

Within a generation, capoeira had gone from being a crime and mark of shame to a source of livelihood. Tourist interest in capoeira has not abated and continues to be one of the most important attractions in the city. In the Salvador airport, guests are often greeted at baggage claim by the sounds of the *berimbau* and two or three young men showing off their moves. Some of the phone booths in the historic downtown area have even been painted to resemble *berimbaus*. When Mestre Waldemar began decorating his *berimbaus* with all colors of the rainbow, this instrument became ubiquitous in tourist shops (Lyrio 2007). They are even produced in miniature, so they can be more easily transported in tourists' luggage. The colorful *berimbau* has now become a recognizable symbol of the city and features prominently on postcards, graffiti, and storefronts.

It is not uncommon to walk through the historic Pelourinho district and see groups of shirtless men in white capoeira pants halfheartedly playing the *berimbau,* showing off a few of their flashier kicks and flips, and then passing the *pandeiro,* using the upturned tambourine as a receptacle for tips. Guidebooks such as *Lonely Planet* (Green 2005: 432) often mention capoeira as a significant attraction in the city of Salvador and give a brief account of its origin myths. The *Lonely Planet* provides a much-abbreviated list of some of the academies where tourists can take classes with instructors that the author deems legitimate and then warns tourists away from the highly visible street acts I just described:

> Be wary of motley bands of hotshots playing capoeira on the Terreiro de Jesus. Not only can you see better capoeira elsewhere, but if you even so much as bat an eyelash in their direction, they will come scurrying across the plaza demanding a contribution. (Green 2005: 416)

In some ways, this caution is well founded, and I myself have been relentlessly hounded for tips. This street hustling was happening even in the 1980s, and D'Aquino (1983) found a direct correlation between the aggressiveness of street performers and the presence of foreign tourists, pointing out that markers of wealth like the expensive cameras carried by many tourists increased the performers' sense of relative deprivation. However, I believe that guidebooks such as *Lonely Planet* largely vilify these performers because they are staging authenticity. The author's suggestion that tourists should instead seek out instruction or observe performances at more formal academies reveals the book's bias toward a particular kind of authenticity. Ignoring the book's warning, I found the *capoeiristas* in the Terreiro de Jesus square to be a convivial bunch quite willing to share their stories. They even offered to buy me beer rather than the other way around, as is the expectation in most foreign/local interactions.

While chatting with these men in the plaza, they stressed the marginalization of *capoeiristas* in Brazilian society. Describing the days when the police heavily persecuted *capoeiristas,* two of the *capoeiristas* lifted their shirts and pant legs to show off the scars from when they had been beaten or had their instruments broken over their own bodies. Their scars could just have easily come from drunken brawls, and such deft hustlers surely know how to make the most of foreigners' sympathies, but this conversation conveyed their sense of being witness to changing times for capoeira. In the past, *capoeirista* was synonymous with vagabond, but now it may provide a way out of the *favela*. Once capoeira was hidden from view; now it is held up as a national symbol. Non-Brazilians' increased exposure to capoeira, through tourism and migration, has caused a number of changes for Brazilian *capoeiristas*.

Local *capoeiristas* are becoming increasingly attuned to foreigners' interest in not only seeing capoeira on the streets or in shows, but actually visiting capoeira academies and perhaps even trying it themselves. In the course of my fieldwork, I made the acquaintance of a young man who was known to be outgoing and made a point of reaching out to foreigners if he suspected that they might be *capoeiristas*. I never did figure out his exact lineage, as he seemed to bounce around from one academy to the next and was equally at home playing *Capoeira Angola* as he was playing *Capoeira Regional*. He had access to studio space in the Pelourinho district and gave private lessons from time to time. He also invited me to accompany him to a *roda* at Mestre Curio's academy in the Pelourinho district, which is technically open to the public but not frequented by pilgrims as often as is the FICA *roda*. This man would charge for his private lessons, but did not attempt to charge money for escorting foreigners to local *rodas*.

Other guides promote the spectacle of capoeira to general tourists who do not have much familiarity with the art prior to their visit. One evening I witnessed a guide bring a family of three to observe a performance at the Forte de Santo Antonio (also known as the capoeira fort). There are several academies housed in the fort, and most welcome visitors at no cost, though they are welcome to leave a donation. This particular academy has a guest book where people can leave remarks and record their country of origin. This particular family seemed to have a general interest in the *roda,* which was already in progress when they arrived, but based on the extensive commentary their guide had to provide, they did not have much prior experience with capoeira.

On two occasions, I witnessed tour guides bringing visitors to FICA Bahia during our regular class sessions. Being located on the periphery of the historic district in a nondescript office building, I was a bit surprised that individuals unacquainted with the social field would be brought to our academy. I was told that this happened approximately once per month, though they did not follow a strict schedule. The guides arrived with their clients prior to the start of class and were given a short lecture in their native language, through a translator, on the history and development of capoeira. Sometimes they were given a short demonstration on the *berimbau*. They were invited to stay through some or all of the class and were encouraged to participate as much as they could. Sometimes they would be separated from the general group and given a private lesson in the back of the room. This was distracting but tolerated by the regular students.

These random visitors had varying degrees of awareness of capoeira prior to their travel. While some know nothing more than what is presented in guidebooks, it is increasingly common for foreigners to have encountered representations of capoeira in films, television, and commercials, as described in chapter 1. However, there is a group of visitors to Bahia that fall somewhere between recreational tourists and the serious capoeira students that I refer to as pilgrims. These individuals have had a meaningful encounter with capoeira prior to their travel, whether they themselves have trained at an academy or have just been exposed to its cultural and historical features as was the case for two college students I met who had studied it in a folklore course. These individuals have chosen to come to Bahia *because of* their interest in capoeira, but for whatever reason, have opted not to seek out a local group and train with them. Sometimes this decision not to train is motivated by fear or insecurities.

One day early on in my 2008 fieldwork, I grabbed a bus to Pelourinho. Five women from a satellite capoeira group in London huddled in the last row of seats. Their instructor is Brazilian and brought a group of fourteen or fifteen students to train with his *mestre* in Fortaleza, also in the northeastern region. Their counterparts at the franchise's flagship academy in Fortaleza gave them a warm welcome, and the women had enjoyed training and playing capoeira with the local students. Following their stay in Fortaleza, the women made it a priority to visit Salvador because it is such an important place in the capoeira cosmology. In Salvador, however, capoeira took a backseat to more general tourist activities. The women had considered playing in a *roda* with a group called Capoeira Axé, but their timing was off and they missed it. Outwardly, they affected an attitude of disappointment, but in actuality, their comfort zone was limited to the Brazilian branch of their own group. Despite their acceptance by the Fortaleza group, they did not feel comfortable in the wider capoeira community. They had not played capoeira with any Brazilians outside of their own group because "[they] didn't want to get killed." Though they had gained legitimacy at the level of the local scene by virtue of their shared lineage, they did not try claiming legitimacy in the social field at large.

I see two primary explanations for travelers such as these that refrain from engaging with the broader capoeira community during their visits. Some lack the confidence to do so, assuming that the Brazilians they meet in other *rodas* will be far superior to them and may play roughly with them. Others are simply uninterested in this kind of external validation. Elsewhere (Griffith 2013b), I have referred to these individuals as "self-assessing pilgrims," arguing that they are content to visit the same sites as other tourists and perhaps participate in one or a small handful of capoeira classes, but improving their skill set and being respected by the locals as a *capoeirista* are not primary motivations for travel.[1]

Showcasing the value of capoeira to a foreign audience is the goal behind a new tour company that I was told about during 2008, which might be particularly appealing for tourists who are a little too intimidated to try and become integrated into the local capoeira scene without significant assistance. The idea for this venture was put forth by a Brazilian *mestre* as a result of his experiences working with *capoeiristas* abroad. Most of the tours to date had been booked as a result of this *mestre*'s interactions with people outside of Brazil. The itinerary is flexible, and the specific things each group does and sees are a result of their unique interests.

The basic idea is for the tour to last about five hours, but some last for an entire day. Some of the items on their itineraries have included visiting the original site of Mestre Pequeno's school, seeing Mestre Bimba's former academy (and meeting the current *mestre*), going to music shops and perhaps even observing the fabrication of music instruments, going to the kiosks in the Terreiro de Jesus where they sell *berimbaus,* observing street *rodas,* visiting the capoeira fort, and basically seeking out aspects of the capoeira culture that cannot be seen just by visiting an academy for an hour or two. The business partner who spoke to me about this new endeavor stressed that the most important aspect of the tour is the chance for guests to interact with local *capoeiristas*. They have been toying with the idea of including homestays with a *mestre* on the itinerary. These interactions would be facilitated by the involvement of a translator, so the guests do not have to be conversant in Portuguese.

Within the capoeira community, there have been mixed reactions to the tours. Some *mestres* were quite happy that this kind of service was being provided for foreign *capoeiristas* and see that it can offer them new opportunities to make money, gain exposure, or just interact with different groups of people. Others, the tour developer thought, are jealous of this new niche they are carving out for themselves. Still others think it is too commercialized. Highly critical of commodified experience, one of the *capoeiristas* in my study criticized non-Brazilian *capoeiristas* who purchase tours to capoeira academies, take tourist-oriented capoeira classes, or content themselves with viewing choreographed capoeira spectacles. She compared them with people who hire prostitutes; they want to "get the goods" without putting in the hard work of developing a relationship with local capoeira teachers and students. For pilgrims such as her, acceptance has to be earned rather than purchased.

## Apprenticeship Pilgrimages to Brazil

The case of non-Brazilian *capoeiristas* who voluntarily leave their homes to undertake extended periods of study with a Brazilian *mestre* in Bahia provides an opportunity to reconsider some of the primary assumptions in the literature on both tourism in general and pilgrimage in particular. Victor Turner's (1974) work is a landmark in the anthropological study of pilgrimage; however, current scholars should not feel constrained by his overriding concerns with liminality and communitas. Indeed, the traditional foci on spiritual fulfillment, communitas, and the power of place should be revised in order to accommodate the wide variety of phenomena to which the label pilgrimage is now being affixed. In this section, I argue that the definition of pilgrimage must be expanded to include journeys to geographic areas that serve as training centers for specific cultural performance forms but, at the same time, restricted to include only those journeys that are sanctioned by one's community.

While some scholars no longer see the utility in distinguishing tourists from pilgrims, and even Victor and Edith Turner remarked upon the overlap between these categories (Turner and Turner 1978), others maintain that there is a distinction. Tourism scholar Erik Cohen (1979), for example, differentiates pilgrimage from tourism by focusing on the direction of one's travels. In his formulation, tourists are connected to the core values of their home societies, but travel elsewhere from time to time to "recharge" and experience a temporary release from these values. Pilgrims, on the other hand, have committed themselves to a value system that is either outside of or extends beyond their geographical home, making their trips a movement toward, rather than away from, their primary commitment system. Although it has been customary to associate the term "pilgrim" with religious travel, many of the more interesting aspects of pilgrimage can be applied to nonreligious travel as well. For example, the liminality often associated with pilgrimage can also be experienced by secular travelers who "depart, geographically and psychologically, from their ordinary social state without entering another state of being" (Belhassen et al. 2008: 673).

In an increasingly secular society (Kosmin, Mayer, and Keysar 2001: 5), acknowledging nonreligious pilgrimages valorizes the transformative experiences of individuals who organize their worldview by nonreligious principles and do not have traditional religious pilgrimages as an option for personal recreation. For some individuals, the center of their worldview will be a specified religious destination, but for others, it may be a cultural icon such as national monuments or an elective center that individuals select for themselves (Cohen 1979: 180). Within increasingly secular societies, a more appropriate way to think of pilgrimage may be as travel to a site "that is revered and sacred within [an individual's] cosmology or belief system" (Digance 2003: 144). Like the traditionally conceived religious pilgrim, these individuals are also concerned with the goal of spiritual rebirth and establishing a new identity (Digance 2003: 144).

In their volume on anthropological approaches to pilgrimage and tourism, Badone and Roseman (2004) took the bold step of declaring that the tourist/pilgrim dichotomy was no longer tenable, if indeed it ever was. Geographer Collins-Kreiner reiterates this point, arguing that "contemporary use of terminology that identifies the 'pilgrim' as a religious traveler and the 'tourist' as a vacationer, is a culturally constructed polarity that blurs travelers' motives" (2010: 442). Within the group of scholars willing to expand the applicability of the term pilgrimage, however, there are two separate, and often oppositional, subsets: (1) those who are focused on the increase of religious tourism, meaning people who visit traditional sacred sites as part of a larger travel itinerary; and (2) those who are interested in personally meaningful journeys to nonreligious sites.

One of the reasons that scholars in the latter group have been so willing to collapse the terms pilgrim and tourist is their perception that humans have a deep, universal need for sacred (or sacred-like) experiences. For example, Badone and Roseman argue that "touristic travel in search of authenticity or self-renewal falls under the rubric of the sacred, collapsing the distinction between secular voyaging and pilgrimage" (2004: 2). What exactly constitutes authenticity will be defined differently by different travelers, which is why Belhassen et al. (2008) call for a reexamination of the concept of authenticity within tourism that focuses on the intersection of place, belief, and action within the pilgrim's experience.

Justine Digance and Carole Cusack (2001) point to the rising interest in alternative religious movements and secular pilgrimages as evidence that people still desire personally meaningful experiences regardless of whether or not they claim to be religious. For Digance and Cusack, "secular pilgrimage, in the mould of traditional religious pilgrimage, is one way that people have been able to regain a sense of the sacred which was lacking in other aspects of their lives" (2001: 218). In such cases, the secular pilgrims are "focused on experiencing something magical that punctuates the normal humdrum patterns of daily life" (Cusack and Digance 2009: 877). This position is similar to that articulated by anthropologist Nelson Graburn (1989), who argues that tourism in general can fill a similar role in modern society as do religious rituals in traditional societies.

There is an unquestioned assumption running through most of the literature on pilgrimage as well as much of the anthropological literature on tourism in general (see Graburn 1989) that everyday life is profane. This is an assumption that should be problematized. Rather than assuming that all people need an alternation of sacred and profane moments to avoid the feeling of alienation that is thought to accompany modernity, it may be more useful to look at the specific reasons that people undertake pilgrimages, religious or secular, at the specific times that they do. Frey (2004) found that many of the pilgrims on the Camino de Compostela were at a crossroad in their lives and used the time and distance away from their normal lives to gain perspective on who they wanted to be and how they wanted to live. This fits quite well with Turner's (1974) model of social drama—a crisis of identity is solved by entering a liminal state that facilitates a transition from one's old, troubled self to a new, reinvented self.

Despite recent scholars' pronouncement that the boundary between tourist and pilgrim is, and always has been, porous (see Badone and Roseman 2004), travelers themselves are sometimes more reluctant to do away with this distinction. For example, on the Camino de Santiago, a well-known Catholic pilgrimage route in Spain, Nancy Frey found that pilgrims making the journey under their own power (by foot or bicycle) defined themselves in opposition to the "tourists" who arrived via modern transportation. From this perspective, "tourists are thought to be people who do not have face-to-face contact with villagers, do not appreciate the spaces of the Camino, and do not suffer the heat and pains of the road" (Frey 2004: 93). In this case, the hardship of the journey, experienced through the body, served as an emic diagnostic for assigning someone to one category or another. Similarly, participants on a mass tour of Western Africa, sponsored in part by the fast-food chain McDonalds, were told that they were "on a pilgrimage, not a safari" (Ebron 2000: 916). This seemed to be an attempt on the part of guides to have the travelers hold themselves to a higher set of standards than what might be expected from a mere tourist without this more reflexive orientation. Therefore, despite my agreement that the tourist/pilgrim dichotomy is problematic, I have opted to call the travelers I studied pilgrims in large part because of their vocal disavowal of the term *tourist*.

For the majority of the *capoeiristas* who I call apprenticeship pilgrims, being considered a tourist is downright insulting. The crass commercial exchanges between hosts and guests in which each party tries to get the best deal out of a very unequal exchange is incompatible with their perceptions of themselves as savvy cultural brokers. By and large, tourists are not greatly transformed by their travels (Bruner 1991); completing a pilgrimage, on the other hand, elevates one to a new status. Therefore, the deep transformation many *capoeiristas* feel as they undertake this journey is more closely aligned with scholarly understandings of pilgrimages than of tourism in general. A female *capoeirista* from the United States told me "it is something more than just a tourist trip for some of us, for a lot of us." As is characteristic of a pilgrimage experience (Turner 1973), this woman entered a liminal state the moment she first stepped foot in Brazil. Describing this experience, she said:

> That very first night I remember I wrote in my journal I felt like I had jumped into the deepest pool I had ever jumped in and realized how far it was to the surface … I had no idea where I was going to go, but I felt like I was in deep. It was disorienting and threatening … All these new

experiences all at once, the language, being with another family that's not mine, everyone's so excited to see one another and I'm over in the corner not knowing what to say or even how to say it. But I think overall what I quickly realized is that a *capoeirista* is a *capoeirista* no matter where, and I realized I could go to a *roda* or go to a training or I could hang out with a *capoeirista* and we had more in common than I have with most Americans because I am so passionate about capoeira.

Despite feeling out of her depths, she soon regained confidence based on her identity as a *capoeirista*. This first night was difficult for her. She had traveled to Brazil with her *mestre* who is Brazilian but has now lived in the United States for more than fifteen years. Her other traveling companion was a black male from Angola, who is similarly an outsider, but whose appearance and fluency in Portuguese facilitated his integration into the local community. She, as a white woman with intermediate language skills, was less comfortable. Nonetheless, she describes a moment in which other identities were stripped away, and everyone was equal under the banner of capoeira. Her excitement about visiting Brazil may have blinded her to some of the inequalities that actually exist within this transnational community and the strategies non-Brazilians must use to claim authority within this social field, but she nonetheless represents the immediate sense of connection that many pilgrims desire when they visit the place of their art's birth.

At this juncture, a working definition of the term pilgrimage is needed. Cusack and Digance define it as: "the undertaking of a journey that is redolent with meaning, which may be associated with an individual spiritual quest operating outside formal religion" (2009: 877). However, this definition is a bit too broad for my purposes, suggesting that any form of tourism could be considered a pilgrimage. While some may grant the title of pilgrim to anyone who undertakes a personally meaningful journey, I qualify this by specifying that the journey or destination have a place of significance within the worldview of one's identity group. While I recognize the immense significance of individual journeys to idiosyncratic locations that are "redolent with meaning," I assign these to a different category than those sites that are treated as obligatory destinations by a group of people. Therefore, within the context of this book, a pilgrim is defined as either a religious or secular traveler who visits a collectively revered site for the purpose of experiencing a specific kind of transformation that is condoned and often prescribed by his or her community of practice.

Although similar in terms of the outcome for the pilgrim, the process through which a secular pilgrimage site is constructed differs somewhat from that of a religious pilgrimage site. These sites become important in the worldview of a group through that group's collective ratification of them rather than through an official pronouncement of the site's holiness. Matthew Lamont (2014) focuses on the process of authentication in sports tourism rather than starting with an a priori assumption regarding the objective authenticity of certain sites. He argues that secular pilgrimages are performative in the sense that by visiting a place, the pilgrim contributes to its authentication, a collective social construction that verifies a site's worthiness within a given community (see Lamont 2014). In other words, the mere existence of a site in and of itself does not make it a pilgrimage destination. A site becomes a pilgrimage destination through the social construction of that site as significant within a particular group's worldview (Belhassen et al. 2008). In the case of capoeira, it is not *just* the number of *mestres* and academies in Salvador that make it a pilgrimage destination, but the subcultural construction of Bahia through capoeira songs, folklore, and teachers' personal narratives that mark it as a significant destination.

The importance of place can be put on a continuum with some pilgrimages being motivated by a particular relic in a particular place while others are motivated by an anticipated internal transformation that can happen in a number of different places. For example, to the *Star Trek* fans studied by Jennifer Porter (2004), the geographic location of the pilgrimage is largely irrelevant; it is the communally constructed atmosphere of the convention that makes this a significant experience. As Porter writes, "the center for the *Star Trek* convention pilgrimage process is a dialogic, rather than a spatial, one" (2004: 168). By focusing on a form of pilgrimage that is "decentered" or unmoored from a specific geographic location, Porter (2004) opens the door to a number of other ways of conceptualizing pilgrimage, including those that are activity-based. At least within *capoeiristas'* pilgrimages, there are a wider number of sites that will fulfill their needs than is the case with traditional religious pilgrimage. For example, a pilgrimage to the Catholic site of Lourdes would be incomplete without seeing the grotto from which healing waters supposedly flow, but a capoeira pilgrim in Bahia has a number of different academies to choose from, any of which can serve her purposes.

Turner (1974) argued that pilgrims enter a state of communitas in which internal divisions are at least temporarily sutured, but subsequent explorations of pilgrimage have contested this claim and instead see pilgrimages as spaces of competing discourse (Reader 1993; Eade and Sallnow 2000; St. John 2001). While there are some cases of contemporary pilgrimages that do exhibit communitas, and the capoeira quoted above seemed to perceive her experience as a moment of communitas, it is not a universal feature of pilgrimage (see Digance and Cusack 2001). To avoid Turner's error of assuming that a single quality, namely, communitas, uniformly appears in all variants, scholars must account for both the individual and societal dimensions of pilgrimage (Reader 1993). For capoeira pilgrims, status markers do not completely disappear, and it would be disingenuous to say that all of the pilgrims who passed through FICA bonded with one another equally. As with most groups, some people found closer connections than others, and on occasion, social cliques did form. Nonetheless, there remained a sense that all of the foreign *capoeiristas* were engaged in a common goal and that served to connect them in a way that would have been largely unimaginable in any other context. Being in Bahia together, whether or not they liked one another, was a physical manifestation of the imagined community of which all *capoeiristas* are a part.

A conversation I had with Gil, an Israeli capoeira instructor, nicely illustrates this feeling of community, if not communitas. After one of FICA Bahia's weekly *rodas,* we joined a group of our fellow students who were going to a barbeque at Mestre Cobra Mansa's home in one of Salvador's outlying neighborhoods. Gil and I lingered slightly behind the rest of the group as we veered off of the sidewalk and carefully navigated a rock-strewn path running parallel to the railroad tracks. Gil has visited other cities in Brazil like Rio de Janeiro and São Paulo as well as other countries to take part in capoeira workshops. He gestured toward the rest of the group in front of us and said that this is what he loves about capoeira. He explained to me that when you are traveling and get to go somewhere with a local *capoeirista,* you get to see the real culture, not just the "touristy stuff." If you go somewhere to train or even just to participate in a *roda,* people invite you into their homes afterward.

A *capoeirista* quoted in the documentary *Intercambio Cultural: Roda Mundo* said that becoming part of this community allows people to travel the world, not as a tourist, but as a *capoeirista* (Vega, n.d.). These comments echo what a fellow *capoeirista* back in Indiana had said about traveling the domestic capoeira circuit, that a *capoeirista* can visit a new city or town but immediately have access to insider knowledge because of his or her relationship with the capoeira community. While Boissevain (1996) and others have commented upon the various strategies locals use to erect barriers between themselves and tourists, shared participation in capoeira seems to override the need for such boundaries. Though they often compare Bahia with Mecca, members of the capoeira community do not typically use the term *pilgrimage* to describe these journeys; nonetheless, they fit the definition of pilgrimage I have outlined here.

Within the larger category of secular pilgrimage, there are several smaller subcategories. To date, much of the work on secular pilgrimage has focused on new age spiritual centers and grave sites of famous people. My discussion of apprenticeship pilgrimage adds a new dimension to secular pilgrimage by focusing on travel to a generalized geographic area where pilgrims seek a particular corpus of knowledge. Apprenticeship pilgrimage can be defined as a journey to a hub of practice that a particular group has "imbued with sacredness because it is a birthplace, the best known, or otherwise remarkable center of practice" (Griffith 2013a).

As I have argued elsewhere (Griffith 2013a), this concept serves as a theoretical bridge between studies of secular pilgrimage and sports tourism. While many of the behaviors of sports fanatics have been likened to those of pilgrims, for example baseball fans who feel that they *must* visit Yankee Stadium before they die (see Gammon 2004), studies of these individuals rarely focus on the personal and social transformations individuals experience as a result of their accomplishment. In his review of sport tourism as secular pilgrimage, Gammon acknowledges both the sacred and the profane permutations of pilgrimage, but argues that "whichever understanding is used, each application of the term will include a journey of some kind to a place (or places) which holds personal and/or collective meaning to the "pilgrim" (Gammon 2004: 40). However, while the sites visited by sports tourists may be extremely idiosyncratic, an apprenticeship pilgrimage site includes two components (1) a specific activity is performed under the tutelage of an individual whose authority has been legitimized by the community; and (2) the study of a particular art happens in tandem with the pilgrim's immersion in the culture that gave rise to that art.

The character of an apprenticeship pilgrimage destination calls for a reexamination of the assumption that pilgrimage sites are simply sacred places. Glenn Bowman (2000) has made progress in this area. Though being in Jerusalem has some significance for Catholic pilgrims, otherwise they would not undertake the journey in the first place, their pilgrimage experience is about more than just seeing sacred sites. Indeed, the group Bowman studied seemed unfazed by their inability to get close to particular sacred sites or objects that were blocked by crowds of other pilgrims. Ultimately, he decides, "it is … the liturgy, in which officiants sanctified by God through the agency of the church pass on to celebrants the redemptive powers of the blood and flesh of Christ, which puts believers into communion with God" (Bowman 2000: 115). In other words, the sacralized site, Jerusalem, is an important backdrop for the cultural text, scripture, which forms the core of this community's value system. A similar observation can be made regarding apprenticeship pilgrims. While the culture in which a training center is housed is an essential part of the pilgrimage experience, it is equally important to participate in an authoritative performance of the cultural form that they have come to study. In both cases, the place and people involved are largely meaningless without the third element, the cultural text.

Apprenticeship pilgrims feel that their training within a particular art or sport will not be complete without actually visiting the symbolic center of their community of practice. This phenomenon can be seen in a number of genres, like yogis seeking out gurus at Indian ashrams (see Strauss 2005) or students of West African dance seeking out instructors in Ghana. It is also quite common in the martial arts, with scores of kung fu practitioners knocking on the doors of the Shaolin Temple. This kind of experience is seen as a graduate school of sorts, the capstone that crowns their years of intense training and dedication (Polly 2007: 41). De Campos Rosario, Stephens, and Delamont (2010: 117) have similarly claimed that "full enculturation into Brazilian *capoeira* necessitates a long stay in Brazil," though they do not take up an investigation of this process. Pilgrims tend to believe that the art is purer in the place of its birth, and they can augment their own legitimacy by traveling to the source. In this type of travel, "the physicality of ... experiences gives the tourist a claim to the locality, visceral memories of which the reality or authenticity cannot be denied, there may even be scars to prove it" (Miller 2010).

Bahia satisfies the requirements of being an apprenticeship pilgrimage destination. Here pilgrims have a number of academies to choose from at which they can undertake study with a well-known *mestre* while at the same time being immersed in the Brazilian culture that shaped capoeira. The importance of the city has been ratified by members of the community and is frequently visited by what one American *capoeirista* described to me as people doing "the hard core *capoeira* tourism thing," or what I call pilgrimage. Whereas the *capoeiristas* described in the previous section are content to just visit Bahia, see the sites, and perhaps observe a *roda* if the opportunity arises, the apprenticeship pilgrims are distinct in both their commitment to capoeira and in the intensity of their desire to become integrated into the local community.

My primary focus here is on foreign *capoeiristas* making pilgrimages to Bahia, but many Brazilians from other parts of the country also make it a priority to visit Bahia. One *capoeirista* at FICA Bahia who lives and trains with the FICA group in Brasilia told me that *capoeiristas* in Brasilia feel compelled to visit Bahia at least once in their lifetimes. It is common for Brazilian *capoeiristas* to come to Bahia to further legitimize their own academies. For example, in 1985 the leader of the Paulista group Cativeiro traveled to Salvador to learn more about traditional capoeira. This pilgrimage was important to him because Salvador "still represented, for capoeira as well as for *candomblé,* the recognized source of authentic tradition, this experience provided him with a new source of legitimacy, both in São Paulo and beyond" (Assunção 2005: 181). For Brazilians as well as foreigners, Bahia is often glorified as a bastion of tradition, even though in actuality it boasts a very dynamic community.

The local population reacts to the presence of these foreigners in a number of different ways. Some see it as a boon to the economy and delight in the announcement of intercultural exchanges and other programs that will bring *capoeiristas* from around the country and the globe into their city. Taxi drivers in particular were eager to engage me on this topic and expressed a great deal of curiosity about the number of women, like myself, who practice capoeira in other countries. Other Brazilians see this as yet another example of how foreigners, mostly white foreigners, are usurping Afro-Brazilian culture. Many of these people assume that pilgrims will find some way to make money off of their experiences, and some of them will in a very roundabout way. If travel to Brazil augments their authenticity, it will open up new possibilities for them to become instructors in their home country. Others take a more balanced view. They are critical of foreigners who take from the culture without giving back, but recognize that many are motivated by a genuine passion for Brazilian culture and want to learn how to do things correctly. A street performer of capoeira told me that he was honestly quite impressed with the capoeira pilgrims because they are dedicated and desire to learn every aspect of capoeira, not just "how to throw their legs around."

While it is heartening to talk with individuals who are willing to judge each pilgrim on his or her own merits, I do not want to discount the concerns of those who think foreigners are exploiting the local culture. Westerners exploiting local knowledge or selling beautiful images of these natural and cultural environments is a story that has repeated itself over and over again, and it is only logical that hosts might be wary of their guests' true intentions. Anthropologists certainly are not immune to these kinds of critiques. Since the 1980s when anthropology took a turn toward self-reflexivity, many of us have become more aware of how the hospitality of people in other countries supports our own career advancement. However, travelers do not necessarily share this self-reflexivity. Many of the pilgrims I knew were upset by these allegations, believing their motives to be completely pure. In fact, they were often angered by the locals' tendency to take advantage of their interest in capoeira by charging them exorbitant rates for training or for charging an entrance fee to watch a *roda,* which happens at some, but not all, academies. This disconnect is not surprising. What the foreigners saw as exploitation was the Brazilians' need to make a living. What the Brazilians saw as gringos stealing their culture was the Western belief that commodification taints authenticity.

## Pilgrims' Hostility to the Commodification of Experience

Discussions of commodification often co-occur with discussions of authenticity. For Vincent J Cheng, who studies the interplay between authenticity and cultural identity, the search for authenticity "is an intrinsically hopeless quest to 'catch' and pin down something already defined as ungraspable" (2004: 34). Here Cheng suggests the imagery of a butterfly being mounted for display; a thing once caught loses the life that made it remarkable. According to this argument, once cultural products have been fixed into a commodity, they lose the ephemeral quality or aura that made them unique (see Jensen 1998). There also seems to be a tipping point in the market for authentic goods. While authenticity can raise the market value of a performance, once too many performers sell their product as unique and authentic, a skeptical public will actually view their marketing technique as a marker of the product's inauthenticity.

One of my favorite scenes from Quentin Tarantino's hit series *Kill Bill* is when Uma Thurman's character has a flashback to her training with martial arts master Pai Mei (Tarantino 2003). Despising white American women, it at first seems uncertain whether or not he will deign to be her master. After painstakingly proving her humility and dedication, however, he not only mentors her, but also teaches her the mythical "five point palm exploding heart technique." This theme of proving one's worth to the master is common in martial arts films. In reality, however, paying the monthly tuition will normally get a student in the door. That student might not learn how to make someone's heart explode with a single blow, that still requires having a special relationship with the master, but the student will have a chance to learn the basics and sweat it out with the rest of the class.

Most martial arts students probably do not want to suffer the humiliation that Thurman's character experienced, but the commodification of the training relationship does make one's admittance into an academy less remarkable. Paying your dues, as Thurman's character had to do, is perceived as being a more authentic experience than paying your tuition. One of the reasons non-Brazilian *capoeiristas* feel compelled to visit Brazil and train with a local group is that they have a deeply held mistrust of commodified experiences. Once a monetary value has been placed on an item or experience, they see it as being less pure. As discussed in the previous chapter, those *mestres* who gain their titles as a result of a financial arrangement with their own teachers are seen as disingenuous and have relatively low status in the capoeira community. Students' distrust of these *mestres* is mirrored in their own desire to have a capoeira experience that money cannot buy.

This is not to suggest that *mestres* should be somehow morally superior to concerns about money. Most members of the capoeira community understand that *mestres* need to earn some degree of financial stability from their teaching; otherwise they would not be able to dedicate themselves to this pursuit in a full-time capacity. On the other hand, when the commercial aspect of advancement within the social field is too blatant, some *capoeiristas* become uncomfortable. This is particularly true of wealthier non-Brazilians who come from a privileged social location. Their participation in capoeira is about their individual identity, and they want to know that they have earned their place in the community. *Capoeiristas* accept a baseline degree of commodification, and it is common practice in Brazil and abroad for students to pay for capoeira classes. However, the purpose of the pilgrimage is to gain access to knowledge and experiences that are not available for purchase.

The economic incentives for local academies to host foreign pilgrims are fairly clear; the economic incentives for inviting them into the backspaces of Brazilian culture are much less clear. When Gil and I went to the barbeque noted earlier in this chapter, we did contribute some funds to help cover the cost of food and drink, but the cost was no more exorbitant than the cover charge one might pay at a college frat party or the cost one would incur if preparing a dish for a potluck dinner. Similarly, on Children's Day, all of the members of FICA Bahia were asked to contribute a gift. The students were told to give whatever they were able to give, even if that was a hand-me-down toy from a niece or nephew. In both cases, non-Brazilians were expected to give slightly more than their typical Brazilian counterpart because of their healthier resources, but the basic expectations and access to special events were the same for both groups. So while there may be some economic benefit accrued by inviting foreigners to these events, it is minimal.

## Conclusion

In today's global marketplace, it is possible for an individual to learn capoeira without ever leaving his or her hometown, even in seemingly remote places like Bloomington, Indiana. However, there will be a limit to what an individual can learn if he or she only trains with the same people year in, year out. Domestic travel, or what one might call a regional pilgrimage, can help non-Brazilian *capoeiristas* feel connected to the larger social field. This kind of travel may also serve as a prelude, or sometimes a substitute, for the more demanding trip to Brazil.

Even if he or she has traveled locally, most serious *capoeiristas* are eventually expected to undertake a trip to Brazil. If an individual is still lacking confidence in his abilities, or if she is uninterested in the local *capoeiristas'* ratification of her legitimacy, the individual may be content to just engage in recreational activities like sightseeing and perhaps observing a *roda*. *Capoeiristas* who undertake this kind of travel are largely indistinguishable from regular tourists. Other individuals, however, visit Brazil with the goal of joining a local group and learning as much as possible from that group's *mestre*. While not always explicitly stated, these individuals are hoping to prove their worth and experience a centripetal movement toward the center of the social field.

It should not be assumed, however, that joining a group guarantees acceptance and entry into the backspaces of capoeira culture that many pilgrims so fervently desire. In many artistic traditions, a legitimate culture bearer must be deemed as having the right "credentials" (Rudinow 1994: 129). Earning these credentials is not a simple process, particularly if they are associated with inherent qualities that the individual lacks. Peterson (2005) uses the phrase "authenticity work" as a way of discussing the effort it takes for individuals to conform to a socially situated definition of authenticity that is subject to change. Performers lacking the expected markers of authenticity within a *genre* must engage in authenticity work in order to convince audiences of their legitimacy (Peterson 2005). In chapters 4 and 5, I discuss two broad categories of authenticity markers: those that are ascribed by virtue of his or her social identities and those more individual characteristics that have to be achieved through what Peterson calls "authenticity work" (1997). Both ultimately contribute to an individual's legitimacy within the capoeira social field.

## Notes

1. The distinction that Belhassen et al. (2008) makes between intrapersonal and interpersonal existential authenticity is equivalent to what I have called elsewhere (Griffith 2013b) self-assessors and externally motivated pilgrims.

## Works Cited

Assunção, Matthias Röhrig. 2005. *Capoeira: The History of an Afro-Brazilian Martial Art, Sport in the Global Society*. London: Routledge.

Badone, Ellen, and Sharon R Roseman. 2004. "Approaches to the Anthropology of Pilgrimage and Tourism." In *Intersecting Journeys: The Anthropology of Pilgrimage and Tourism,* edited by Ellen Badone and Sharon R Roseman, 1–23. Urbana: University of Illinois Press.

Belhassen, Yaniv, Kellee Caton, and William P. Stewart. 2008. "The Search for Authenticity in the Pilgrim Expeirence." *Annals of Tourism Research* 35 (3): 668-689.

Boissevain, Jeremy. 1996. *Coping with Tourists: European Reactions to Mass Tourism.* Providence, RI: Berghahn Books.

Bowman, Glenn. (1991) 2000. "Christian Ideology and the Image of a Holy Land: The Place of Jerusalem Pilgrimage in the Various Christianities." In *Contesting the Sacred: The Anthropology of Pilgrimage,* edited by John Eade and Michael J Sallnow, 98–121. Urbana: University of Illinois Press.

Bruner, Edward M. 1991. "Transformation of Self in Tourism." *Annals of Tourism Research* 18 (2): 238–50.

Cheng, Vincent J. 2004. *Inauthentic: The Anxiety over Culture and Identity.* New Brunswick, NJ: Rutgers University Press.

Cohen, Erik. 1979. "A Phenomenology of Tourist Experiences." *Sociology* 13 (2): 179–201.

Collins-Kreiner, N. 2010. "Researching Pilgrimage: Continuity and Transformations." *Annals of Tourism Research* 37 (2): 440–56.

Cusack, Carole M, and Justine Digance. 2009. "The Melbourne Cup: Australian Identity and Secular Pilgrimage." *Sport in Society: Cultures, Commerce, Media, Politics* 12 (7): 876–89.

D'Aquino, Iria. 1983. "Capoeira: Strategies for Status, Power and Identity," PhD dissertation. University of Illinois.

De Campos Rosario, Claudio, Neil Stephens, and Sara Delamont. 2010. "'I'm Your Teacher, I'm Brazilian!' Authenticity and Authority in European Capoeira." *Sport, Education and Society* 15 (1): 103–20.

Digance, Justine. 2003. "Pilgrimage at Contested Sites." *Annals of Tourism Research* 30 (1): 143–59.

Digance, Justine, and Carole M Cusack. 2001. "Secular Pilgrimage Events: Druid Gorsedd and Stargate Alignments." In *The End of Religions?: Religion in an Age of Globalisation,* edited by Carole M Cusack and Peter Oldmeadow, 216–29. Sydney: Department of Studies in Religion, University of Sydney.

Eade, John, and Michael J Sallnow. (1991) 2000. "Introduction." In *Contesting the Sacred: The Anthropology of Pilgrimage,* 1–29. Urbana: University of Illinois Press.

Ebron, Paulla A. 2000. "Tourists as Pilgrims: Commercial Fashioning of Transatlantic Politics." *American Ethnologist* 26 (4): 910–32.

Frey, Nancy L. 2004. "Stories of the Return: Pilgrimage and Its Aftermath." In *Intersecting Journeys: The Anthropology of Pilgrimage and Tourism,* edited by Ellen Badone and Sharon R Roseman, 89–109. Urbana: University of Illinois Press.

Gammon, Sean. 2004. "Secular Pilgrimage and Sport Tourism." In *Sport Tourism: Interrelationships, Impacts and Issues,* edited by BW Ritchie and D Adair, 30–45. Clevedon, UK: Channel View Publications.

Graburn, Nelson H. 1989. "Tourism: The Sacred Journey." In *Hosts and Guests: The Anthropology of Tourism,* edited by Valene L Smith, 21-36. Philadelphia: University of Pennsylvania Press.

Green, Molly. 2005. "The Northeast." In *Lonely Planet Brazil*, edited by Lonely Planet, 409-474. Oakland: Lonely Planet Publications Pty Ltd.

Griffith, Lauren Miller. 2013a. "Apprenticeship Pilgrimage, An Alternative Analytical Lens." *Annals of Tourism Research* 41: 228–31.

Griffith, Lauren Miller. 2013b. "Apprenticeship Pilgrims and the Acquisition of Legitimacy." *Journal of Sport and Tourism* 18 (1): 1–15.

Jensen, Joli. 1998. *Nashville Sound: Authenticity, Commercialization, and Country Music*. Nashville, TN: Vanderbilt University Press.

Joseph, Janelle Beatrice. 2006. "Capoeira in Canada: Brazilian Martial Art, Cultural Transformation and the Struggle for Authenticity," MS thesis. University of Toronto.

Kosmin, Barry A, Egon Mayer, and Ariela Keysar. 2001. *Religious Identification Study*. New York: The Graduate Center of the City University of New York.

Lamont, Matthew. 2014. "Authentication in Sports Tourism." *Annals of Tourism Research* 45: 1–17.

Lyrio, Alexandre. 2007. "Martir da Capoeira." *Correiro da Bahia,* 25 February.

MacCannell, Dean. 1976. *The Tourist: A New Theory of the Leisure Class*. Berkeley: University of California Press.

Miller, Lauren. 2010. "Martial Arts in Tourism." In *Martial Arts in Global Perspective*, edited by Thomas A Green and Joseph R Svinth, 411-416 Santa Barbara, CA: ABC-CLIO.

Peterson, Richard A. 1997. *Creating Country Music: Fabricating Authenticity*. Chicago: The University of Chicago Press.

Peterson, Richard A. 2005. "In Search of Authenticity." *Journal of Management Studies* 42 (5): 1083–98.

Polly, Matthew. 2007. *American Shaolin: Flying Kicks, Buddhist Monks, and the Legend of Iron Crotch: An Odyssey in the New China*. New York: Gotham Books.

Porter, Jennifer E. 2004. "Pilgrimage and the IDIC Ethic: Exploring Star Trek Convention Attendance as Pilgrimage." In *Intersecting Journeys: The Anthropology of Pilgrimage and Tourism,* edited by Ellen Badone and Sharon R Roseman, 160–79. Urbana: University of Illinois Press.

Reader, Ian. 1993. "Introduction." In *Pilgrimage in popular Culture*, edited by Ian Reader and Tony Walter, 1-28. Houndsmills: The Macmillan Press Ltd.

Rudinow, Joel. 1994. "Race, Ethnicity, Expressive Authenticity: Can White People Sing the Blues?" *The Journal of Aesthetics and Art Criticism* 52 (1): 127–37.

St. John, Graham. 2001. "Alternative Cultural Heterotopia and the Liminoid Body: Beyond Turner at ConFest." *The Australian Journal of Anthropology* 12 (1): 47–66.

Strauss, Sarah. 2005. *Positioning Yoga: Balancing Acts across Cultures*. Oxford: Berg.

Tarantino, Quentin. 2003. *Kill Bill Vol. 1.* Directed by Quentin Tarantino. Santa Monica, CA: Miramax.

Turner, Victor. 1973. "The Center Out There: Pilgrim's Goal." *History of Religions* 12 (3): 191–230.

Turner, Victor. 1974. *Dramas, Fields, and Metaphors: Symbolic Action in Human Society*. Ithaca, NY: Cornell University Press.

Turner, Victor, and Edith Turner. 1978. *Image and Pilgrimage in Christian Culture*. New York: Columbia University Press.

Vega, Louis. n.d. *Intercambio Cultural: Roda Mundo*. Brazil: Virtual Capoeira Media. DVD, 110 min.

# Chapter 4

# Preparing for the Pilgrimage

The protagonist in a popular capoeira song proclaims that his love called him to the Ilha de Maré, so when some of the pilgrims at FICA found out that this was an actual place in the Bay of All Saints, we just had to go. Our trip had very little to do with capoeira. We sat on the shore, swam in the sea, and drank beer as we watched the tide for which the island is named roll in. On the boat ride back home, however, people reflected on their experiences training capoeira. One woman said it was hard to date another *capoeirista* because if the couple broke up, the woman was typically expected to leave the group to avoid any post-breakup awkwardness. Indeed, this had happened in my own group back in the United States. But one of the men in the group said he would never date a non-*capoeirista* again because they just could not understand the depth of his passion for training. Another woman agreed, saying she had received too many ultimatums from past boyfriends who said, "it's capoeira or me." For her, it was an easy choice.

## Introduction

Time and again, I heard Brazilians describe the local capoeira scene as a tower of Babel. The amount of diversity found at the FICA academy on any given day can be stunning. At this academy alone, I met pilgrims from twenty-five countries in only six months. They tend to be young; most are in their mid-twenties to mid-thirties. With a few exceptions, most are unmarried and have the freedom to travel abroad without worrying about family commitments. Because most of them stay for a period of several weeks to several months, and some even longer, they all have a degree of flexibility in their schedules. It is common to find college students in Bahia during their summer break, but it is also routine to meet people who have just left a job or whose employment allows them to work remotely. Still others have found ways to make money while in Brazil, most often by teaching English or providing translation services in an under-the-table arrangement.

*Capoeiristas* are encouraged to visit Brazil as part of their development, but the timing of their trip may be influenced by a number of factors such as an upcoming obligation that would impede future travel opportunities or a crisis/transition period during which individuals are looking for something to fill a personal void. Capoeira becomes such an all-consuming passion for some that they have even sacrificed personal relationships in order to further their training. One individual in my study made the decision to take an extended trip to Brazil to the detriment and eventual dissolution of his marriage. Many of them are experienced travelers, and some have already lived abroad for extended periods. What is most striking is how they have spent months if not years assembling their identities as *capoeiristas* through intentional acts like dedicated physical training, learning to speak a foreign language, or even using graduate study as an opportunity to learn about this history and culture of capoeira as was the case for at least three of the pilgrims I met.

Making a pilgrimage to Bahia is a major event in a *capoeirista*'s development, and he or she will likely have spent a significant amount of time preparing for it. This chapter addresses how capoeira fits into the pilgrims' sense of self and why making this trip is so important to them on an existential level. I also describe some of the anxieties that pilgrims may feel when thinking about interacting with Brazilian *capoeiristas*. Finally, I discuss the ways in which a pilgrim's lineage can facilitate his or her entrance into the Brazilian capoeira scene.

## The Role of Existential Authenticity

Pierre Bourdieu's work has been criticized for overstating the tendency toward reproduction of norms and habits within a social field (Chaney 1996). While I believe that recognizing the tendency for power to be reproduced must be central to our understanding of society, I also recognize an individual's agency to construct his or her identity from a plethora of possibilities that grows daily with each exposure to new cultural forms. Seen in this way, our actions are not mere executions of the behaviors dictated by society, but creative projects that are constrained by these rules while at the same time testing their limits. In other words, people have the ability to determine what leisure activities they find most appealing, but those preferences tend to be an outgrowth of the institutions in which they were socialized. It is not surprising when a child of the elite gravitates toward polo while an inner-city child prefers basketball. These performances of one's class background go unnoticed by the social actors themselves because the system has become naturalized. By the same token, many observers would find it "natural" for a poor Afro-Brazilian boy to take up capoeira, but to see a white American woman doing it seems to require a bit more explanation.

Subscribing to a lifestyle implies knowledge about consumption and knowing which goods to consume if an individual wants to further his or her status in the eyes of others who subscribe to the same lifestyle (Chaney 1996: 57). This leads Chaney to conclude that consumerist choices within a lifestyle will form a consistent whole, but those with sufficient cultural capital have the freedom to experiment with the boundaries of taste (1996: 63–64). Consumption habits will tend to reproduce many aspects of the social field in which individuals are embedded, but they are not perfect copies of those who came before them. As globalization brings more and more tangible and intangible goods within easy reach, the consistency of our consumption habits begins to erode.

Chaney uses the concept of *lifestyles* to explain how consumer behaviors aid in the process of identity construction. The idea that one is what he or she buys is characteristic of modernity. These identity-building projects are reflexive in the sense that they display to us and to our audience who we are, who we think we are, or who we want to be (Chaney 1996: 37). Recalling the work of Georg Simmel, Chaney argues that the need for people to differentiate themselves comes only with a multiplicity of available styles of living (1996: 52). Lifestyles are, in part, a display of consumer competence (Chaney 1996: 97). A hippie who shops at Wal-Mart rather than the local co-op just would not be taken seriously. The modern identity-building project is one of managing surface appearances and presentation of self in order to signal belonging in a group of like-minded others (Chaney 1996). Aligning individual consumption with the overarching sensibilities of taste current in a lifestyle group took on a quasi-sacred importance in modern life (Chaney 1996: 129).

In the postmodern era, however, identity becomes a more individualized project. The decentralizing of leisure, aided by the development of personal technology devices like CD players or iPods, makes identity construction a private process whereas it used to be a result of communal participation in culture (Chaney 1996). The process of identity construction today exhibits the same extreme relativism that can be seen in other permutations of postmodernity. Lifestyles and subcultures are still important, but there is more room for eclecticism. I can listen to both classical music and rap without (most) of my colleagues wondering if I have a multiple personality disorder. Reading the latest tabloid will not ruin my scholarly aura. In postmodernity, the individual rather than the community becomes the final arbiter of whether or not one is properly living out his or her identity.

Apprenticeship pilgrims epitomize the postmodern identity builder who looks to herself as the ultimate authority of whether or not a practice is suitable, but for most individuals, external validation of her internal sense of self is also important. While this may seem to be contradictory, I understand these dueling desires as an indication that belonging to a community still matters even in an era of eclectic individualism. Interest in existential authenticity stretches back to Rousseau and his belief that people should indulge the desires of their true inner selves (Lindholm 2008). What I am referring to as existential authenticity, Armstrong refers to as "first person authenticity" (2004: 337), Taylor discusses it as "self-reflexivity" (1992), and Peterson writes about "authenticity to constructed self" (2005). Existential authenticity is what makes firsthand experiences in Brazil and the validation from Brazilian *mestres* matter to *capoeiristas*. Because they feel that capoeira is such an integral part of who they are, they are highly invested in claiming legitimacy.

Apprenticeship pilgrims exhibit a high degree of devotion to their chosen sport or art, and spending six or more hours per week training is considered normal. The Estrela do Norte group in Indiana, for example, holds three two-hour practices a week and occasional weekend trips and performances. On top of this, many *capoeiristas* also train independently on the days when they are not training with the group. For most individuals used to "doing their own thing" and not being beholden to anyone, especially as college students, this demonstrated a significant commitment. The cost of weekly classes is not prohibitive for *most capoeiristas*, but traveling to Brazil is another matter. To undertake a journey that demands such an investment of time and financial resources is an indicator that a pilgrim's practice is more than a mere hobby.

The individuals who have committed themselves to the practice of capoeira have opted to become part of this community because they think it reflects who they are at the core of their being. However, it is not always easy to understand why they have made this connection. Consider these questions raised by Cheng:

> What is it, after all, that composes our genuine, authentic personal identity? Is it our lived experience, the sum total of how we each have (individually and collectively) lived? Or is it our cultural, ethnic, or racial heritage, an inherited past but not one that has been necessarily lived or experienced? (Cheng 2004: 178)

Some of the American *capoeiristas* with whom I have worked look to capoeira, an Afro-Brazilian art, as a way of intensifying their ethnic identity. However, this is a very small percentage as the groups with which I have worked are predominately white. Others express a belief that capoeira "fits" with their personality, and that Brazilian culture is more comfortable for them than is the culture of their home society be it American, European, or Asian. Like the existential tourists Cohen describes (1979), these individuals feel that their personal value system is out of alignment with their home culture and they have found an alternative that resonates with them more deeply. Thus, their time spent at home is experienced as a period of exile, and they orient themselves toward the future trips they will make to Brazil.

D'Aquino stresses that to really become a *capoeirista*, and not just someone with a passing interest, is a lifelong commitment bordering on obsession. She writes, "it is not a part time proposition even if an individual can only dedicate part of his [*sic*] time to it" (D'Aquino 1983: 91). It is all consuming. The depth of these individuals' commitment to capoeira is genuine, but it still warrants asking whether or not they have the right to claim capoeira as their own. To play devil's advocate for a moment, one might point out that Afro-Brazilians have endured a great deal of suffering in order to protect this art, the embodiment of their cultural heritage, from being snuffed out by repressive regimes characterized by racial prejudice. Indeed there area some capoeira groups, particularly in the United States, who limit the participation of whites because of this history (see chapter 5). On the other hand, from the 1960s onward, white *capoeiristas* from Brazil and beyond have taken a significant role in protecting and promoting the art.

Such questions of identity and appropriation are increasingly important as the world becomes more interconnected, boundaries become more permeable, and people have more options than ever before for constructing their identities (see also Cheng 2004). The implications of cultural appropriation are vast and varied, depending in great part upon the power dynamics involved. The local and global stand in tension with one another, reaffirming long held identities while simultaneously allowing people to sample new ones. Yet when the local becomes a commodity for sale on the global market, Westerners who sample from far-flung cultural tables are said to be appropriating.

Despite the negative charges that could be levied against anyone attempting to perform the Other, this practice can potentially generate an increased self-reflexivity in the performer (Johnson 2003: 209). The dissonance felt when embodying a performance style from another culture may cause the performer to look at the practice more critically to determine which aspects are okay to embody and why. Granted, not everyone will engage in such introspection, and many will instead just ask themselves if a practice feels right and pursue it based on that self-evaluation.

The reasons that nonblack and non-Brazilian individuals pursue the practice of capoeira in the first place are as varied as the practitioners themselves, with some being attracted to the physicality, some to the artistry, and others to the sociability provided by training. Yet others conform to MacCannell's (1976) expectation that the sense of alienation that accompanied the rise of modernity leaves many Westerners in search of an authentic Other that will fill this void. As institutionalized rituals lose their place in modern life, people initiate their own quests for existential authenticity (Lindholm 2008). Such individuals attempt to do this through the consumption of goods and experiences, either through tourism or appropriation of cultural forms. Existential authenticity motivates pilgrims to claim legitimacy according to the dominant definition of authenticity protected by the social field, or the "duly authorized" standard (see Bruner 2005).

Tyrell was among those who felt that capoeira had become an integral part of his identity; denying himself the opportunity to deepen his connection with

Brazil would have been detrimental to his well-being. He had reached a point where he felt that "[he] was truly incapable of continuing [his] life in the United States." His passion for capoeira had become "all consuming," and he felt like he was "living a lie" in his nine-to-five existence. One day he said, "Why don't I just do it, all out. Get it out of my system, kind of calm down, then maybe I can have a 'normal' life, I'm putting this normal in quotes. ... big air quotes." For Tyrell, the only way to achieve balance and conform to the generalized expectations of a thirty-something American was to temporarily engage in this quest. Yet his very presentation of the word normal, stressing that it needed to be put in "air quotes," indicates that he does not quite know what normal means or what characteristics he is supposed to embody as a young American adult.

Like Tyrell, Bridget felt that something was missing in her life back home in the United States. She said,

> at this point in my life I'd rather be [in Bahia] than in the United States. And it's largely because of capoeira ... I don't think I'd necessarily be in Brazil if it weren't for capoeira, maybe I'd be somewhere else in the world. But I think that I have, there was an insatisfaction [*sic*] with living in the United States that has kept me here again and again and will probably keep me here through the next year. Brazil fulfills that insatisfaction [*sic*] with living in the United States and then capoeira is that icing on the cake.

Again, much like Tyrell, Bridget was at the early stages of a lucrative career when she decided to temporarily walk away from it. She holds a baccalaureate degree and a master's degree from elite institutions, but still has not accommodated to what are considered typical middle-class, American norms and values. She says that she sees a lot of people turning to *Capoeira Angola* precisely because they are "looking for more in life than what ... society offers you." She thinks this is especially true of the non-Brazilians who become *capoeiristas*.

Tyrell and Bridget are not anomalies. I heard similar stories over and over again. These individuals were clearly bright, highly educated, and hard workers, as evidenced by their success in mastering a very difficult art. Perhaps this is just evidence of wanderlust or prolonged adolescence, but for whatever reason, these individuals chose to opt out of entering the American rat race and instead sought an adventure that was related to an identity they chose for themselves rather than one that was imposed on them by the institutions of their upbringing. While careful to point out that contemporary, white-collar working conditions in Canada are not the same as what African and Afro-Brazilian slaves experienced, Janelle Joseph, a scholar of sport who has studied Canadians' participation in capoeira, nonetheless indexes a parallel between the way that *capoeiristas* in Western societies might feel trapped by their workaday routines and seek freedom in the counter-hegemonic space of the *roda* (2012: 1087). This may help to explain why so many well-educated pilgrims like Tyrell and Bridget temporarily left promising careers to pursue their study of capoeira in Brazil.

## Anxieties about Meeting Brazilians in the *Roda*

In a blog dedicated to discussing capoeira, Eurico Vianna (2011) raised an interesting question about inclusivity in the larger capoeira community. This blogger points out that when an individual joins a group, he or she is included at the local level, but there are still tensions between Brazilians and non-Brazilians. Vianna references a passage from Edward Said's (1984) work on exile, which claims that people in exile tend to exaggerate the boundaries between themselves and their fellow exiles and those in the larger society. This, Vianna writes, helps to explain the hostility and superiority some Brazilian capoeira teachers outside of Brazil exhibit toward non-Brazilian teachers. A number of readers commented on this post, confirming that Vianna's experiences of discrimination and conflict are not unique and that many Brazilians "conceive [of foreigners] as eternal students."

When training in the United States, I have been told that foreigners must train hard in preparation for their visit to Bahia because Brazilian players will test them and try to humiliate them in the *roda*, possibly even injuring them. As mentioned previously, I had heard the cautionary tale of a female student whose arm was broken by a *mestre* wanting to show his superiority. Similarly, Joseph stresses the latent violence in Brazilian capoeira and compares this with the ludic form of capoeira practiced among her research population in Canada. She says, "Canadian players are reminded that when they encounter 'real' Brazilian capoeira, they must be prepared for a fight" (Joseph 2006: 62). The *capoeiristas* in Joseph's study trained vigilantly to prepare for potential encounters with Brazilians. In my experience, however, games between Brazilians and foreigners were not necessarily more aggressive than what I had experienced at home.

With all of the things about which a non-Brazilian *capoeirista* might feel anxious—for example, their skill-level, their fluency in Portuguese, the likelihood that they will stand out as a naïve foreigner, and so on—it is almost surprising that they would even *want* to make a trip to Brazil where they will have to defend their legitimacy as outside practitioners of an art that figures prominently in Brazilians' national identity; but they do. Traveling domestically to participate in workshops and train with other groups is a useful technique for tapping into the extended capoeira community, but for most non-Brazilians, nothing beats going to Brazil. Because Brazil and Brazilian capoeira are positioned as the standards against which foreigners must measure their practice, foreigners like those studied by Joseph might approach Brazilian *rodas* with trepidation knowing legitimacy would only be bestowed if he or she could withstand the competition. In some cases this may be true; however, this oversimplifies the issue, and in reality, there are a number of factors that can predict whether one will be roughly handled or, alternatively, coddled in the *roda*.

## Before You Go, It's Who You Know that Matters

A pilgrim's lineage influences his or her access and acceptance by the local capoeira community. As a player enters the *roda,* his or her teacher is also metaphorically present. An experienced player could tell from a mile away that my style has more in common with that of Mestre João Pequeno than that of Mestre João Grande, both of whom are *Angoleiros* who had an affiliation with Mestre Pastinha prior to his passing in the 1980s. That embodied history will have a bearing not only on how well one performs in the *roda,* but also on how well one will be received in any given academy.

During my first game with Mestre Valmir, which I described in the introduction, Mestre Iuri was also physically in attendance. As we knelt in front of the *berimbau* and Mestre Valmir led the group in song, he cried out "long live my *mestre,* long live your *mestre*" and gestured in Iuri's direction. To this day, I have not decided if this was genuine respect, a bit of good-natured ribbing, or a combination of the two. The way Mestre Valmir tossed me around in the *roda* certainly did not seem to indicate any degree of reverence. On the other hand, the very fact that he sought me out for special attention indicated that he at least saw my humiliation as a worthy use of his time, which could be interpreted as a gesture of respect to my teacher.

The capoeira community is highly fractured and decentralized in large part because of its evolution in the shadows of respectable society, but lineage orients *capoeiristas* in an otherwise disorderly social field. Apprenticeship under a *mestre* legitimizes a *capoeirista* within this community (Downey 2005: 63 & 70). Entering into a training relationship admits practitioners into his or her teacher's lineage. In capoeira, as in most martial arts, prestige is associated with tracing one's ancestry back to the founder of the style. *Capoeiristas* commonly try to trace their descent back to Mestre Bimba or Mestre Pastinha, depending upon which style of capoeira they claim to play.

Among pilgrims there is a widespread belief that "to be a 'true' *Angoleiro* you must be recognized by the *Capoeira Angola* community, including connecting yourself in some way to *Capoeira Angola*'s lineage from Mestre Pastinha" (Timbers 2000: 151). Some groups buttress this legitimacy by tracing their lineage even further. For example, GCAP not only stresses Mestre Moraes's descent from Mestre Pastinha via Mestre João Grande, but also stresses that Pastinha himself learned capoeira from an African, Tio Benedito. Thus, "at the same time that Pastinha is a source of authority, his historically recent receipt of capoeira from an African strengthens the group's assertion that capoeira originated across the Atlantic" (Downey 2005: 70). By faithfully replicating the movement style of their forbearers, the group gives their political discourse bodily form (Downey 2005: 70).

A *capoeirista*'s lineage defines his or her orientation to the larger capoeira community. Teachers expect fidelity unless they have granted a student special permission to train with another teacher (De Campos Rosario, Stephens, and Delamont 2010: 104). A FICA student from Brasilia told me that in Brazil, students should have a *mestre* and only train with that *mestre*. He was referencing loyalty, perhaps in contrast to foreigners who come to Bahia and train at many different academies. This kind of behavior is tolerated in tourists, but it jeopardizes the pilgrims' chance of becoming completely accepted in the Brazilian capoeira community. Pilgrims can play in other *rodas* but are expected to remain loyal to their *mestre* in training. One of the first questions a capoeira pilgrim is asked upon arriving in Brazil is, "who is your *mestre?*" *Capoeiristas* affiliated with a recognized group will generally seek out the *mestres* in their lineage to train with in Brazil.

Capoeira pilgrims who have a preexisting relationship with an international franchise will typically not find it difficult to gain entrance to a Brazilian academy. They already know which academy they will be training with, and the Brazilian *mestre* will generally have little trouble locating the pilgrim within his mental framework of the capoeira community. The pilgrim's teacher may or may not be in the *mestre's* direct lineage, but affiliation with the franchise legitimizes the pilgrims' request to join the group. However, this is not to say that someone from outside an established lineage would be turned away; after all, even a completely unqualified pilgrim still represents tuition dollars. It is the case, though, that a pilgrim who does not come from one of the franchise's satellite groups is an unknown element. This was my predicament in 2008 when I approached Mestre Valmir at FICA about joining the group and conducting my research there. I felt fortunate that Mestre Iuri was also in Salvador at the beginning of my fieldwork and was present at the first *roda* I attended at FICA, which gave Mestre Valmir a sense of my lineage and allowed him to place me within the larger capoeira community.

Most unaffiliated pilgrims have to work a bit harder to gain acceptance into their new group than will someone with an established connection to a well-known teacher or franchise. Their first task is to decide upon which group they want to join. Bridget had come to Brazil a few times before I met her in 2008. On one of her earlier trips she had been training with a lesser-known group that was fairly distant from the historic area where FICA is located. She said that she just kind of "fell into" training with them because of the contacts she had made, but probably would have sought out FICA if she had known that they existed. This was prior to her involvement with a FICA group back home in the United States. Another woman who was talking with us agreed that people generally align themselves with whatever group seems most convenient because novices do not understand the nuanced differences between groups. I later spoke with a German pilgrim who was planning to stay in Bahia for two months. In addition to attending classes very regularly at FICA, she was also taking classes at two other nearby academies. She preferred the style of FICA, but found that it was sometimes easier to interact with people at the other academies, all of whom she thought were very nice. She thought that it was more difficult for her to become integrated into the FICA academy because she, unlike Bridget, was not affiliated with one of their satellite groups.

A large percentage of the *capoeiristas* who trained at FICA Bahia during 2008 were members of other FICA groups such as FICA Stockholm, FICA Paris, FICA Atlanta, FICA Oakland, and FICA D.C. Not only did these students share a similar movement style, they were also accustomed to the practical expectations of the group like how class is run, the prohibition against drinking water during class, and the expectation that students contribute to the upkeep of the physical space. I myself was only familiar with the prohibition against drinking water because I had committed that error when I attended a workshop in Austin that was led by Mestre Jurandir of FICA Seattle. When he saw what I had done, he quickly disassembled my *berimbau* and swept the stick back and forth underneath my feet making me hop over and over and over until I eventually was too slow and landed on the stick, which resulted in me crashing to the floor. One student who had not trained with FICA prior to her arrival broke this rule during a particularly hot day. When the *mestre* saw her at the water cooler, he stopped class and had everyone turn and watch her before pointing out her mistake and publicly scolding her for it.

*Capoeiristas* in the same lineage will exhibit many common characteristics. Most academies in the Pastinha line wear black and yellow, but sometimes wear all white in honor of the slave heritage in capoeira when men split canvas bags, sewed them into pant legs, and tied them tightly with cotton ropes. Other groups have different traditions, like Mestre Lua's students who wear blue and white or the group in Feira de Santana who wear leather sandals to honor their regional heritage as leather producers. At the very least, a *capoeirista* is normally expected to wear a T-shirt proclaiming his or her capoeira lineage. This takes on special significance when a *capoeirista* plays at a *roda* outside of his or her group. One evening, a Romanian capoeira pilgrim sat in the circle, waiting for the GCAP *roda* to begin. Mestre Moraes was not there, but his *contramestre* adhered closely to the etiquette prescribed by Moraes. The *contramestre* saw the Romanian's plain gray T-shirt and asked him where his uniform was. His tone was accusatory as if it were an insult for someone to attend this *roda* without announcing his or her lineage. Without this declaration, the *contramestre* had no way of situating the Romanian pilgrim within the social field. Incidentally, the primary reason this student was in Brazil was to find a *mestre* who might be willing to oversee his group in Romania, which was at the time without a leader.

Training with a *mestre,* or even a lower-level teacher like a *contramestre,* is important for a number of reasons. First, this individual serves as the group's visionary and gives cohesiveness to the group. Even chapters of FICA, arguably the most unified *Capoeira Angola* organization, have floundered when they did not have an authorized leader at the helm. In her master's thesis on capoeira, Caroline Timbers connects the presence of a *mestre* with the maintenance of authenticity in capoeira groups outside of Brazil by claiming that "American groups without *mestres* may begin to re-shape even Capoeira Angola's most central ideas" (Timbers 2000: 171). She is suggesting that without the guidance of a *mestre,* American students will, perhaps unwittingly, let their own cultural lens disrupt the traditions of capoeira. Whether or not this is really a problem is an entirely separate debate, which will gain more and more importance as the population of non-Brazilian *capoeiristas* grows.

Second, a *mestre* gives stylistic coherence to the group. Mestre Valmir's stylistic influence on his group is immediately apparent. Valmir's two sons would teach classes at FICA Bahia from time to time, and the way they moved in the *roda* looked so much like their father that it was a bit surreal. Stylistic similarities characterize *capoeiristas* from the same lineage; however, that is not to say that every teacher exhibits identical traits. A *capoeirista* from Thailand said that one of the things he liked about classes at FICA Bahia was that different teachers took turns leading the classes. During my time with the group, five different Brazilian teachers led classes on at least a semi-regular basis, and two Americans also had the opportunity to teach one class each. This variety can be in part explained by the frequency with which Mestre Valmir, the primary leader, is invited to teach workshops abroad. He was frequently away from the academy during my time there.

My acquaintance from Thailand appreciated that all of these teachers had the same basic foundation, which is essential for preserving the stylistic unity of the FICA franchise, but exhibited their own personal style too. During one session, Marcelo, who is Mestre Cobra Mansa's son, taught a slightly modified version of the *negativa* movement (a defensive posture in which the player lowers his/her body until it is parallel to the floor, almost touching the ground, with one leg outstretched and the other bent under the chest where both hands are placed for support). After class he said that João Pequeno uses this movement a lot, but not everyone in FICA does it. When someone pointed out that one of FICA Bahia's assistant teachers uses it, Marcelo said that is because he used to train with Mestre Jogo de Dentro, who descends from Mestre João Pequeno. Someone else pointed out another move that Marcelo had just taught and said that Mestre Cobra Mansa does it a lot, but it is not necessarily characteristic of the FICA style. Marcelo said yes, he does that because he is a close friend of a *mestre* who uses it, and they train together.

The seeming contradiction between the importance of lineage and the variability within lineages can be resolved by recognizing that while many elements of style are passed vertically down through the generations of *capoeiristas* via apprenticeship, style is also transmitted horizontally as peers train together and incorporate movements that they learn from their friends. Vertical transmission from master to apprentice is responsible for the continuities in a group's style while training with peers from other schools introduces variation. Brazilians are more likely to be the recipients of this horizontal transmission because they have more opportunities to play with *capoeiristas* from other schools. Non-Brazilians spend much more time training with members of their own group; the relative smallness of their community means they have less access to peers who train with different teachers. At FICA Bahia, it was possible for horizontal transmission to occur between foreigners and locals, and there were a few instances of Brazilians adopting, or at least experimenting with, elements of very skilled foreigners' style. Yet even with this degree of idiosyncrasy, *capoeiristas* are more similar to others within their lineage than those outside of it.

It is not only movement style, but also etiquette that students cultivate as a result of their lineage. For example, *Angoleiros* are supposed to conform to a particular style of dress, which may seem overly modest to women who are accustomed to working out in tank tops or sport bras or to men who are accustomed to going shirtless. I was taught early on that showing my shoulders would be disrespectful to the ancestors. Similarly, a *Capoeira Regional* student who attended class at FICA Bahia was warned that if she wanted to go to any *Capoeira Angola* *rodas* over the weekend, she would need to wear shoes and a shirt with sleeves. Mestre Valmir told this German woman, "if you go to an academy for a *roda* and you are wearing a sleeveless shirt, the *mestre* might ask you who your teacher is and then tell everybody that your *mestre* isn't keeping the tradition." In a similar example, an Israeli woman played in Mestre João Pequeno's *roda* one evening. She first started training capoeira with the famous group Cordão de Ouro in Israel, but now trains *Capoeira Contemporania* in the United States. Like many *Capoeira Regional* and *Capoeira Contemporania* players, she was wearing a close-fitting, short T-shirt. She tried to keep her shirt tucked into her pants, but every minute or two it slipped out of her waistband, exposing her midriff. Every time this happened, she and her partner were called back to the *berimbau,* and she had to fix it. After the fourth or fifth time, the man in charge of the *roda* called an end to their game. Clearly he had little tolerance for people that did not know, understand, or respect the customs at their academy. Adhering to tradition is an important way that students both mark themselves as insiders in this subculture and show respect to their lineage.

If a group or individual is not affiliated with a *mestre,* it is more difficult for them to develop relationships in Brazil. For example, the German woman who had violated the norm of covering her shoulders and wearing shoes typically trains with a *Capoeira Contemporania* group back home, but she trained primarily with FICA while in Brazil because her group did not have an ongoing relationship with a group in Bahia. She thought the people at FICA were nice, but she was unaccustomed to the amount of acrobatics in their games. She said she felt good about being part of FICA, but that it takes time to become integrated into a new group, especially if you are not already part of the international FICA system. She felt that it was more difficult for her to become integrated in the group than other foreigners who had a preexisting relationship with FICA.

Some of the members of Estrela do Norte felt a similar sense of alienation after severing ties with the parent group from which Mestre Iuri had originated. In a sense, we became capoeira orphans. When visiting Bahia in 2008, Iuri worked hard to seek out training opportunities for us, such as attending the kids' class at the Pierre Verger Foundation, attending a *roda* with Mestre Pele in the capoeira fort, and organizing private training sessions with an independent capoeira teacher. Despite his hard work, however, we were still a bit untethered in comparison to those pilgrims with a predefined base of operations. The consequences of this situation remain to be seen, but in all likelihood, pilgrims whose teachers have severed ties with their *mestres* who wish to become integrated into the core of the social field will have to work extra hard to claim a place in the local community.

Oftentimes, a student from a weaker lineage is assumed to be weak him- or herself. To be seen as legitimate, a *capoeirista* needs to be able to prove his or her descent from a teacher who is considered legitimate. After a *roda* at GCAP that I observed, Mestre Moraes gave a short lecture on globalization and its effects on capoeira. He, like so many others, questions the legitimacy of many teachers abroad. Three French *capoeiristas* had participated in this *roda,* though he only knew one of them personally. He asked the two others who their teacher was. He claimed that the only worthwhile teachers in France would have descended from his lineage. In an act of dismissal, he told them that the other French student could put them in touch with someone better, someone from his school.

Many *mestres* jealously defend the honor of their school. The politics of capoeira are complicated, and many relationships between *mestres* are wrought with tension, particularly when one group breaks away from its *mestre*. It is publicly known that Mestre Cobra Mansa established FICA after breaking away from GCAP, taking many talented *capoeiristas* with him. Both FICA and its sister group Nzinga originated out of GCAP. Though the FICA *mestres* maintain their distance from GCAP, their rivalry does not extend to the students. FICA students, particularly foreigners, frequently attended *rodas* at GCAP because it is such a well-known group of high quality. Some of my consultants suggested that petty feuds between *mestres* also weakened the Associação Brasileiro de Capoeira Angola (Brazilian Association of Capoeira Angola), which used to be the overriding organization for *Capoeira Angola mestres*. Today, however, this organization's activities are restricted to hosting weekly *rodas* where *mestres* from a variety of schools sometimes come to play one another. They also operate a capoeira store and rent out their upstairs space to various capoeira teachers who do not have a permanent space of their own.

Lineages serve to preserve tradition and legitimize *capoeiristas,* but they are not static. Lineages frequently split due to conflicts, like that between the *mestres* of GCAP and FICA, but may also expand in previously unforeseen directions as a result of new opportunities. Like the Romanian individual I described previously, some pilgrims come to Bahia because they are exploring the possibility of inviting

Brazilians to visit their countries, hopefully to establish a satellite outpost of their franchise. For example, two pilgrims with whom I trained were in the process of relocating to Holland. There is a capoeira teacher currently working there, but these pilgrims were hoping to lay the groundwork for eventually establishing a FICA chapter in Holland. For the most part, these were exploratory visits, and the pilgrims were not in a position to sponsor a Brazilian teacher's visa or financially support his relocation to another country, but it does demonstrate the value pilgrims place on being able to train with a teacher who is seen as legitimate by virtue of both his nationality and lineage.

The *mestres* of tomorrow are already well on their way to gaining prominence in the capoeira community. During one *roda* for which Mestre Valmir was absent, his two sons knelt at the *berimbau* and prepared to play the first game of the morning. During the *chula* (formulaic call and response song), they gestured to one another as they sang "*viva meu mestre, quem me ensinou*" (long live my *mestre*, who taught me). This playfulness indexed their shared learning under their father who is a *mestre*, but also seemed to slip into the subjunctive. They gestured to one another as if they were already *mestres*, and indeed with their heritage and training, it is not unlikely that they will one day become *mestres*.

Lineage is important because it determines a *capoeirista*'s style and positions him or her within the social field. As the Romanian pilgrim learned at the GCAP *roda*, some *mestres* will not acknowledge a pilgrim unless they know his or her lineage. Merely being adopted into a lineage does not guarantee legitimacy, which is predicated upon execution of proper form. However, without being affiliated with a lineage, a *capoeirista* will have a harder time gaining acceptance in a Brazilian capoeira academy. Their plight is not hopeless, however, and there may still be a chance that he or she can gain entrance to the community by either displaying the right forms of traditional cultural capital, with which one is born, or by adopting the right forms of charismatic capital (achieved characteristics that augment one's standing in the field), which are much more subject to change over time. In the end, the Romanian was just too earnest and eager to learn that the group could not help but welcome him into the community despite him being a free agent from a country completely outside of the African diaspora.

## Conclusion

The capoeira community has become incredibly diverse since being introduced to new audiences outside of Brazil. While many celebrate this diversity, it may also be seen as threatening by those whose power in the field may be challenged by outsiders. This, along with allegations that some of the capoeira instruction taking place abroad is subpar, is grounds for questioning the legitimacy of non-Brazilian *capoeiristas*. As I established in the previous chapter, travel to Brazil is one way that foreign *capoeiristas* can move to a more central position in this social field.

Not all *capoeiristas* will be engaged in this kind of identity work. Being seen as legitimate is most important to those individuals for whom capoeira has become a key piece of their existential authenticity, who they feel themselves to be at the core of their being. Their confidence in this identity is what they believe gives them the right to embody a tradition that comes from a culture other than their own. However, as I have argued in this chapter, local *capoeiristas* often need more than just a proclamation of a pilgrim's sincerity in order to validate his or her claim on the identity. Having the right lineage is key to gaining acceptance at the local level. Yet this is not the only factor that matters, and in chapter 5, I turn to the more overt, bodily markers of authenticity that may give *capoeiristas* a leg up in their quest for legitimacy.

## Works Cited

Armstrong, Edward G. 2004. "Eminem's Construction of Authenticity." *Popular Music and Society* 27 (3): 335–55.

Bruner, Edward M. 2005. *Culture on Tour*. Chicago: The University of Chicago Press.

Chaney, David. 1996. *Lifestyles*. London: Routledge.

Cheng, Vincent J. 2004. *Inauthentic: The Anxiety over Culture and Identity*. New Brunswick, NJ: Rutgers University Press.

Cohen, Erik. 1979. "A Phenomenology of Tourist Experiences." *Sociology* 13 (2): 179–201.

D'Aquino, Iria. 1983. "Capoeira: Strategies for Status, Power and Identity," PhD dissertation. University of Illinois.

De Campos Rosario, Claudio, Neil Stephens, and Sara Delamont. 2010. "'I'm Your Teacher, I'm Brazilian!' Authenticity and Authority in European Capoeira." *Sport, Education and Society* 15 (1): 103–20.

Downey, Greg. 2005. *Learning Capoeira: Lessons in Cunning from an Afro-Brazilian Art*. Oxford: Oxford University Press.

Johnson, E Patrick. 2003. *Appropriating Blackness: Performance and the Politics of Authenticity*. Durham, NC: Duke University Press.

Joseph, Janelle Beatrice. 2006. "Capoeira in Canada: Brazilian Martial Art, Cultural Transformation and the Struggle for Authenticity," MS thesis. University of Toronto.

Joseph, Janelle Beatrice. 2012. "The Practice of Capoeira: Diasporic Black Culture in Canada." *Ethnic and Racial Studies* 35 (6): 1078–95.

Lindholm, Charles. 2008. *Culture and Authenticity*. Malden, MA: Blackwell Publishing.

MacCannell, Dean. 1976. *The Tourist: A New Theory of the Leisure Class*. Berkeley: University of California Press.

Peterson, Richard A. 2005. "In Search of Authenticity." *Journal of Management Studies* 42 (5): 1083–98.

Taylor, Charles. *The Ethics of Authenticity*. Cambridge: Harvard University Press.

Timbers, Caroline C. 2000. "Building an International Quilombo: Meaning, Marginality, and Community in Capoeira Angola and Its Practice in the United States," MA thesis. Georgetown University.

Vianna, Eurico. 2011. "Random Thought: Capoeiras in Exile," Capoeira Thoughts, blog.

# Chapter 5

# A World in Which the Black Brazilian Man Is King

One of my favorite songs in capoeira is *"Navio Negreiro."* The opening lines proclaim: "Slave ship from Angola arrived, full of blacks, bringing King Nagô." It has always struck me as simultaneously sad and proud. That ship after ship would dock in Bahia's port and empty its human cargo is profoundly disturbing and stomach turning. To think that even a king would be reduced to chattel is deflating. Yet at the same time, this song explains that the slaves were not defeated by what had been done to them, and they managed to recreate their culture in a foreign land under the noses of their oppressors. And while I love this song, I also wonder what it means for me, as a white woman, to sing it in the company of those who are part of the African diaspora and to play alongside men who descended from kings.

## Introduction

The very title of this chapter acknowledges the intersectional nature of identity; the ideal *capoeirista,* at least in popular imagination, is not *just* black, Brazilian, or male, but is all three simultaneously. Other *capoeiristas* embody some or none of these characteristics. In some situations, these markers of identity are relatively unimportant, but in other contexts, one or more of these categories may become central. For example, for those *mestres* who feel called to defend the Brazilianness of capoeira, non-Brazilian *capoeiristas* may be seen as interlopers, but in a context that stresses the African roots of the art, those same *mestres* may feel an affinity with black *capoeiristas* of any nationality.

In conducting an intersectional analysis, "discussing multiple categories is only the first step" (Hancock 2008: 18). Understanding how these various categories contribute to the experienced privilege or oppression of an individual in any given scenario is a far more complex task. It is for this reason that Patricia Hill Collins advocates for a "strategy of *dynamic centering*, a stance of foregrounding selected themes and ideas while moving others to the background" (2008: 68). In this chapter, then, I first discuss the building blocks of this idealized *capoeirista* identity before examining the areas of intersection that cannot be easily separated.

After explaining why the body is so central to conceptualizations of authenticity, I discuss the importance of blackness in capoeira. This includes a discussion of many pilgrims' discomfort with discussing race, primarily because it calls attention to one of the most visible differences between themselves and the local population, as well as scattered resistance to white participation in capoeira. I then focus on the issue of nationality and why many *capoeiristas* think that it will be harder for a non-Brazilian to become a skilled *capoeirista*. Ultimately, however, race and nationality must be discussed together. Finally, I discuss the changing role of women in capoeira as well as the differences in achievement between Brazilian and foreign women.

## The Body's Role in Authenticity

Despite their confidence that capoeira "fits" who they are at the core of their being, many *capoeiristas* are also quite invested in external validation of their identity, which is closely associated with the body and bodily experience. The body's surface becomes a canvas upon which people display their identities. Terence Turner (2012) identifies a cross-cultural fascination with the decoration of the body, either through clothing or other forms of adornment such as body paint or piercings. Furthermore, he writes, "the surface of the body seems everywhere to be treated ... as the frontier of the social self" (Turner 2012: 486). *Capoeiristas* decorate their bodies in distinctive ways through their choice of clothing, as described previously in conjunction with my discussion of lineage, but may also tattoo their bodies with the image of the *berimbau*. Beyond the surface of the body, one's identity as a *capoeirista* can also be discerned from the movement of his or her body. I will never forget the day that my undergraduate thesis advisor told me I had traded a bit of my ballet dancer's uptightness for the *capoeirista*'s swagger. Nor will I forget the day I went shopping with a female capoeira pilgrim in Bahia who complained that capoeira gave women broad backs and overly muscular thighs, but said she would not trade her experience and expertise for a more streamlined physique.

Physicality brings a seemingly incontrovertible proof to experience. Physical challenges fit into an individual's self-making project in ways that overly constrained workaday routines cannot (Wang 1999: 363). This engagement confirms beyond any doubt for the tourist that his or her experiences are authentic because the body as medium of experience is beyond doubt (Lindholm 2008: 48). The pilgrims in my study had clearly conformed to this notion, and physical engagement with the capoeira community was the focus of their travel activities, but the implications of this concept extend far beyond the apprenticeship pilgrimage phenomenon. Parallels can be seen in such wide-ranging subsets of tourism as gastronomic tourism and sex tourism. In the first example, the tourist is literally consuming *terroir,* the taste of a place as expressed in culinary products. In the latter, the tourist is symbolically consuming the land through intimate contact with a representative of the land. Indeed, the female pilgrims I met were occasionally approached by men in Brazil who said that having sex with them could be their souvenir.

Because of the body's centrality in tourists' attempts at claiming an authentic experience, some seek to alleviate the burden of modernity by intentionally subjecting themselves to the physical hardships associated with nature or less-developed lifestyles. Lindholm compares these tourists with religious pilgrims, "practicing austerities along the way to ensure the validity of their religious experience" (2008: 42). Tourists may embrace hardship as a way of intensifying their experience and take pride in their accomplishment. For example, anthropologists Frederick Errington and Deborah Gewertz (2008) recount an experience in Papua New Guinea during which they were drawn into a competition with young backpackers over who had endured a rougher, and hence more authentic, travel experience. In such cases, it is the physicality of the tourists' experiences, and the marks left on their bodies that verify their encounter with otherness.

The body is more than just a physical presence; its semantic density influences others' perceptions of us. This is especially significant for individuals wishing to embody a tradition, like capoeira, that has traditionally been associated with the black, male body. Since the beginning of the Transatlantic slave trade, the black, male body has been objectified and denigrated, but is given special status within capoeira. Many of today's *capoeiristas,* however, do not fit this stereotypical image, and their bodies instead more closely resemble those of the oppressors who have tried to not only repress capoeira, but also destroy the culture responsible for it. These are sensitive issues to raise, even in a community that often professes its Afrocentricity. Unfortunately they cannot be avoided. In this martial art, the body becomes the center of attention in the *roda* where it is both an index of a player's heritage and the object upon which others' hostilities and aggression can be enacted.

Authenticity that is granted by virtue of one's ascribed characteristics is more irrefutable than are achieved qualities that must be legitimized by an external authority like a teacher or licensing body (Peterson 2005: 1086). In such cases, the individual does not need to do any additional work to qualify his or her group membership; membership is automatic. At first glance, it may seem strange to discuss ascribed authenticity within the context of a performance genre. I have not yet come across any infants who were born with the ability to deliver the perfect *rabo de arraia* ("stingray tail" kick) or play the *berimbau.* However, some genres do become so closely associated with a particular racial/ethnic group or nationality that it is difficult to be perceived as a legitimate performer without exhibiting these qualities. I call these ascribed characteristics, which serve as markers for legitimacy within a particular social field, traditional forms of cultural capital.

Traditional forms of cultural capital offer the simplest routes to authenticity because they are noncommodifiable qualities inherent to the individual; however, they are not sufficient in and of themselves to guarantee legitimacy. Final legitimacy rests upon mastering the form, but traditional forms of cultural capital may help individuals get their foot in the door with a particular teacher or academy, which will help them master the form. This is particularly true in groups that limit participation based on ascribed characteristics like race. While academies like this represent a minority within the capoeira social field, they have not gone unnoticed by the capoeira community. *Capoeiristas* at FICA typically argue that personal qualities like having a positive attitude or being outgoing are more important than one's race or nationality when it comes to gaining legitimacy in the field. Nonetheless, small occurrences at the academy point toward a naturalized tendency to favor *capoeiristas* who are rich in traditional forms of cultural capital. In this chapter, I ask whether or not the three stereotypical components of traditional capoeira identity—race, nationality, and gender—are still requisite characteristics for contemporary practitioners.

## Blackness and Authenticity

From minstrels to blues artists, from boxers to basketball players, the black male body has been historically objectified as a primitive spectacle (see Johnson 2003). This objectification of racialized bodies not only dehumanizes them, but also primes cultural performances for appropriation. Blackface, for example, can be seen as an attempt on the part of whites to both enjoy what they perceived as the licentiousness of black culture while simultaneously distancing themselves from it (Lott 1993). The marginality of performance in the Western intellectual tradition, due in large part to its association with the body, naturalizes whites' fascination with an objectified primitive display. This racist tendency fixes a simplified notion of what black culture is in the white public's mind, and this oversimplification leads many audiences to use race as an authentication device when viewing performances of hip-hop, gospel, jazz, blues, or capoeira.

Traditionally, most *capoeiristas* were poorly educated, black men from the lower strata of Brazil's socioeconomic system. And while it is still commonly practice among this demographic, capoeira is also becoming prevalent among the middle and upper classes. Mestre Valmir acknowledged that the world of capoeira is changing, and today there are doctors, lawyers, and professors playing capoeira, whereas in the past it was stevedores and fishermen. As Assunção writes:

> A capoeira roda allows one to log into the homepage of an epic past and a glorious present. As such it is still a powerful marker of ethnic (black),

regional (Bahian) and national (Brazilian) identities, despite its expansion
to new constituencies that are none of these three. (2005: 212)

In many *rodas* today, it is common to find blacks and whites, Brazilians and
foreigners, rich and poor, men and women. However, that is not to say that each
is given equal value in this economy of authenticity.

Joseph notes that this "tacit confluence of blackness and Brazilianness cannot
be ignored" within capoeira (2008: 203). Repeatedly in her study, Canadian teachers, both black and white, chided Canadian students for moving like stiff "whities"
and told them to move more like blacks (Joseph 2008: 203). Though De Campos
Rosario, Stephens, and Delamont were speaking of *maculele,* a complimentary Afro-
Brazilian art form, their observations about students' anxiety are also relevant to
capoeira. Writing of the British students in their ethnographic study, they report,
"some students may ... be self-consciously embarrassed at the spectacle of rather
unskilled light skinned Europeans attempting a pale shadow of an African-Brazilian
slave dance" (De Campos Rosario, Stephens, and Delamont 2010: 113). These
anxieties conflate physical skill with racial identity, which largely comes from the
longstanding and widespread erroneous belief in the physical superiority of one "race"
over another. These myths tend to persist in society despite anthropologists' and
others' best efforts to explain how race is a social construct without biological validity.

Behind the discourse of equality that is prevalent in capoeira, and Mestre
Pastinha's claim that capoeira is for "*homen, menino, e mulher*" (man, child, and
woman), black Brazilian men inhabit a naturalized place of authority in capoeira.
While poor Afro-Brazilian men often occupy marginal positions in Brazilian society at large, they are simultaneously assumed to occupy the highest rungs of the
legitimacy hierarchy within capoeira. Joseph has identified "a socio-ethnic hierarchy that is the reverse of mainstream Canadian society" (2006: 51). She found
that dark-skinned, poor, and newly immigrated Brazilians who also had a high
skill level inhabited the upper realms in the Canadian capoeira hierarchy (Joseph
2006: 51). This suggests that all things being equal, those rich in traditional claims
to authenticity will claim a privileged position in the social field, at least in its
non-Brazilian outposts.

## Pilgrims' Discomfort with Discussing Race

Many of the pilgrims that I interviewed were uncomfortable with my questions
about race. They were shocked that I would even ask about the importance of
race because they believe race has no place in the practice of capoeira. Yet most
of those who expressed such shock were not black. There was only one African
American (U.S.) individual in my study population who trained consistently at
FICA, though one black woman from France did visit for a few weeks. In contrast to the underrepresentation of non-white foreigners among capoeira pilgrims,
there are, understandably, a large number of Afro-Brazilians who train capoeira

in Bahia. One of the teachers at FICA said it might seem like blacks dominate in capoeira, but his reasoning was pragmatic; capoeira originated in an area with a high density of African descendants, so their numbers naturally predominate. Indeed, the social and demographic characteristics of place are important for shaping the expectations of a social field.

Though many practitioners do not like to talk about it, race is ever present in debates around authenticity in capoeira, whether as part of a black pride agenda or as a problem to be explained away by white participants. Within the context of various African diaspora arts, white privilege often gives rise to the luxury of color blindness (Harrison 2008). White participants are able to claim that because they practice a stereotypically black art, they themselves cannot be racist.[1] This helps them sidestep uncomfortable allegations about inappropriately coopting the art (Harrison 2008). However, in capoeira, this color blindness is often advocated by Afro-Brazilians themselves as they encourage their students to adopt the *mestres* and African slaves as their own ancestors.

Nonblack capoeira pilgrims underplay the racialized aspects of capoeira in a number of ways: (1) by espousing the view that all people come from Africa; (2) by developing an intellectual identification with the African diaspora through historical and cultural studies; and/or (3) by referencing their own painful histories as a source of identification with oppressed peoples. Nonetheless, they often fail to grasp the severity of the racial inequalities playing out in front of their eyes. The fervor of their attachment to this Afro-Brazilian art, especially in the case of *Capoeira Angola* practitioners, would lead one to expect more politicized aspects of their engagement with Brazilian culture, but these are largely absent. While several of the pilgrims I worked with had volunteered to teach capoeira to underprivileged youth in the *favelas,* their empathy did not appear to extend to all poor Afro-Brazilians. This became painfully clear when my own whiteness and nationality became the center of attention.

After an evening training session, I walked approximately three blocks to the bus stop, as was my habit. Normally I walked with a few other students who were also catching the bus, but on this particular evening, attendance at the class had been slim and those few students who had attended were on their way out to a nightclub. As I walked, three children surrounded me. It was difficult for me to determine their ages, as they were all very malnourished and sickly looking. One held a butcher knife inches from my chest while the other two took all of my belongings, including the *berimbau* that I was carrying. Frightening as this incident was, it is not uncommon for foreigners and locals alike to be mugged. Once I moved past my fear and anger, I was actually able to develop some amount of sympathy for these children who were either orphaned or chose to live on the streets because it was an attractive alternative to their home life (see Hecht 1998). When I mentioned this incident at the academy, it was the first sustained dialog I witnessed regarding race and racism.

A capoeira teacher that anthropologist Margaret Wilson studied under had no sympathy for tourists who get robbed, saying "they can afford it ... And they're stupid. They just come to take what they want and get it cheap" (quoted in Wilson 2007: 19). I found my own teachers to be much more sympathetic, but it was the reaction of my fellow students that interested me the most. I took a day off from training to deal with a few of the practical matters like reporting the crime, to no avail, and canceling my credit cards. When I returned to the academy, a foreign woman who had lived in Bahia for a significant amount of time and who had heard about the incident entered the dressing room and started talking animatedly. She said that people here hate foreigners, and this is the root of problems like my mugging. She said they look at me, "*uma rainha*" (a queen), "*bonitinha*" (pretty), and see that I have all these things and they hate me for it. They wonder why I should have all these things while they are hungry. She said people hate her too because she makes more money than they do, but she has worked hard, mastered the language, and deserves the money she makes. Her hard work got her to where she is now, and poor people hate her for it. The grammatical construction she used for this, "*ter raiva*" (to have rage), conveys extreme sentiment. I agreed that it did not seem fair to me that I should have life so easy just because of who my parents are and where I was born, but the anger she and others felt toward people holding such attitudes struck me as a bit extreme.

Another capoeira group in Bahia that hosts a significant number of foreign pilgrims has a loosely articulated policy on caring for foreign guests. If there was an "un-Brazilian looking" foreigner among the group, the *mestre* insisted that someone walk with him or her to wherever he or she needed to go. I found this phrasing to be a bit unusual, but in Bahia where the majority of the population is of African descent, my consultant's phrasing can be interpreted as meaning "white." Sometimes the *mestre* would personally drive students home because he felt it was just a matter of time before they would be robbed. White foreigners, or gringos as they are generally called, are known to be *alvos* (targets) for muggings; clearly I was no exception.

After being mugged and seeing what intense emotions it evoked, I started collecting similar narratives from capoeira pilgrims. There was a man who had been mugged at knifepoint like myself in nearly the same spot, a woman who had been stabbed in the hand after resisting her muggers, another woman who had been mugged at gunpoint by someone in a car while waiting for a bus with another *capoeirista*. My list became sadly long. Yet rather than directing their outrage toward a racial hierarchy that positions Afro-Brazilians at the very bottom of the social strata, creating a desperation that leads some children and young adults to engage in petty crime and theft as well as some of these more serious, physical confrontations, most of my fellow pilgrims felt that the *children* were the racist ones. In other words, they are racist because they target white foreigners who they assume to be rich.

I use a much more limited definition of racism, which holds that while anyone can be prejudiced or discriminate against others, only those who have the power to oppress others because of their so-called race should be labeled racist. Nonetheless, the pilgrims passionately held to their position that the children were racist and associated whiteness with wealth, which is why whites were the target of such attacks. And while most pilgrims are not rich by the standards of their home countries, the gap between their standard of living and that of the street children is almost unfathomable.

I can recall very few conversations with non-Brazilian *capoeiristas* that seriously addressed these inequalities.[2] More often than not, I would either hear complaints about being asked to pay the "gringo price" for classes (meaning higher fees than locals were expected to pay) or about the hassle of dealing with beggars on the streets. Either these individuals were not aware of their white privilege, or they felt that their voluntary association with an African diaspora art gave them a pass from recognizing their collusion in this system.

At a capoeira gathering in Indiana, Mestre Iuri told his students that "many students ask [him] how they, as whites, can sing *ladainhas* (litanies) and *chorridos* (choruses) that talk about slavery and 'my time of captivity,' but [he tells] them, 'you are a *capoeirista* now.'" It is as if by virtue of their participation in an Afro-Brazilian cultural art form, white students have adopted Africa as their philosophical, if not actual, motherland. Statements such as these are often accompanied by very basic discussions of mitochondrial Eve and the fact that if people trace their ancestry back far enough, everyone can claim African heritage.

Similarly, in her master's thesis on capoeira in the United States, Timbers relates an incident in which she was singing a song in class. The *mestre* told her she had forgotten two lines of the song: *Capoeira veio da Africa/Africana eu sou* (Capoeira comes from Africa/I am an African). Believing that proper singing in capoeira requires conviction, she questioned how she, a white American woman, could sing about herself being an African. She had this to say about her experience:

> Clearly, being a white American singing this song, I was twisting the meaning of the words. However, as I sang, I realized that the words were also twisting my self-conception. At that moment, I felt a much closer connection to Capoeira Angola's "African" roots, which I had never really considered before. I was forced to think how calling myself an "African" and having others around me accept this idea re-worked the word. Its use to describe a physical location or to reference certain cultures became secondary, while the idea that its use made me part of something exclusive, separate from the dominant societal paradigm, as well as subversive [became primary]. (Timbers 2000: 125)

This suggests that there is some degree of imaginative work that must be done in order for white *capoeiristas,* primarily *Angoleiros,* to reconcile their competing beliefs that capoeira is inseparable from blackness, but can also belong to them.

This leads me to ask, perhaps crudely, is Africa a state of mind? In some ways, this seems to be the way that many *capoeiristas* operate. White *capoeiristas* frequently allude to the sense of connection they now have with Africa despite their privileged position in the dominant societal paradigm, and some *mestres* encourage students to identify with Africa in this way. However, these students do not share the lived experience of someone born into the African diaspora and tend to be ignorant of the blatant and more covert acts of racism to which people of color are subjected.

## Capoeira and Political Activism

*Capoeiristas* today generally recognize the important role played by Africans in the creation of their art; however, this recognition does not imply that all *capoeiristas* are activists. Oftentimes their statements of recognition are no more than lip service ironically papering over the persistent injustices that Afro-Brazilians experience on a regular basis. For example, Bahian cultural minister Juca Ferreira was recently quoted as saying "the step of recognition [of capoeira] brings the society closer to a racial democracy, valuing a typically black cultural manifestation, but that today has international dimensions" (Carmezim 2008, translation mine). This followed a pronouncement in 2008 that capoeira had been named part of Brazil's intangible cultural patrimony.

By valuing the black origins of capoeira, individuals index themselves as nonracist (Downey 2005: 15), while also positioning themselves as part of a global community. This was made particularly clear in another statement Ferreira made, claiming that the recognition of capoeira will remove the stain of slavery in Brazil by recognizing the African contributions to the country (Ribeiro 2008). In reality, it will be a long time if it is indeed ever possible to remove this stain. Here I do not mean to target Ferreira or discount his appreciation of capoeira, but to demonstrate that the overly optimistic view that Brazil can be a racial democracy has permeated official discourse. Proclamations that valorize Afro-Brazilian contributions to the nation's patrimony are nice, but it will take considerably more action on the ground to make any real difference in the lives of Afro-Brazilian people.

Many capoeira groups that take an Africanist stance toward its creation do advocate for black rights and prioritize fighting discrimination as a central mission of their group. The GCAP mission, as stated by founder Mestre Moraes, has an explicit Afrocentric agenda. Their purpose is to preserve *Capoeira Angola* as well as spread awareness of its African roots and Afro-Brazilian expression that embodies political, cultural, and racial struggles. Reflecting on the constitution of GCAP, Ferreira notes with pride that people of all races, ages, and nationality come together, and their only difference is in personal ability (Ferreira 1997). Ferreira's association with GCAP began in the 1980s, at which time he felt the city of Salvador come alive with black consciousness (Ferreira 1997), which created the right environment for GCAP's message of black pride to gather a following. Moraes (1997) argues that prejudice against Afro-Brazilians must be surmounted in order to appreciate the beauty inherent in the aesthetics of capoeira. Mestre Cobra Mansa, figurehead of an international capoeira organization, interprets Mestre Moraes's strong agenda as a necessary recognition of the art's heritage, which is sometimes swept under the rug by instructors teaching capoeira abroad because of their own discomfort in raising racial issues with students of different ethnic backgrounds (Taylor 2007: 151).

## The Importance of Place in Authenticity Work

It was the first week of my 2008 trip to Brazil. Camille, Jerome, and I had accompanied Mestre Iuri to a children's capoeira class at the Pierre Verger Foundation. I had visited once before, but it was a new experience for my two fellow students. Camille in particular, perhaps because she is a mother, really enjoyed meeting the children, talking with some of their mothers, and learning more about the organization's goals. Here underprivileged kids were given expert instruction in traditional Afro-Brazilian arts like capoeira and dance while also having access to a library, job training programs, and, perhaps most importantly, a hot meal. We happily played with the children before class began. They were fascinated by my camera, and I made the mistake of turning it over to them, thinking how great it would be to capture some of this experience through the eyes of children. I got some great shots; then it broke. Many of these children were only eight or nine and most had never used a camera with a zoom lens, so I should not have been surprised. Others were in their early teens, but there was still a vast age difference between them and us.

We started the session by running a few laps around the room and then did some calisthenics, not that our muscles really needed to be warmed up in such muggy, tropical conditions. I attribute this quirk of training to the push for institutionalization and the physical education pedagogies that were imported to Brazil from much colder climates like Scandinavia. Truth be told, I was exhausted before we even started with the capoeira training, and I was a well-conditioned 25-year-old. I assumed that the children must have been tired too because their attention gradually flagged. When a critical mass of them had stopped participating, they were admonished with a shout of, "look, even the Americans are doing better than you!" Clever, I thought, to tap into their competitive side to get them back on track. But then again, we probably *should* have been better than them. We were much older and had been training for longer than most of them. Even if years spent training were not a factor, our greater maturity allowed us to reflect on our training and self-direct our learning in a way that is largely out of reach for children. Nonetheless, in this case, nationality seemed to trump age and time spent training as a key marker of legitimacy in the field.

In trying to understand one another, Brazilians and foreigners often relied on national stereotypes. For example, Japanese students were coveted because they were reputed to prioritize the collective over the individual (see Fujita 2009: 57 on this stereotype). Brazilian *capoeiristas* at FICA Bahia generally had a hard time differentiating the American and British pilgrims from one another. All English speakers were lumped together. This was not based on ignorance or ill will, but was an understandable reaction to the complexity of interacting with so many people from different cultures. Hanging out in the academy during lunch one day, Mestre Valmir, Valmir's son Aloan, who also teaches at FICA Bahia, and a female pilgrim from Mexico were laughing about the different habits foreigners bring into the academy. Hygienic practices in particular were cause for amusement, but Mestre Valmir pointed out that when you travel somewhere else, there will be some things that you get accustomed to and adapt to, but other ingrained habits are hard to change. In another instance, when I expressed concern that Mestre Valmir did not like me because he picked on me during training, another American woman said that a lot of teaching in capoeira involves humiliation, and it is a "very Brazilian" way of dealing with students. Stereotypes like these, while often incorrect, at least provided a basis for common interaction if not real understanding.

Ways of moving and carrying the body, or corporeality, are associated with different cultural values and are often indicative of the spaces in which one's enculturation has taken place, whether those spaces are in the homeland as would be the case for Brazilians learning capoeira at home or in the transnational arena, which is the case for non-Brazilians learning capoeira in their own nations (Joseph 2008). Though humans everywhere have "the same basic sensory capacities," the development of these capacities will be directed by one's culture and, to a lesser extent, the elective training one pursues (Howes and Classen 2014: 9). There is a pervasive sense that while it is not impossible for non-Brazilians to learn capoeira, it will be significantly more difficult for them than it would be for a Brazilian. Mestre Moraes claimed that "learning Capoeira Angola was not impossible for [foreigners] … but a German would have to 'sacrifice more' to achieve proficiency" because his or her body was not accustomed to the habits demanded by the Afro-Brazilian aesthetic (Downey 2005: 196). Similarly, a Brazilian teacher working in London conveyed that "the habitus of *capoeira* is … quintessentially Brazilian. Brazilians are born into that aspect of the habitus, but others are not" (De Campos Rosario, Stephens, and Delamont 2010: 110).

In discussing the racial dimensions of the fifty-two hand blocks, a fighting style typically associated with African Americans, Thomas Green explains that "it is less a matter of 'white guys can't flow' than it is that in general at the microsocial level of culture they do not flow" (2013: 138). Anyone could potentially learn the habitus associated with this fighting style, but "white guys" rarely do because they are not immersed in the cultural context (prisons and inner cities) where this habitus is constructed through repeated opportunities to fight in close quarters. Likewise, it is not impossible for non-Brazilians to cultivate the bodily habits of a *capoeirista,* but it is difficult and will take intentional cultivation, typically with the help of a Brazilian teacher. In this sense, capoeira can be said to be as much a Brazilian space as it is a "black space," meaning that both blackness and Brazilianness confer a special type of legitimacy on practitioners without them having to exert any special effort (see Downey 2005: 15). This gives Brazilians a naturalized position of authority within the capoeira social field, which provokes anxiety among some non-Brazilian practitioners who question their own legitimacy in relation to their Brazilian counterparts.

## Resistance to Non-Brazilians' Participation

Debates over the importance of nationality are becoming more intense with the increasingly rapid globalization of capoeira. While some *mestres* view the globalization of capoeira as a positive development and recruit foreign students with an evangelical zeal, not everyone shares their rosy outlook. At the 1990 World Samba Capoeira Meet held in Rio de Janeiro, many *mestres,* some of whom had relocated to teach capoeira abroad, gathered to debate the future of the art. One topic of concern is whether or not Americans in particular would usurp control over the future of capoeira's development. Nestor Capoeira quoted the esteemed Mestre Jelon Vieira, who was among the first Brazilians to perform capoeira abroad, as saying:

> There are several American students (sociology, anthropology, Afro-studies, etc.) doing graduate studies with capoeira as their topic. Americans have the tradition of going into a specific area with determination, embodying everything. Some believe and try to prove that capoeira is exclusively African without any Brazilian influence. With time, some may believe Brazilians have to go to the U.S. to do their research, making Brazilian capoeira a secondary thing. (Capoeira 2002: 300–301)

As an American (U.S.) anthropologist, I am aware of the irony of including Vieira's critique in my own book. Clearly, some *mestres* are preoccupied with the growing dominance of Americans in the study of capoeira and with good reason. Throughout history, whoever has had the ability to shape discourse has managed to foist their vision of how society should work on those in more marginal positions. Despite the seeming durability of Brazilians' positions in the capoeira hierarchy, it is conceivable that this could change over time as Brazilian *mestres* cede more and more control to foreigners.

African Americans in particular were discussed at this gathering as posing a particular challenge to Brazilian authority. African Americans who claim affinity with Brazil based solely on race may come into conflict with Brazilians of all races who resent such presumptions (Downey, personal communication 2005). Several *mestres* at this conference expressed concerns that globalization would open the door for special interest groups to coopt capoeira for ideological purposes. Several alleged that African Americans were reframing capoeira as an African diaspora art, rather than a Brazilian one.

Indeed, capoeira has been used by African Americans who are anxious to invent traditions and symbols they can use to confront a white world (Sansone 1997). This is not a new phenomenon coinciding with the arrival of capoeira from Brazil; rather, it is a continuation of the colonial era practice of African Americans using sport to forge a sense of shared cultural identity in the face of white oppression (Green 2003). Though black nationalists in the United States could have turned to any number of martial arts as a focal point for community building, and kung fu has been adopted by some groups, many have gravitated toward combative forms with African roots or created an Afrocentric narrative to compliment their practice of other forms. These groups stress the African roots of capoeira, largely ignoring Brazilian innovations.

In an attempt at regaining control over the representation of their art as a uniquely Brazilian creation, several of the *mestres* at this event publically disregarded deeply held Africanist beliefs about the origins of capoeira. For example, Nestor Capoeira incited intense, emotionally charged debate by publicly refuting the *N'Golo* thesis, which holds that capoeira originated from a specific dance form found in Angola (see Capoeira 2002). This idea has been around for quite some time and is fervently defended by many *Capoeira Angola* schools, though no one has been able to definitively prove or disprove it. Quite predictably, deadlock ensued between the Africanists and the Brazilianists.

Mestre Acordeon, a *Capoeira Regional mestre* who is generally aligned with the Brazilianist position, viewed this debate as an opportunity to come to consensus on a unified version of capoeira that could be presented to outsiders. In his experience teaching American students, he "perceived a tendency in some Afro-American radical minorities to use capoeira and other arts of African origin to support private interests or certain ideologies. And in doing so, they distort capoeira's essence and diminish Brazil's role in capoeira's history and origins" (Capoeira 2002: 299). Nestor Capoeira further quotes Mestre Acordeon as having said "If we don't mark our position, these [radical Afro-American] minorities will do it for us, distorting capoeira as we know and practice it" (2002: 299).

The same range of attitudes toward foreigners being expressed by these *mestres* was also in evidence at various capoeira academies throughout Bahia.[3] Although FICA was quite welcoming of students from all over the globe, some academies had the reputation of marginalizing foreigners. And "why not?" one of my interview subjects asked. She admits that her group sometimes marginalizes Brazilians who attend classes and events at their academy in London. She said they do not like it when certain Brazilians show up at their academy because they are arrogant and claim to know everything about capoeira by virtue of their heritage, which is why the British students marginalize them. Therefore, she is not surprised when Brazilians behave in a similar manner, marginalizing foreigners who presume to know their traditions.

At a public forum in 2008, a group of *mestres* agreed that one of the biggest challenges for the preservation of capoeira in contemporary society was getting foreigners to understand the fight as something more than physical movements done to the accompaniment of the *berimbau* (Portela 2008). Mestre Cobra Mansa framed the problem in even more specific terms. He lamented that foreigners have trouble understanding the essence of capoeira because they want to think of it in terms of their own culture, not Afro-Brazilian culture. He said the hardest things to teach are the slang, the proper way to be a *malandro* (tough guy), and the *malícia* that must be expressed with the body, but "when these students go to Brazil they are able to understand. It is like something clicks" (Portela 2008). These are essentially embodied attitudes that arise out of the history of marginalized populations in Brazil and are reinforced in Brazilian popular culture.

Thus it is not the technique that is so difficult to transmit to foreigners, it is the feeling behind the technique that is difficult for them to grasp because they have not been steeped in the same folklore as a Brazilian. These elements of performance are similar to the paralinguistic elements that make talk meaningful. Words, by themselves, can only communicate so much. Yet when coupled with intonation, pitch, gesticulation, and facial expressions, they become much richer and more clear. In much the same way, the paratechnical features of capoeira performance separate those who have an embodied understanding of Brazilian culture from those who do not. Fortunately, as Mestre Cobra Mansa points out, pilgrims can adopt these paratechnical elements of performance once they visit Brazil.

## The Race and Nationality Duet

Just as it would be impossible to have a capoeira *roda* without two partners in the ring, it is ultimately impossible to disassociate race and nationality in discussions of *capoeiristas'* identity. As I have been arguing in this chapter, there is a great deal of slippage between the categories of race and nationality, which is why they must ultimately be discussed in tandem. Distinguishing the relative weight of race versus nationality in capoeira is particularly challenging because Brazilian national identity is so closely intertwined with a belief about racial or ethnic heritage. Despite the persistence or racial inequalities in Brazil, Brazilians frequently claim that their national character is forged from African, European, and Indigenous practices.

In comparing various countries where people now practice capoeira, one of Taylor's interview subjects said "if you are going to jump to Europe, where they don't have a background that's African, sometimes it can be double difficult for them to learn, but when they do learn sometimes they see a few things that we cannot see" (in Taylor 2007: 390). In this quote, it is hard to know here whether the teacher is really referencing race or nationality. He seems to take for granted that Brazilians would have a familiarity with African-derived traditions simply because of their nationality. However, this oversimplifies the real nature of race relations in Brazil. Since the birth of the regionalist movement in the early part of the twentieth century, elite Brazilians have often paid lip service to African traditions without really valuing it or permitting their children to engage in them. It is thus conceivable that a European could have had more direct exposure to Africans and African traditions than a white, upper-class Brazilian, but this would run counter to the racial democracy myth that has been part of the Brazilian worldview for so long.

When practitioners debate who "owns" *Capoeira Angola,* they attribute different values to the concepts of race and nationality. Some argue that Brazilians own capoeira while others believe that it belongs to anyone in the African diaspora. Still others feel that capoeira rightfully belongs to those who dedicate themselves to its preservation in any country. According to one of my consultants, the FICA DC group practiced exclusionary racial politics until Mestre Cobra Mansa deliberately intervened and integrated their practice by reaching out to nonblack students. Since that time, many in the extreme Afrocentric camp have since fallen away from the group. My consultant used this as evidence that capoeira belongs to whoever dedicates him- or herself to the art. Joseph uses the phrase "kinesthetic citizenship" to capture the sense of entitlement many *capoeiristas* feel to represent a Brazilian art (2008: 205). While recognizing that they are not actually Brazilian, many *capoeiristas* do feel that they have a right to train in Brazil and claim the art as their own by virtue of their extreme dedication.

On a few occasions during my time in Brazil, I was told that during the height of these debates, a satellite capoeira group in Philadelphia hosted an all-black *roda* to kick off a weekend-long event. On the surface, this story seems to be about race, but upon closer inspection it reveals the complex interrelations between race and nationality. White members of the group were allowed to attend, but their role was limited to behind-the-scenes support. What made this situation particularly awkward was their invitation of a white Brazilian *mestre* to the event. Fortunately for them, the *mestre*'s flight was delayed, and he thus arrived the day after the *roda,* allowing the group to conveniently skirt the issue of barring a white Brazilian *mestre* from their African American *roda.*

Whether or not the white members of the group colluded in this plan was not clear from these stories, and that omission is actually quite telling, but at least one white female was uncomfortable enough about the racial politics to leave the group. One *capoeirista* who shared this story with me argued that these individuals fail to understand the way Brazilians handle race. She acknowledged that many Brazilians claim a black identity and identify with the black power movement, but claimed that they do not tend toward the same racial isolationism that she sees practiced in some African American communities. While the scholarship on race in Brazil is beginning to acknowledge that the white/nonwhite dichotomy is more salient in Brazilians' lives than previously believed (see Sansone 2003), my consultant's impression that race has been conceptualized differently in Brazil than in the United States is nonetheless accurate.

Racism in Brazil has tended to be of a much subtler variety than its counterpart in the United States (Telles 2004: 2). This should not, however, be taken as an indication that its effects are any less disastrous than the more blatant forms seen in the United States. In many cases, the more subtle forms of racism are even harder to fight than the clearly institutionalized forms because the perpetrators and victims alike often deny or overlook its existence. One piece of evidence to which Brazilians point when defending the racial democracy myth is their long history of interracial interactions. This integration is most visible in the institutions that were raised to the level of a national symbol under the Vargas regime and continue to do this symbolic work today: soccer, carnival, and capoeira (Telles 2004). Even *Candomblé,* an explicitly African religion, has a long history of accepting white members. Whether this inclusivity was motivated by a true desire to welcome fellow believers into their houses of worship or a more strategic interest in building a reputable clientele with powerful connections in the government, however, is debatable (see Telles 2004).

In contrast, racial relations within the United States have often been exclusionary. Whereas Brazil promoted a discourse of miscegenation and racial democracy, the United States enforced Jim Crow laws. While official segregation has ended, informal practices of exclusion are still evident in many areas of life. These exclusionary tendencies become visible when one group is either formally or informally barred from participation in a domain associated with another racial or ethnic group.

Based on the comments of certain *mestres* at the World Samba Capoeira Meet and the actions of certain Afrocentric *Capoeira Angola* groups in the United States, some students from the United States do interpret capoeira as a black practice. Livio Sansone, for example, argues that capoeira in the United States has "little or no room for non-black practitioners" (Sansone 2003: 87). While my own participation in this social field, and that of the many nonblack practitioners I have met in various parts of the country, would seem to refute Sansone's position, it remains the case capoeira in the United States is often interpreted through a racial lens. This also appears to be the case in Canada (Joseph 2012).

These different historical trajectories give weight to my consultants' assertions that U.S. and Brazilian students interpret the racial politics of capoeira differently. The legacy of slavery is an important aspect of capoeira for most Brazilian players, but repudiation of the Portuguese colonists' gross transgressions have not led most Brazilians to treat capoeira as a black-only space. Yes, they may from time to time denigrate the foreign gringos who infiltrate their spaces, but this anger is generally not aimed at white Brazilians. Extremely Afrocentric groups in the United States, on the other hand, have occasionally imposed segregationist tendencies onto this imported genre. Although this is outside the scope of what I am discussing here within the framework of apprenticeship pilgrimage, an important avenue of future study would be the ongoing conflicts between Brazilians who claim ownership of capoeira as part of their national patrimony, like the *mestres* at the World Samba Capoeira Meet, and African Americans who claim ownership of capoeira by virtue of common roots in the African diaspora.

Sometimes the conviction that capoeira is essentially a black art is manifest in practitioner's self-consciousness about their ability to embody a particular aesthetic. This is a rather common, if disturbing, attitude. I have heard even some of my most liberal and enlightened friends make fun of themselves for "dancing like a white girl." Taylor also describes the attitudes of some nonblack and non-Brazilian *capoeiristas* he has met:

> There are quite a few non-Brazilian students, many of them white, who view their own efforts at gingando, at *malícia*, at trying to develop an African Brazilian way of being with a healthy dose of ironic self-mockery (given the impossible nature of the task). Of course, there are many African American, African Caribbean, and Black European students who can find a greater degree of identification, though even when people have strong points of cultural reference, there are going to be qualitative differences in expression and understanding due to differences in geographical location, social class, and the age in which we live. (Taylor 2007: 220)

Taylor is pointing out the difficulties of adopting the *habitus* of another culture, a point with which several of the previously cited *mestres* would likely agree. For him, however, the solution is more complex than just making a pilgrimage to Brazil. His comment points out that there are both racial, national, and temporal differences between the contemporary European practitioners he studies and the men who originally developed capoeira. While he says that adopting this *habitus* is an impossible task, I see no reason why a white, non-Brazilian *capoeirista* cannot develop the sway, the deceitfully mischievous way of moving, epitomized in capoeira. It may take years of study, but it is possible. Likewise, there is no reason to assume that a European of African descent would have any more natural facility in this way of moving simply because of a shared ancestry hundreds of years past.

Sometimes non-Brazilians of any race are so intimidated by the prospect of trying to adopt this *habitus* that they settle for lower levels of proficiency than they could reasonably attain with some practice. A U.S.-born capoeira teacher in California writes:

I have ... frequently encountered capoeira students here in the United States with little to no ambition to reach any real level of proficiency, particularly tragic when it's a student with potential. This type of student may believe that simply because he or she was born here and not in Brazil that he or she is less gifted when it comes to capoeira. I have heard my mestre say countless times that the secret of capoeira is this: train capoeira! (Essien 2008: xvi)

Whereas this teacher's own *mestre*, a Brazilian, stresses dedication as the primary way to become a better *capoeirista*, many non-Brazilian students limit their ambition because of their own preconceived ideas about the impossibility of adopting an Afro-Brazilian aesthetic.

## The Uniqueness of Brazilian Capoeira

With the globalization of so many sports like soccer or cricket with enough standardization that there can be international tournaments, it is worth asking just how different capoeira in Brazil is from capoeira played elsewhere. *Capoeiristas'* opinions on this differ. Whereas the pilgrim whose diary entry I shared at the beginning of this book found that the familiarity of the capoeira *roda* was the one thing that helped her feel at home when she arrived in Brazil, several of the *capoeiristas* Timbers interviewed claimed to see significant differences between capoeira as it is played in Brazil versus the United States (see Timbers 2000: 61–62). Some cited the energy of the *rodas* in Brazil, some referenced the greater weight of history present in Brazil, but the most instructive comments referenced the different styles of play. One interviewee told her that Americans "fight at capoeira" whereas Brazilians "play" (Timbers 2000: 61). This stands in contrast to what Joseph's Canadian consultants told her and what I myself heard when training in Indiana.

The prevailing discourse holds that Brazilian capoeira is more violent, or at least more prone to violence, than variants found elsewhere, but the members of FICA DC that Timbers interviewed were specifically referencing the ludic aspects of Brazilian *rodas*. Her explanation of this comment echoes what the *mestres* at Ginga Mundo's 2008 gathering said about non-Brazilians needing to learn that capoeira is about more than movements done in time to music. It is about a sensibility, a playfulness, that makes the extreme skill necessary for "moving around one's opponent quickly and nimbly" appear effortless (Timbers 2000: 62). Novices, whether they are foreign or Brazilian, will have a difficult time executing the nuanced movements necessary for achieving this aesthetic of playfulness. Timbers seems to be suggesting that the necessity of playing with *malícia* must be taught to foreigners whereas it comes more natural to Afro-Brazilians because of the culture in which they are immersed. Following this line of reasoning, one could claim that because capoeira is part of Brazilians' quotidian experience in a way that it will never be for U.S. students, naturalness emanates from Brazilian *rodas* more so than their own *rodas* in Washington, D.C. However, it is possible that these skills have less to do with the cultural environment than with the density of practitioners in Brazil. According to this reasoning, the embodied sensibility of capoeira must be deliberately taught to foreigners because they do not have the opportunities to see advanced players who carry off such artistry (see Royce 2004) on a regular basis simply because their social field is much smaller.

Foreigners' insecurities are matched by some Brazilians' amazement when foreigners display any level of proficiency. In an issue of *Praticando Capoeira,* a popular Brazilian magazine for *capoeiristas,* the editor expressed his staff's amazement and delight at finding out that foreign *capoeiristas* were so passionate and respectful in their practice of capoeira (De Carvalho n.d.). Mestre Itapoan, a well-respected *capoeirista* from Bahia, was referenced as saying that not only the quantity, but also quality, of *capoeiristas* abroad is growing. This, he says, shows that the teachers are doing right by their students. The high quality of foreign *capoeiristas* is thus interpreted as evidence that the so-called VARIG *mestres,* or at least some of them, are indeed qualified to be teaching.

The theme running through this magazine was the florescence of capoeira outside of Brazil as well as the remarkable skill exhibited by many of these foreigners (De Carvalho n.d.). While the magazine writers treated this as a good thing, sometimes recognition of foreigners' skill is accompanied by a wave of anxiety that they are becoming too good, and many supplant Brazilians in the capoeira hierarchy. This was the case for Amity, a white British woman in her late twenties, who had an uncomfortable encounter with a local woman. Amity told me that she felt the local *capoeirista* was annoyed by her advanced level. She felt like this local woman wanted a justification for disparaging her, but could not find it because of her proficiency.

This theme also came up to some extent when people at the academy found out that I had been mugged. The female pilgrim who was so outraged by the children's hatred of me drew an explicit connection between this hatred and the globalization of capoeira. As we discussed the incident, she reminded me that some people think foreigners cannot play capoeira. She said some people hate Mestre Cobra Mansa because he has taken capoeira abroad, and they believe "this is a lie." At the time, I found it difficult to interpret her meaning. Upon greater reflection, however, I realized that the alleged falsity of capoeira abroad is a reference to its inauthenticity. She said people who hold this attitude want to hurt foreigners in the *roda.* She said FICA was different, but this attitude prevailed at other academies. "There is a lot of racism in capoeira," she said, "but no one wants to talk about it." It is worth noting that in her commentary, she conflates race and nationality, which is common in actual discourse.

In some cases, locals' discrimination toward foreigners may be unintentional. A novice Brazilian joined us one evening for class at FICA Bahia. Like so many, he tried it for a few sessions and was never seen again. On his first night, he was introduced to the other students there. Mestre Valmir said, "we have a lot of temporary people, but we have a base group too." He pointed to three of the Brazilian students, including one that everyone called "*maluco*" (crazy) who only showed up at the academy a handful of times during my fieldwork, typically with red eyes and dirty clothing. He did not include in this category either of the Japanese men who had been with the group for longer than some of the "base" members. In fact, the Japanese men attended classes more regularly than did anyone else during my time in Bahia. Despite all this, it was only the Brazilians who were introduced as being part of the base group. One of the Brazilians with teaching responsibilities at FICA Bahia told me that capoeira exists for all people equally, but there must be a Brazilian base in order for the group to be maintained. He says:

> I believe that the people that come from abroad come to learn, they come to give a little, they come to interact, but whatever capoeira group wants to remain … it has Brazilians or it won't be maintained, it won't have an identity, it won't have any of this.

In other words, the foreigners have a marginal role in the group because with their transient status, they are unable to contribute to the cohesiveness and identity of the group in the same way as the Brazilians can. Most pilgrims would not disagree. Their anxiety about detracting from this cohesiveness was sometimes manifest in whispered questions regarding whether or not the *mestres* had revealed to me how they really felt about the presence of so many foreigners in the academy.

Despite listing only Brazilians among the base group when introducing the new students to us, Mestre Valmir was always quick to appreciate the presence of foreigners in the academy. For example, FICA Bahia held a special end-of-year *roda* in mid December 2008. Mestre Valmir thanked several key people in the organization including his two sons and another teacher who had led classes during his various trips abroad. He also thanked Bridget and Tyrell, capoeira pilgrims from the United States who had each taught a class in December, as well as Daisuke and another Japanese *capoeirista* who had been integral members of the group. His special recognition of these pilgrims is significant and suggests that they were successful in transforming their cultural capital into legitimacy, but he also recognized the rest of the pilgrims in a more generic sense. He thanked them for leaving our homes, their countries, to come to Bahia for a week, a month, or more, letting them know that he valued their contributions to the energy of the *roda*.

At FICA, foreigners were generally well received. A female pilgrim from Russia told me that the marginalization of foreigners is a problem at some academies, but not at FICA. At FICA, she said, "everybody is equal," and that is why she has returned to train there on all of her visits to Brazil. At other academies, resentment of foreigners was more palpable. Typically, this became clear in how *rodas* operated. The first game of a *roda* sets the tone for the event, and some *mestres* are particular about who can play in this first game. At FICA Bahia, it was common for foreigners to start *rodas,* which suggests that foreigners and locals were treated equally. At other academies, the *rodas* would always start with two Brazilian players.

In practice, it was often difficult to determine whether or not aggression in any particular game was due to foreign/local conflict or whether it was based on other factors like lineage affiliation or position in the capoeira hierarchy. One game stood out to several witnesses as being particularly aggressive, and it was even more notable because it took place at Mestre João Pequeno's academy, a *mestre* who is known for encouraging his students to play slow, controlled, and beautiful games. Perhaps this case of aggression is not surprising because this academy is a requisite stop for many pilgrims, and one man from the United States suggested to me that locals go there with the intent of picking on foreigners in the *roda.*

A very skilled Israeli man and a local *contramestre* from another academy entered the *roda.* There was nothing unusual about the beginning of their game. The Brazilian called a *chamada,* a brief interlude in which players depart from the typical question and answer structure of the game. After traversing the floor several times, the Israeli tried to reinitiate the game, but the Brazilian refused his move and continued the *chamada.* Shortly thereafter, the two paused briefly at the foot of the *berimbau.* The Brazilian gave the Israeli a headbutt, which is not an illegal movement, but it was an odd context in which to initiate this attack. The man controlling the *roda* leaned down and reprimanded him. As they reentered the circle, the Brazilian untied the Israeli's shoelace, which is considered to be a cheap shot. Having reached the limit of his patience, the Israeli responded by giving him a leg sweep that knocked him to the ground. While the variables in this interaction are too numerous to say whether or not nationality was at issue, when he was given the opportunity to lead a song, the Brazilian sang:

Paranaê, Paranaê, Paraná
Estrangeiro vou apanhar, paraná

The Brazilian player took a well-known song and inserted his own lyrics, modifying the second line of the verse by saying "Foreigner I'm going to get you." In all likelihood, he probably did not expect his Israeli opponent or the *estrangeira* (foreigner) in the audience to understand what he said, but we did.

Despite the egalitarian ethos, Bridget told me that sometimes this foreign/local aggression emerges in FICA *rodas* too. Sometimes the *treinels* will enter the *roda* and "really give it to the new gringo guys." Despite touting capoeira as the foundation for an international community of practitioners, not everyone shares this imagined solidarity (see Timbers 2000: 177). Timbers explains that American *capoeiristas* feel an affinity toward Brazil and Brazilian culture because they have invested so much of themselves in their practice of capoeira; however, Brazilians are not as likely to share this view of Americans, whom they assume to be less knowledgeable about capoeira (Timbers 2000: 177).

Timbers quotes an American *capoeirista* who acutely felt this prejudice when she visited Bahia in 1999: "while the physical space of the *roda* may have the potential to create an 'equal playing field' for all Angoleiros and knowing how to execute the movements, play the instruments, and sing songs beautifully and skillfully may have an 'equalizing' effect, Capoeira Angola will always be Brazilian (as well as African and Afro-Brazilian)" (Timbers 2000: 178). The dominant discourse in capoeira recognizes Africans and Afro-Brazilians as the genitors of the art but denies the importance of race for advancement. However, there is also an undercurrent of anger and frustration expressed in racial terms when a *capoeirista*'s advancement is curtailed in a field he or she claims as his or her own. Timbers justifies Brazilians' indifference toward American and other non-Brazilian capoeira groups by explaining that interactions between the groups take place relatively infrequently. However, as more and more foreigners embark upon extended pilgrimages to Bahia, engaging in exchange with foreigners is becoming the norm rather than the exception.

## Eu Sou Homen; Não Sou Mulher (I Am a Man; I Am Not a Woman)

Two men are in the center of the *roda*. One, clearly the more advanced player, executes a perfectly timed leg sweep. The other man was in the middle of a spinning, half-moon kick when the aggressor swept his base foot right out from underneath him. The pain of hitting the ground while his body is still torqued from this kick is significant. Dueling emotions cross the face of the man now lying on the floor. His eyes are damp with unshed tears, an automatic reaction to the pain, but at the same time his lip curls just slightly as he thinks about how he is going to strike back. Both crying and lashing out in frustration run counter to the prevailing ethos in capoeira that a player must take his or her licks with good humor. The *mestre* starts singing the song, "I am a man; I am not a woman," reminding the audience of how a man is supposed to deal with defeat in the *roda*.

The title of this section comes from a capoeira song that may be invoked when a player is doing something "wimpy" or otherwise unmasculine in the *roda*. It reminds the player that *capoeiristas* should be manly and not act like women. The inclusive practice of accepting people who exhibit characteristics that are stereotypically associated with another gender has not yet become the norm in the world of martial arts. What makes this particularly problematic, however, is that capoeira songs are structured in a call and response format, which "forces the audience to assent to an interpretation of capoeira's past with which they don't agree" (Downey 2005). Therefore, every time someone sings this song, male and female players alike are expected to echo back: "I am a man, I am not a woman." First of all, this statement is technically incorrect for a growing number of *capoeiristas* who *are* women and identify as such. More disturbingly, it calls into question the legitimacy of women in the *roda*. If women cannot sing this and have the statement hold true, one might ask whether or not they should be in the *roda* at all.

Not everyone passively accepts this hegemonic discourse. I have heard some women subvert the message embedded in this song by singing "*não sou homen, eu sou mulher*" (I am not a man, I am a woman). This maintains the structure of the line and is hardly noticeable in a chorus of mostly male voices. Some groups have entirely rewritten the lyric to say that capoeira "*é pra homen e pra mulher*" (it is for men and for women), which fits the rhythm of the song without imposing outdated gender expectations on participants. Both of these variations change the original intent of the song, which is to reprimand a player for becoming emotional in the *roda*.

Eradicating the sexism embedded in the full canon of capoeira songs will take time. Take, for example, the following song that chides a boy for crying:

| | |
|---|---|
| O menino chorou | The boy cries |
| Nhem, Nhem, Nhem | Wah, Wah, Wah |
| É porque não mamou | It's because he wasn't breastfed |
| Nhem, Nhem, Nhem | Wah, Wah, Wah |
| Cale a boca menino | Shut your mouth boy |
| Nhem, Nhem, Nhem | Wah, Wah, Wah |
| É menino chorão | It's the boy that cries |
| Nhem, Nhem, Nhem | Wah, Wah, Wah |
| Sua mãe foi pra fonte | Your mother went to the fountain |
| Nhem, Nhem, Nhem | Wah, Wah, Wah |
| Ela foi pra Cabula | She went to Cabula |
| Nhem, Nhem, Nhem | Wah, Wah, Wah |

The underlying message is that being a *capoeirista* demands a particular *habitus,* one that does not admit weakness (see also Lewis 1992: 165). Like the first example, it is also sung when a player starts becoming emotional in the *roda*. I have heard it sung when both adults and young children were playing. According to the logic of this song, a man should not cry even if he has been abandoned or if a woman has erred in her treatment of him (such as denying him the opportunity to breastfeed). This reinforcement of traditional gender roles makes it difficult for women to achieve equality and acceptance in the *roda* (Assunção 2005: 109).

These two examples reference women as a foil for proper male behavior, but there are some songs that focus on a woman as the main character. Most, however, either portray female *capoeiristas* as deviant because they are daring to cross gender lines, or they portray women as the object of male desire. Even in a group like FICA Bahia that typically had a progressive attitude toward gender equality, these songs would sometimes appear. During 2008, the FICA Bahia *roda* was often visited by a particularly well-respected and elderly *mestre* who no longer maintained his own group. He supported himself financially in part by visiting other *rodas* and selling CDs of himself performing capoeira songs. On more than one occasion, he was leading the song when it was my turn to play. No matter what song was being sung beforehand, he would start a chorus of "*leva, morena, me leva,*" which is a song asking the woman to take the man to her bungalow. This *mestre's* song choice can be interpreted in multiple ways. On the one hand, it could be seen as a statement on the female's sexual desirability as the details of what might occur in the bungalow are clearly implied, though never specified. On the other hand, there are a relatively limited number of songs that specifically reference women, so a *mestre* may choose this song simply because the player is a woman, regardless of whether or not he intends to highlight her sexuality. Regardless of the intent, songs such as these contribute to the reification of men as macho and women as frail conquests, and the call-and-response format obligates all participants to ratify this message.

When anthropologist Ruth Landes was conducting research for her landmark work on women in the Afro-Brazilian religion *Candomblé,* capoeira was clearly a male domain (Delamont 2005). Jorge Amado, in his novels that vividly capture Brazilian life, also portrays capoeira as a male domain by portraying the *capoeiristas* themselves as tough guys and lovers (Lewis 2000). This has changed to some degree in recent years. D'Aquino reports that by the early 1980s, capoeira was no longer an exclusively male domain and that in the cities of São Paulo and Rio de Janeiro, females may comprise as much as one third of academy enrollment (1983: 188). However, by and large, it was uncommon for women to be considered "serious" *capoeiristas* during this period (D'Aquino 1983: 188). Most female *capoeiristas* with whom D'Aquino talked reported encountering some resistance to their participation from family and friends (D'Aquino 1983: 188). Although today, more than thirty years after D'Aquino's fieldwork, female participation is more common, full equity has yet to be achieved.

Reflecting on her own experiences conducting fieldwork on capoeira, Delamont asserts that "being female is not a problem" for *capoeiristas* currently practicing in Europe, North America, Australia, and most parts of Brazil (2005: 309). MacLennan also downplays the importance of gender in capoeira, claiming that *capoeiristas* do not bother with divisions, like the sex segregation seen in mixed martial arts competitions or the weight classes one might see in wrestling, because there is too much individual variation to make such subgroupings useful. Both Delamont and MacLennan draw their data from the study of *Capoeira Regional,* which may explain why they see fewer barriers to female participation than I saw in my study of the more traditional *Capoeira Angola,* but I nonetheless recommend accepting any general statement about gender equality in capoeira with caution. Despite a discourse of equality, gender remains a salient category for many female *capoeiristas.* Based on her research in Goiânia, Green found that female participation in capoeira can empower women by providing them with "a philosophy of resistance to oppression," but can also paradoxically reinforce the very gender inequalities and paternalistic attitudes that oppressed women in the first place (2009: 9). While there are significantly fewer barriers to female participation than there were during Landes's era, females still encounter microagressions in everyday practice that reinforce capoeira as a male space.

All of the non-Brazilian women I met during the course of this study were in their twenties and thirties. This is a generation of women who largely grew up being told that they can be anything they want to be. In my experiences both as a professor and researcher, I have seen that many women in this age range are unaware of the continued inequalities experienced by women, so for many it is shocking when they encounter sexist attitudes in the Brazilian capoeira community. Others, who have encountered sexism prior to their pilgrimage, have come to expect this as part of what it means to be a female *capoeirista,* even if they do not condone it. In fact, every female pilgrim I talked to mentioned gender as one of the most important factors that influenced her ability to navigate the Brazilian capoeira scene.

Women in capoeira continue to be objectified and are "not taken seriously" by many of their male counterparts (Essien 2008: 58). With a few notable exceptions, women were almost entirely absent from capoeira until well into the twentieth century. Up through the 1930s, Afro-Brazilian men and women's activities were segregated by gender; men played capoeira, and women were involved with *Candomblé* and/or the Catholic Church (Landes 1947; Taylor 2005: 216). Then, alongside the emergence of feminist thought in the 1970s, female participation in capoeira increased (Capoeira 2006: 179).

Women remain all but invisible in street *rodas,* and even in academies, women continually struggle against the hegemonic dominance of male *capoeiristas* (Lemle 2008); however, the droves of female capoeira pilgrims descending upon the city has raised the visibility of women in capoeira to some extent. Not only are women becoming more visible in capoeira based on their numbers, their skill is beginning to be recognized. From his personal experiences, Essien believes "that female capoeiristas in the States play at a higher level than they do in Brazil" (2008: 74). This sentiment was expressed multiple times by the foreign women I interviewed. One of the pilgrims told me that the greatest honor she received was a young, female Brazilian *capoeirista* saying she hoped to play like her one day. However, this is not to suggest that women have reached full equality with men.

Feminist scholars of sport have come to see the martial arts as a domain in which a woman can embody resistance of male domination by rejecting societal expectations of women as passive and frail by instead training herself to resist anyone's attempt at physically dominating her (Channon 2013a). However, this ideal is not always realized. Joseph (2012) recounts a frightening scene of male domination in which the instructor and his spouse, also a *capoeirista,* played a game in which he publicly humiliated her. Her inability to match his skill resulted in her using cheap shots like punching and scratching to defend herself. The scene horrified many of the students, but tradition prohibited them from ending their teacher's game. Joseph tells this story to point out that "relatively even numbers of male and female capoeiristas ... do not necessarily reflect equality of power" (2012: 1089). In other words, despite the fact that female *capoeiristas* are growing in number, and many of them are becoming superb players, men continue to have a dominant place in the capoeira hierarchy. There is a quote popularly attributed to Mestre Pastinha that capoeira *é pra homen, menino e mulher* (capoeira is for man, child, and woman), but in everyday practice, female *capoeiristas* are often marginalized in subtle ways.

There are several female *mestres* in *Capoeira Regional,* but fewer in *Capoeira Angola.* Taylor argues "it is only a matter of time before the large number of women now doing Capoeira Angola begin to break through that final barrier" (2007: 210). I, however, am not as sure about this progression. Women like Mestre Janja show that it is not an impossible goal. Likewise, Contramestre Gege has also achieved international renown for her skills as a player and teacher. However, most Brazilian women are not encouraged to become dedicated *capoeiristas,* and those who do display an interest and aptitude often find it difficult to balance training with other responsibilities. The general expectation that women will be responsible for domestic duties like cooking and cleaning contribute to the lack of Brazilian women who seriously train capoeira (Green 2009).

Recent studies have suggested that mixed-sex sports provide opportunities to challenge the hegemonic assumption of males' physical superiority (Channon 2013b). Sports that divide the sexes, on the other hand, contribute to the "*naturalization* of inequitable sexual difference" (Channon 2013b: 1293). As such, martial arts like capoeira that allow men and women to train and play/spar together should destabilize discourses of male superiority. However, this does not mean that the academy is a gender-neutral space. The non-Brazilian women I met reacted to these inequalities in different ways. Some, who were acutely aware of the unequal status of men and women in the *roda,* worked hard to present themselves as asexual within capoeira. This was particularly evident in speaking with Bridget, who was among the most talented of students, male or female, Brazilian or foreign, training at the academy. Bridget says that she sometimes sees a line being drawn between being a *capoeirista* and being a woman, and still does not know how to overcome this kind of thinking. In other words, she finds it difficult to perform her femininity in and around the academy for fear that men will see her as a potential sexual conquest rather than a peer to be respected.

The conflict Bridget was describing became very clear one evening when Mestre Valmir asked her to help him demonstrate a training sequence. She lumbered forward. Valmir watched her for a moment and then parodied her walk, which by her own admission is less than ladylike. Seeing that he was making fun of her, she backed up and came forward again with an exaggeratedly feminine walk, shoulders back and hips rolling sensuously. We burst into laughter. Moments of levity like this were always welcome in an otherwise intensely focused environment, but this incident was all the funnier because Bridget works so hard to downplay her gendered identity. After they finished demonstrating the movement sequence, Valmir kissed her hand and gave her a little twirl. This exchange could be interpreted in multiple ways. On the one hand, it is possible that our *mestre* was simply poking fun at one of our classmate's habits and she played along, wordlessly admitting that she could be more ladylike. I, however, see something more subversive in her actions. The sexy strut was a slap in the face to the males in the room who, intentionally or not, inhibit a woman's full expression of herself as both a *capoeirista* and a sensual being. It was as if Bridget had said, "I know this is what you want me to be, but my training is more important than your desire."

In her review of the existing literature on women in the martial arts, Giovanna Follo (2012) found than female practitioners are by and large still expected to temper their adoption of a masculine body culture with performances of femininity. This feminine apologetic, in which "the female athlete dresses and behaves according to feminine expectations" as a way of making her athleticism acceptable to a society with rigid gender norms, is in operation among many female martial artists (Follo 2012: 710). Though she may not have realized it, Bridget's performance of exaggerated femininity was an index of the feminine apologetic in capoeira. This performance was similar to those observed by Carly Giesseler (2014) in her study of Roller Derby skaters. She found that the skaters took pleasure in using their bodies and performances to subvert mainstream societal expectations of female sexuality. In many cases, they did this by performing "exaggerated sexualities," which Giesseler argues, "reveals the construction of institutional ideals of women and desire; the parody as imitation and woman as performer mocks expectations of women athletes and sexualities" (Giesseler 2014: 759).

As Bridget's actions show, it is oftentimes very challenging for women to present themselves as skilled players while still embracing their femininity. I occasionally attended the *roda* at the Nzinga academy, which is considered FICA's sister group because the *mestres* of both groups descended from the GCAP group. Nzinga is known for promoting the role of women in capoeira and, in fact, offers women-only classes a few mornings per week. The *mestres* of Nzinga also take an active role in nurturing the neighborhood children's development as *capoeiristas* and as responsible citizens by giving them significant responsibilities in caring for the physical space of the academy.

Mestre Janja is one of the three leaders of this group. On one of the nights that I was present, Janja approached a non-Brazilian player and said she needed to work on adding more variety to her game. This particular woman always proactively attacked the other player in the *roda* before her opponent could launch an offensive, and her games tended to be more adversarial than cooperative. Janja wanted this woman to add more playfulness to her game instead of always being so focused on the attacks. Janja said this was especially important when playing with children, but she was also trying to help this woman see that she does not need to adopt an aggressive aesthetic in order to be respected as a *capoeirista* and that women do not have to play like men just because men set the original parameters of the game.

Janja acknowledges that some men will devalue a female *capoeirista* because she is a woman but says, "when I need to pick up a knife, I pick up a knife." She was suggesting that aggression is justified in some cases, but women do not need to have that as their default attitude just because men might play that way. Yet when aggression is justified, a woman should know how to wield a knife well. I do not agree that aggressiveness should necessarily be seen as a masculine trait and rather side with Chapman in noting that "there are women who actively compete in their chosen sport with this kind of confrontational aggression" (2004: 322). Nonetheless, Janja's point was that it is okay for men and women to adopt different styles in the *roda* provided that a woman is ready and able to diffuse male aggression when it arises.

Janja used her position as a *mestre* to promote equality for women. One evening she brought a petition to the *roda* for men to sign, pledging their support to fight domestic violence. At the next *roda,* she brought white ribbons for men to tie around their wrists if they would promise not to commit violence against women. She explained this in terms that the younger boys in the group would understand. In December of 2008, she was given an award for her contributions to women's rights. When she received her award, she said that for a long time, women have been made invisible in capoeira. She pointed out that women within capoeira are a recent phenomenon. In this time, there have been many political interventions that have arisen from within capoeira. However, she pointed out, even within capoeira, it is common to find the same "violences" against women that occur in Brazilian culture more generally. Some of these violences are quite literal, but others are symbolic, such as the restrictions placed upon the ways in which a woman can express her femininity in the *roda.*

In other martial arts, there are ways for women to emphasize their femininity while participating in an activity that is primarily associated with masculinity such as their choice of clothing that is made for the female form or gender-coded gear like pink boxing gloves (Channon 2013b). However, this was not encouraged among the *Angoleiros* with whom I worked. Instead, the teachers promoted a discourse of gender neutrality, even if their actions and the actions of other students blatantly contradicted this. For example, the female body was occasionally at issue in discussions of students' uniforms. In *Capoeira Angola,* players wear T-shirts, which must be tucked into the waistband of their pants. The practical reason for this is that players spend so much time upside down, in cartwheels, handstands, and so on, that a loose shirt could obstruct one's vision and be dangerous. A sneaky, win-at-all costs player might also grab a loose shirt and use it to pull another player off of his or her feet.[4] However, an incident that happened at one of the group's evening training sessions suggests that *Angoleiros'* sartorial rules are about more than just the aforementioned practicalities.

A Polish woman who trained at FICA in July and August of 2008 wore a particularly short shirt that kept rising up and exposing her stomach. Once would have been forgivable, but it happened with such regularity that our teacher finally had to address it. He said, "it is fashionable for young women to wear short shirts and show off their bellybutton rings and they want things to fit just right." As he said this last part, he sensually ran his hands down the length of his body and over his hips in an imitation of feminine comportment. He said he understands this and likes it; it is pretty. "But if a woman's shirt comes up and she is showing things, she might distract her adversary." Apparently a woman using her sexuality to distract an opponent in the *roda* would constitute an unfair advantage, and therefore needs to be curtailed, which is ironic considering that *capoeiristas* pride themselves on manipulating any situation to their benefit.

Despite the fact that most of the foreign women would have been well versed in the discourse around victim blaming and the lame argument that men cannot control their desire when they see a woman's body dressed in a sexy manner, this comment did not appear to evoke any anger in the women who were there that night. Perhaps they were all too committed to upholding tradition, or the *mestre's* authority, to offer any resistance to this line of thinking. The basic gist of the conversation was this: all *capoeiristas* tuck in their shirts because in the *roda*, there are no male bodies or female bodies, there are just bodies. However, the way in which the female body was referenced during the conversation actually highlighted the differences between male and female bodies and did so in a very objectifying manner.

The differences between male and female *capoeiristas* were also exaggerated during the ritual of shaking hands during class. Before and after each partner exercise, *capoeiristas* are supposed to shake their partner's hand. This ritual reinforces respect across skill levels and was normally taken for granted by the students. During one class, I approached a male Japanese student so we could work together on the sequence our teacher had just demonstrated. We greeted one another with the handshake/fist bump combination that has become so popular among young Brazilians. The teacher saw this and expressed his surprise. "What is this?" he demanded. He made a big show of walking up to me, giving me a devastatingly alluring smile, gently taking my hand, and kissing it. The class laughed; my partner muttered "cultural differences" under his breath. He was clearly not pleased with being made the butt of the joke and attempted to brush it off as an example of Brazilian machismo that is outside of his frame of reference for gendered interactions.

When we switched partners, as we frequently did, my next partner started to give me a fist bump as well. The teacher caught his eye and gave him a reproachful look, so my partner quickly kissed my hand in an attempt at performing genuinely what the teacher had done in jest. But when he absentmindedly wiped his mouth afterward, the class erupted into another round of raucous laughter. Now I felt like the butt of the joke. At the end of class, our teacher explained that he had not kissed my hand because I was a woman, but because I am a *capoeirista* and he has respect for all *capoeiristas*. Of course I did not see any men kissing each other's hands, so I remain a bit skeptical of this gender-blindness. This is another case in which actual practice falls short of the discourse of equality in capoeira.

Gendered dynamics can often be observed not only in training, but in the *roda* as well. Local men often took an attitude of superiority toward foreign women regardless of the latter's skill level. Sometimes these mixed-gender games were characterized by playfulness, often bordering on flirtation, especially when the male was a Brazilian and the female was a foreigner of a lower ability level. In these games, the machismo attitude tended to manifest itself in both being the dominant partner and making sure that the female was not unduly harmed or humiliated. Bridget said people will coddle a foreign woman a bit until they know what she can do.

Channon (2013a) explains male reluctance to spar with women in terms of a deep-seated moral imperative not to hit a "girl," which is in and of itself a form of oppression because it implies that females are weak and in need of protection. This socialization of which he writes is culturally specific and it would be irresponsible to assume that it explains men's reluctance to treat women as equal adversaries in all martial contexts; however, the similarities with capoeira are striking. In both cases, women tend to be underestimated, and as one of Channon's consultants explained, "you sort of have to prove yourself to [men] before they'll spar you with any kind of commitment" (quoted in Channon 2013a: 102).

There were also cases in which the foreign woman was clearly the stronger player, but the Brazilian man adopted an attitude of superiority nonetheless. For example, Bridget outplayed a Brazilian in a *roda* at Mestre Joao Pequeno's academy one evening, clearly displaying her superior skill. The man then approached her after the *roda* and offered to give her private capoeira lessons. She attributes this arrogance to the fact that she is a woman. Presumably, a foreign male probably would not have been solicited in this way. One of the older men at FICA was known for this kind of arrogance and constantly tried to "teach" foreign women, even when they were more advanced than him. When a woman proves herself to be more capable than a man in the *roda,* it can be a source of amusement, and the man might be mocked for his shortcomings. That people laugh or express surprise when a woman knocks a woman down in the *roda* provides evidence of the ongoing disregard that many have for women's abilities to play capoeira at the same level as men (Green 2009).

Hope for more gender equality may be on the horizon, though it will take time for this to become a reality. Women's events are becoming more popular in capoeira. In August of 2008, I observed a women-only *Capoeira Regional roda* held in conjunction with an international co-ed capoeira event. The presiding *mestre,* who was a woman, said they wanted to host this *roda* to combat the prejudice against women in capoeira. The first song they sang commented on how each instrument in the orchestra was being played by a woman. Similarly, FICA hosts an annual event in the United States that combines capoeira workshops and *rodas* with presentations and discussions about the changing role of women in capoeira.

In March of 2007, nine members (five females and four males) of the Estrela do Norte group flew to Atlanta, Georgia for one such workshop hosted by the local chapter of FICA. Jerome and Camille were both in attendance. Both men and women were welcome at the event even though the theme was focused on the role of women and female empowerment in capoeira. Mestre Cobra Mansa attended the event in a supportive capacity, but Janja led the majority of the classes and was assisted by a number of female *treinels.* The program for this weekend included several intense training sessions, a music class, a dance class, nightly *rodas,* lectures, and a panel discussion. During the panel, Janja and several other women, both Brazilian and American, discussed their experiences with capoeira and the obstacles they had faced as women in a male-dominated sphere of activity.

Some women's events, such as the *Capoeira Regional* event in 2008, are exclusive and may inadvertently contribute to the idea that men and women compete at different levels. Events like that hosted by FICA, on the other hand, are inclusive. Men and women train and play in the *roda* together, signaling that both sexes have an equal right to participation. What is not clear, however, is the lasting effects of these events. Further research should be done to determine whether or not the discourse around gender equality, which is promoted by these events, is transforming actual practice. In 2009, well after the event we attended in Atlanta, Jerome told me that after we returned to Indiana, he did some soul searching about our group and the role of women in it. He started questioning why the men always start the *rodas* and take primary roles in performances. However, there were not any noticeable changes to our group's operation or composition as a result of having attended this conference. The most lasting effects were related to the new movements and songs we learned, not the thematic programming, thought provoking though it was.

Chapman (2004) argues that although sport participation has been used in many cultures to naturalize the physical superiority of men, studying individual experiences within athletic and martial communities elucidates the ways in which people often challenge gender norms. Chapman writes, "there is the potential for each person to come to a personal understanding of training which both confirms yet questions social expectations" (2004: 332). I agree that individual performances can challenge societal stereotypes about the gendered nature of sport (Chapman 2004). At the same time, however, it bears recognizing that the individual's conception of him- or herself as a gendered being will be shaped by the messages he or she receives daily in the training hall.

## Conclusion

The widespread popularity of capoeira has united people from vastly different parts of the world together in their practice of this art, radically changing the original demographics of capoeira. Whereas *capoeiristas* were traditionally assumed to be Afro-Brazilian men from the lower classes, this is no longer the case. The relatively stable characteristics like race, nationality, and gender over which individuals have little or no control have been explored here as traditional claims to legitimacy. Despite the changing demographics of practitioners, blackness, *Brasilidade* (Brazilianness), and masculinity remain at the top of the capoeira hierarchy.

Afro-Brazilian males are often assumed to be superior *capoeiristas* because of their cultural background, growing up in a cultural milieu saturated with the sounds of the *berimbau* and with easy access to capoeira instruction. Capoeira, associated with blackness because of its history, has also been claimed by African Americans in the United States who find resonance in its association with their homeland. However, some Brazilians, particularly those who do not identify as Afro-Brazilian, see African Americans' usage of capoeira as contentious and fear that their claims to the art will eventually override Brazilians' control of racial discourse.[5] Some academies in the United States only admit black students, but they are the exception rather than the norm. In Bahia, it is more common for complaints about foreigners' race or nationality to be expressed subtly, through performance in the *roda*. Oftentimes this marginalization is not intentional, but the result of naturalized assumptions about what it means to be at the core of the capoeira social field.

The involvement of women in capoeira is a recent phenomenon. Women have to work hard to prove that they are credible inheritors of the genre. I am not aware of any academies that explicitly bar women, but several factors contribute to their marginalization. Many female *capoeiristas* pilgrims find it difficult to embrace both of their identities, woman and martial artist, particularly when forced to negotiate the expectations of male *capoeiristas* from other cultures. Chapman acknowledges that "gender is only one of the varied attributes that comprise personal identity" and one's experiences in the training hall (2004: 317). The same could be said of virtually any embodied activity, which necessitates taking an intersectional approach to identity, as I have done here. In this chapter, I have argued that both women and foreigners, particularly those who are not of African descent, come up short in the realm of traditional claims to authenticity, meaning that they often have to rely upon achieved characteristics, or what I call charismatic forms of cultural capital, to help them gain legitimacy within the capoeira community.

## Notes

1. Much of the engagement Westerners have with the artistic styles of the African diaspora are at a very surface level. To extend Browning's (1998) metaphor of "infectious rhythms," many Westerners/whites are titillated by the flirtation with these contagions without fully experiencing what it means to be a carrier. From a place of global privilege, Western/white consumers can listen to global pop or experiment with something like capoeira without being subjected to racial discrimination or having their own interpretations of the art muted by more powerful individuals

2. In describing the development of her NGO in Bahia, Margaret Wilson (2007) says that she was initially confused by what appears as passive acceptance of gross inequalities in Bahia, and was keenly aware that she embodied privilege, with her white skin and well-nourished body, that her friends in Bahia would never enjoy. Although she is discussing the passive acceptance by local Brazilians, I felt similarly confused and frustrated by my fellow pilgrims' seeming lack of engagement with this social justice issue. This is an issue that deserves further study, but my preliminary conclusion is that admitting one's racial and national privilege would undercut the imagined solidarity that pilgrims have forged with Brazilian *capoeiristas* and would therefore be threatening to their sense of self as a *capoeirista*.

3. Accounting for these different orientations would be a monumental task involving many interacting variables, but students often replicate the views held by their *mestre*. When confronted with examples of foreigners having been marginalized, the younger and more progressive *mestres* attribute this to the "ignorance" and "prejudice" of their older counterparts.

4. In *Capoeira Regional*, male players often go shirtless and women wear a sports bra and/or a tightly fitting tank top, eliminating the problems posed by a loose T-shirt.

5. Margaret Wilson's research assistant was annoyed by African American *capoeiristas* who assert the rights of blacks to play capoeira over those of white Brazilians and ridiculed their assumption of familiarity with Afro-Brazilians based on skin color alone. Though recognizing that both Afro-Brazilians and African Americans share a history of enslavement, he argues that the similarities end there (Wilson 2007: 54).

## Works Cited

Assunção, Matthias Röhrig. 2005. *Capoeira: The History of an Afro-Brazilian Martial Art, Sport in the Global Society*. London: Routledge.

Browning, Barbara. 1998. *Infectious Rhythm: Metaphors of Contagion and the Spread of African Culture*. New York: Routledge.

Capoeira, Nestor. 2002. *Capoeira: Roots of the Dance-Fight-Game*. Berkeley, CA: North Atlantic Books.

Capoeira, Nestor. 2006. *A Street-Smart Song: Capoeira Philosophy and Inner Life*. Berkeley, CA: North Atlantic Books.

Carmezim, Vitor. 2008. "Ê Camara, a Capoeira é Patrimonio Cultural!" *A Tarde*.

Channon, Alex. 2013a. "'Do You Hit Girls?': Some Striking Moments in the Career of a Male Martial Artist." In *Fighting Scholars: Habitus and Ethnographies of Martial Arts and Combat Sports*, edited by Raul Sanchez Garcia and Dale C Spencer, 95–110. London: Anthem Press.

Channon, Alex. 2013b. "Enter the Discourse: Exploring the Discursive Roots of Inclusivity in Mixed-Sex Martial Arts." *Sport in Society* 16 (10): 1293–1308.

Chapman, Kris. 2004. "Ossu! Sporting Masculinities in a Japanese Karate Dojo." *Japan Forum* 16 (2): 315–35.

Collins, Patricia Hill. 2008. "Reply to Commentaries: Black Sexual Politics Revisited." *Studies in Gender and Sexuality* 9 (1): 68–85.

D'Aquino, Iria. 1983. "Capoeira: Strategies for Status, Power and Identity," PhD dissertation. University of Illinois.

De Campos Rosario, Claudio, Neil Stephens, and Sara Delamont. 2010. "'I'm Your Teacher, I'm Brazilian!' Authenticity and Authority in European Capoeira." *Sport, Education and Society* 15 (1): 103–20.

De Carvalho, Leticia Cardoso. n.d. "Das Senzalas Para a Europa." *Praticando Capoeira.*

Delamont, Sara. 2005. "No Place for Women Among Them? Reflections on the Axe of Fieldwork." *Sport, Education and Society* 10 (3): 305–20.

Downey, Greg. 2005. *Learning Capoeira: Lessons in Cunning from an Afro-Brazilian Art.* Oxford: Oxford University Press.

Errington, Frederick, and Deborah Gewertz. 2008. "Tourism and Anthropology in a Postmodern World." In *Tourists and Tourism: A Reader,* edited by Sharon B Gmelch, 91-114. Long Grove, IL: Waveland Press.

Essien, Aniefre. 2008. *Capoeira Beyond Brazil: From a Slave Tradition to an International Way of Life.* Berkeley, CA: North Atlantic Books.

Ferreira, Juca. 1997. "Experiência de Cidadania." *A Tarde.*

Follo, Giovanna. 2012. "A Literature Review of Women and The Martial Arts: Where Are We Right Now?" *Sociology Compass* 6 (9): 707–17.

Fujita, Yuiko. 2009. *Cultural Migrants from Japan: Youth, Media, and Migration in New York and London.* Lanham, MD: Lexington Books.

Giesseler, Carly. 2014. "Derby Drag: Parodying Sexualities in the Sport of Roller Derby " *Sexualities* 17 (5/6): 758–76.

Green, Aimee Beth. 2009. "Empowerment through Cultural Practices: Women in Capoeira," MA thesis. University of Florida.

Green, Thomas. 2013. "White Men Don't Flow: Embodied Aesthetics of the Fifty-Two Hand Blocks." In *Fighting Scholars: Habitus and Ethnographies of Martial Arts and Combat Sports,* edited by Raul Sanchez Garcia and Dale C Spencer, 125–40. London: Anthem Press.

Green, Thomas A. 2003. "Surviving the Middle Passage: Traditional African Martial Arts in the Americas." In *Martial Arts in the Modern World,* edited by Thomas A Green and Joseph R Svinth, 129-38 Westport, CT: Praeger.

Hancock, Ange-Marie. 2008. "Intersectionality, Multiple Messages, and Complex Causality: Commentary on *Black Sexual Politics* by Patricia Hill Collins." *Studies in Gender and Sexuality* 9:14-31.

Harrison, Anthony Kwame. 2008. "Racial Authenticity in Rap Music and Hip Hop." *Sociology Compass* 2 (6): 1783–1800.

Hecht, Tobias. 1998. *At Home in the Street: Street Children of Northeast Brazil.* Cambridge: Cambridge University Press.

Howes, David, and Constance Classen. 2014. *Ways of Sensing: Understanding the Senses in Society.* New York: Routledge.

Johnson, E Patrick. 2003. *Appropriating Blackness: Performance and the Politics of Authenticity.* Durham, NC: Duke University Press.

Joseph, Janelle Beatrice. 2006. "Capoeira in Canada: Brazilian Martial Art, Cultural Transformation and the Struggle for Authenticity," MS thesis. University of Toronto.

Joseph, Janelle Beatrice. 2008. "'Going to Brazil': Transnational and Corporeal Movements of a Canadian-Brazilian Martial Arts Community." *Global Networks* 8 (2): 194–213.

Joseph, Janelle Beatrice. 2012. "The Practice of Capoeira: Diasporic Black Culture in Canada." *Ethnic and Racial Studies* 35 (6): 1078–95.

Landes, Ruth. 1947. *The City of Women.* Albuquerque: University of New Mexico Press.

Lemle, Marina. 2008. "Maestria Reconhecida." *Revista de História da Biblioteca Nacional.*

Lewis, J Lowell. 1992. *Ring of Liberation: Deceptive Discourse in Brazilian Capoeira.* Chicago: University of Chicago Press.

Lewis, J Lowell. 2000. "Sex and Violence in Brazil: Carnaval, Capoeira, and the Problem of Everyday Life." *American Ethnologist* 26 (3): 539–57.

Lindholm, Charles. 2008. *Culture and Authenticity.* Malden, MA: Blackwell Publishing.

Lott, Eric. 1993. *Love and Theft: Blackface Minstrelsy and the American Working Class.* Oxford: Oxford University Press.

Moraes. 1997. "Arte de Soma." *A Tarde.*

Peterson, Richard A. 2005. "In Search of Authenticity." *Journal of Management Studies* 42 (5): 1083–98.

Portela, Maira. 2008. "Lingua da Capoeira." *Correio da Bahia,* 5 May.

Ribeiro, Perla. 2008. "Capoeira Se Torna Patrimonio Cultural." *Correiro da Bahia.*

Royce, Anya Peterson. 2004. *Anthropology of the Performing Arts: Artistry, Virtuosity, and Interpretation in a Cross-Cultural Perspective.* Walnut Creek, CA: AltaMira Press.

Sansone, Livio. 1997. "O Olhar Estrangeiro." *A Tarde.*

Sansone, Livio. 2003. *Blackness without Ethnicity.* New York: Palgrave Macmillan.

Taylor, Gerard. 2005. *Capoeira: The Jogo de Angola from Luanda to Cyberspace.* Vol. 1. Berkeley, CA: North Atlantic Books.

Taylor, Gerard. 2007. *Capoeira: The Jogo de Angola from Luanda to Cyberspace.* Vol. 2. Berkeley, CA: North Atlantic Books.

Telles, Edward E. 2004. *Race in Another America.* Princeton, NJ: Princeton University Press.

Timbers, Caroline C. 2000. "Building an International Quilombo: Meaning, Marginality, and Community in Capoeira Angola and Its Practice in the United States," MA thesis. Georgetown University.

Turner, Terence S. 2012. "The Social Skin." *HAU: Journal of Ethnographic Theory* 2 (2): 486–504.

Wang, Nina. 1999. "Rethinking Authenticity in Tourism Experience." *Annals of Tourism Research* 26 (2): 349–70.

Wilson, Margaret. 2007. *Dance Lest We All Fall Down: A Journey of Friendship, Poverty, Power and Peace.* Nashville, TN: Cold Tree Press.

# Chapter 6

# How the Rest of Us Get Our Foot in the Door

I was sitting by myself on the floor in the back of the room stretching before class started. Minutes before noon, an incredibly vibrant woman burst through the doorway. She was already talking a mile a minute in Portuguese before she even set down her bag. Between her white skin and slight accent, I thought she might be a foreigner, but I could not be entirely sure. Therefore I was surprised when most of the Brazilian students got up to hug her and welcome her back. She asked one man if he remembered her, and he said that of course he did. After greeting the people she knew, she put her things away and took her place at the front of the room. This is how I met Bridget, whose warm welcome on this, her sixth trip to Brazil, set the bar in my mind for the legitimacy a foreigner could attain given the right set of personal qualities.

## Introduction

In the previous chapter, I explained how having certain social identities, specifically those that have been traditionally associated with capoeira, tend to facilitate one's entrance into a training relationship. This is not particularly surprising. Having the same nationality as one's teacher, and sharing much of the same cultural background as a result of that, can give a student a sense of belonging that cannot be assumed for a foreigner. The same could be said for being of the same gender or racial group. Yet nonblacks, non-Brazilians, and women *do* manage to enter into training relationships with local *mestres*. I have found that, regardless of one's ascribed social identities, an individual's charisma can open the door to deeper relationships with *mestres,* creating more learning opportunities during which he or she can master the nuanced form of capoeira.

Charisma, according to Max Weber, is either divinely bestowed or otherwise "inspires personal devotion by virtue of extraordinary individual qualities" (Titunik 2005: 144). Weber applied this concept to schemes of domination, which is not the objective of capoeira pilgrims. Yet it is applicable in terms of understanding how pilgrims use their personal characteristics to ascend through the legitimacy hierarchy by developing close bonds with key players. Charismatic leaders are often thought of as having an unnamable mystic essence. It is indeed challenging to enumerate the qualities that give someone an aura of charisma; however, the recurrence of several qualities among charismatic capoeira pilgrims allows me to begin such a sketch.

For my purposes, I define charisma as the uncommodifiable proclivities of an individual that facilitates his or her popularity within a local scene. Enactment of these proclivities may involve economic exchanges such as paying for Portuguese lessons, but these impulses and commitments themselves are not commodifiable. These are different than the ascribed characteristics like race or gender that were discussed in the previous chapter because the individual has some measure of control over them and because they are not automatically passed down from parent to child. People are drawn to charismatic individuals because of these traits, tend to trust them (Titunik 2005: 144), and help them achieve their aims. These proclivities could just be labeled as "likability," but it is a particular kind of likability that aligns with culturally constructed values.

Using charismatic factors to gain acceptance within a community requires a significant amount of initiative on the part of the individual. Peterson calls this type of work "inventive" or "elastic" (2005: 1087), an apt characterization because it stretches the boundaries of the social field to incorporate people other than direct inheritors who are rich in traditional claims to authenticity. Different communities will prioritize different personal characteristics, and it is important for anyone trying to operationalize charisma to take note of what qualities a particular community values. In this chapter, I describe four different personal qualities that facilitate a pilgrim's integration into the local capoeira scene: attitude, speaking Portuguese, capoeira travel, and, to some extent, volunteerism. Of these, attitude is clearly the most important. The remaining qualities can be considered supporting evidence that a *capoeirista* has the proper attitude.

## It's All in the Attitude

Out of all the strategies pilgrims might use to facilitate their acceptance into a local capoeira group, I would recommend that they go out of their way to be open and engaging with the local *capoeiristas*. This encompasses talking with other students before class (in Portuguese I might add), greeting teachers appropriately and enthusiastically, and making oneself available to assist the academy in any way possible. Above all, pilgrims must be willing to engage in *troca de informação* (information exchange) with local *capoeiristas*. A pilgrim should not just take knowledge from the locals, but also share his or her experiences and insights on a variety of topics. All of these practices fall under the designation of attitude. As I came to see during interviews with both local and foreign *capoeiristas*, as well as in my own engagement at the academy, attitude is discernable both in daily comportment and through performance. It is the central element of a *capoeirista*'s charisma and is manifest in all of the elective practices that deepen one's engagement with the local scene.

Upon entering an academy, one's attitude will initially be gauged by his or her openness, which is commonly assumed to be difficult for foreigners. Being open, or *aberto,* is a blanket term for exuding warmth, friendliness, and approachability. It also implies a degree of ease and confidence. This can be difficult for newcomers to project, though it tends to be easier for members of satellite academies in a franchised organization because they already have a sense of belonging in the flagship academy and a baseline understanding of how the academy works.

Members of the academy where I trained believe themselves to be incredibly open to foreigners, and I believe they are sincere in their desire to welcome others. However, that does not mean that every foreigner will feel comfortable at the academy or find a level of true acceptance that goes beyond being permitted to enroll in the academy. A female pilgrim from Mexico who had been living and training in Brazil for months before I arrived in Bahia told me that the burden for facilitating intercultural relationships falls upon the foreigner to a greater extent than the Brazilian. She explained this by saying that "the ones that traveled to know the country were us, they didn't leave their country." For her, this means that the pilgrim has to adopt an open attitude "because [Brazil] is an open country."

Being *fechado* or closed is the biggest barrier to a foreigner's acceptance. Unfortunately, this is one of the key descriptors used for North Americans and Europeans. These individuals are often assumed to be reserved and standoffish whereas Brazilians are assumed to be more open. Openness is manifest in many small ways, such as smiling, making eye contact, talking with other students before class, and so on. Many of the behaviors that are associated with being *fechado* could be related to someone being an introvert or just not being comfortable in a new environment, especially if their language skills are poor. But regardless of why one acts in this way, being closed will be a barrier to a pilgrim's acceptance.

After initially establishing contact with a group, perseverance becomes an important way for a pilgrim to demonstrate his or her attitude. In capoeira (like most martial arts), the willingness to suffer through difficult training scenarios with a smile trumps a novice's lack of skill. Just think of the karate kid's diligent repetition of "wax on, wax off" despite his lack of understanding as to how these seemingly mundane chores actually contributed to his training. The long-suffering apprentice is a common theme in personal narratives of martial arts training. Take, for instance, this reflection from Sam Sheridan's account of his time spent in a Thai training academy. He writes of a Swede named Blue.

You had to give Blue credit. He wasn't there to fight, and he didn't have much form, but he tried. There was a trainer for the Limpini fighters who in all my time there never spoke to me or looked at me once; he didn't have any time for or interest in the silly farang [foreigner]. But he would talk to Blue. Blue had won them over by nearly killing himself training, by a show of heart. (Sheridan 2007: 32)

Even though he was not particularly skilled, Blue's spectacular dedication allowed him access to trainers who were otherwise off-limits to foreigners. Talking with capoeira pilgrims similarly confirms that perseverance and dedication are far more important than skill in becoming integrated with the group. However, not all demonstrations of dedication are received equally among *capoeiristas*. There is a clear difference between the kind of personal dedication that is solely focused on becoming a good capoeira player and the kind of dedication that is oriented toward the capoeira community at large.

The first type of dedication is very personal in nature; the individual works to improve his or her own physical and musical skills. Some of the capoeira pilgrims with whom I was working attended up to eighteen hours of class per week and participated in multiple *rodas* over the weekend. On top of this are additional hours they spend practicing both their moves and their musical skills at home and the time they spend discussing capoeira with others. Some pilgrims are able to maintain this pace over the course of several months spent in Brazil, but most will have a limited amount of time to dedicate to this kind of intensive training. One evening a new Brazilian student had joined our class, and Mestre Valmir introduced the rest of the group to him. Valmir remarked that all of the foreigners present were "running in front of the question," a poetic way of saying that the pilgrims were all in Bahia to experience as much capoeira as they possibly could in the time available to them. This often leads to cramming, with pilgrims spending more than one half their waking hours focused on capoeira. Most local *capoeiristas* do not have the luxury of this much free time, even if they had the desire, to think about capoeira 24-7.

The other type of dedication includes personal training as well as commitment to bettering the group. The latter is far more important for an individual's legitimacy within the local capoeira scene, especially at the level of individual academies that are the direct recipient of a pilgrim's efforts. There are many small ways in which foreigners can show their dedication to the group. After classes at the Washington, D.C. branch of FICA, "students do various chores around the space, because, as Cobra Mansa reminds them, the space is theirs (not his) and they are responsible for its maintenance" (Timbers 2000: 121). This expectation gives the students a sense of ownership over the space and a greater investment in the maintenance of the group. Students must pay dues in order to be members of FICA; however, requiring the students to do chores disrupts the prevailing capitalist mentality that when someone pays for something, those who are paid should serve him or her. This sense of responsibility, and resultant sense of ownership, carries over to the behavior of non-Brazilian FICA students when they visit FICA Bahia. Foreigners who are not aware of this convention must learn it quickly or risk being viewed as someone who only wants to "take" from the group. Generally, these expectations are not taught directly and must be learned by emulating more experienced students who already understand these norms (see Stephens and Delamont 2013).

Capoeira is not unique in its emphasis on dedication to the group as a route to acceptance and integration. In her study of *Nihon Buyo,* a form of traditional Japanese dance, Yamazaki found that students were reluctant to engage in any additional activities that would siphon away time normally spent at school. This would seem to be similar to the first kind of dedication identified among capoeira pilgrims, but in fact is more related to their sense of group identity. According to Yamazaki, it is the student's intense devotion toward their teacher and school that explains their reluctance to cultivate outside interests (Yamazaki 2001: 36). Any additional obligation might be experienced as a betrayal toward the teacher and an indication that the student is not as dedicated as her peers. Similar to what is seen among the *capoeiristas* who help care for the space, among *Nihon Buyo* students, there is a shared sense of ownership for the school, which is symbolized by all students possessing keys to the academy (Yamazaki 2001: 42). It is also manifest in their willingness to help with chores and treating their teacher's home as if it were their own.

Taking initiative and not waiting to be asked to do something is a key indicator of how successfully a pilgrim will be able to integrate with the group. It is not coincidental that those individuals who regularly took it upon themselves to help clean the academy were those most closely integrated in the group. Frequently before and after class, students would sweep and mop the floor, complete small tasks related to the manufacture of *berimbau* strings, and wash the plastic cups that were made available to students near the ten-gallon water dispenser. The majority of Brazilians who regularly attended classes participated in these activities; the foreigners who had attended classes consistently at the academy or were familiar with these expectations from their prior engagement with the franchise also helped out with these chores, but casual attendees who took classes for only a few weeks generally did not. This attitude of humility, particularly in a setting where class status is often marked by domestic service, contributes to a pilgrim's acceptance. However, this type of service is not the only measure by which a pilgrim's attitude will be assessed.

## Can't You Even Answer the Phone

Some people would like to think that it is possible to have meaningful interactions with people from another culture without speaking the same language. Some pilgrims try to apply this same logic to capoeira: because all players understand the corporeal language of capoeira, and *capoeiristas* trade physical questions and answers in the *roda,* there is really no need to speak. That might work for some who are content to pay their money, take class, and leave, but it will not endear a pilgrim to the local community. Before class one day, I was stretching and warming my muscles. The phone rang, and I was the one nearest to it. I just let it ring because I did not feel like I was enough of a member of this group to answer their phone. The teacher asked me incredulously, "can't you even answer the phone?" I thought doing so would have been presumptuous, but I was rebuked for not doing my part to support the academy. Yet there was another reason I did not answer the phone. For while I was conversant enough in Portuguese to conduct face-to-face interviews, I was still a bit nervous about speaking on the telephone because I would not be able to fall back on pantomime if my words failed me.

Learning to speak Portuguese is seen as evidence of a capoeira pilgrim's dedication to both his/her individual practice *and* to the group. There are very important reasons for speaking Portuguese, all of which ease a pilgrim's integration into the group: (1) speaking Portuguese helps students understand the nuance behind movement because they can ask questions and participate in debriefing discussions, (2) it unlocks the poetic mysteries of capoeira songs, and (3) it facilitates *troca de informação* between capoeira pilgrims and locals, particularly *mestres.* Local *capoeiristas* value foreigners' attempts at speaking Portuguese, but capoeira pilgrims vary greatly in their facility with speaking Portuguese. Most pilgrims have some knowledge of the language, but those who succeed in becoming integrated into local groups tend to be quite fluent.

An inability to speak Portuguese does not necessarily preclude foreigners from participating in the physical dialogue that is at the center of the *roda,* but it can lessen the experience. Often, pilgrims can get through training sessions without speaking Portuguese because being able to read body language is sufficient to understand the lesson. For example, participants of Ginga Mundo's Fourth International Encounter, a capoeira event that draws participants from a large number of different groups to take part in several days' worth of capoeira classes, *rodas,* and lectures, concluded that it is not necessary to speak Portuguese to enter the *roda* because muscle memory and the physical language of capoeira transcended speech (Portela 2008). The transition is made easier because, as Mestre Cobra Mansa pointed out, *mestres* teach in more or less the same manner. When a foreigner enters the *roda,* he or she already knows how to carry out the movements (Portela 2008). Sometimes, verbal cues are not used at all when making corrections in a student's execution. Rather, the *mestre* will demonstrate the correct movement directly in front of the student or physically move the student's body into place. This approach to teaching will probably be familiar to anyone who has taken a ballet class and had his or her posture corrected by the teacher adjusting the student's shoulders or realigning the student's pelvis. Many body cultures are taught in this way. However, for students wishing to go beyond mere mimicry of movements demonstrated by the instructors, speaking Portuguese is essential for one to understand the nuance and logic behind the proper execution of the movements.

Being able to understand and communicate in Portuguese is also needed to fully appreciate capoeira music, which is an essential part of the art. While lyrics provide players with a historical record of the past, they do much more; "they, together with the sound of the berimbau and gestures like the chamada, encourage players to imagine across the gap between the past and present, to experience the resonance of events through time" (Downey 2005: 113–114). The internalization of these historical memories and landscapes, achieved by viscerally participating in the reproduction of a canon of songs, also allows non-Brazilian players to "imagine across the gap" between their home and Brazil. This reinforces their sense that they are part of the greater capoeira community rooted in Brazil even if they do not share the same markers of identity that the original *capoeiristas* had.

Being unable to speak Portuguese is a considerable handicap when it comes to appreciating the music. At the Ginga Mundo international event, it was said that though they do not know Portuguese or even the meaning of the songs, the foreign *capoeiristas* know how to sing them well (Portela 2008). But aping the sounds of the music is not the same as critically reflecting on what the song means for one's own participation in a cultural group. Mestre Cobra Mansa says it is important for foreigners to understand the context of the songs, whether they are playful or provocative, pushing the players to intensify their game (Portela 2008). Even though *mestres* all over the world rely on the same form, and foreigners can enter Brazilian *roda*s without speaking Portuguese, it remains important to be able to understand the context provided by capoeira songs, which are almost universally sung in Portuguese.

Among native speakers of Portuguese, there tends to be more improvisation with both *ladainhas* and *chorridos*. Recall Mestre Valmir singling me out at my first *roda*. He stopped the performance, dragged me to the foot of the *berimbau*, and improvised a *ladainha* that, among other things, said it was his responsibility to lead me. On other occasions he used the *ladainha* as a time to mock players, and very often he interspersed corrections and commentary into the *chorridos*. Foreigners who did not speak Portuguese or did not understand it well enough were left out of these exchanges.

Not speaking Portuguese also limits pilgrims' participation in music class. At FICA Bahia, it was generally assumed that students already knew how to play the instruments and just needed practice refining their technique and rhythm. Because the *berimbau* is the most important and most difficult instrument, students were encouraged to bring their own to class. It was only if someone did not have their own and there were not enough academy-owned *berimbaus* to go around that we incorporated the other instruments. Part of the class might be dedicated to learning new rhythms on the *berimbau,* but much time was also spend practicing songs. Students often took turns leading the rest of the group in call-and-response choruses. Sometimes students were allowed to have these verses memorized word-for-word, but other times they were asked to improvise new verses on the spot. There was a clear impetus to be as creative as possible in improvising new lyrics, which demands familiarity, if not fluency, in Portuguese. Rhyming may come easier in Portuguese than in English because of its structure, but this is still a pretty daunting task when struggling to properly execute a new *berimbau* rhythm.

On top of this, all but the most novice students were also expected to be able to lead a *ladainha*. This is the longest type of song performed in capoeira and does not have as much repetition or rhyming as do choruses, meaning that there are fewer structures to support recall. This is performed as a solo so when it is a student's turn, all eyes and ears are on him or her. It is difficult to hide one's lack of fluency in such a situation. Lewis writes that "only rarely will foreign players feel confident enough to sing a solo ladainha litany, let alone improvise a new one" (1992: 161), but this is precisely what students, domestic and foreign alike, were being trained to do at FICA Bahia. After class one evening, Aloan commented on three of the students' performances, all of whom were foreigners from Germany, Israel, and Martinique. He said that the *ladainha* is supposed to be a story or instruction to the two players preparing to enter the *roda*; therefore, they need to be sung with good enunciation. The *ladainha* should be authoritative and inspiring. He said that all three of these students speak Portuguese well, so they have no excuse for not pronouncing their words clearly.

Pilgrims' reliance on English or other languages can hinder their development as Portuguese speakers. During one class in mid December 2008, Mestre Valmir called all of the students to sit together in a circle. Several of the foreign students had been training at the academy for four or more months, though the group also included some relative newcomers who had only been in Brazil for about one month. With a single *pandeiro* as accompaniment, Mestre Valmir asked us to take turns playing capoeira inside the circle. While playing, each pair was to select a song and take turns leading verses. We were allowed to use some stock verses but were expected to improvise some new verses of our own. Two foreign men, one from Colombia and the other from Japan, were the first to take their turn. The Colombian has spent several years on and off living in Bahia. The Japanese had been in Bahia for nearly a year. Their movements were slow and clear, their singing good, and their improvisations funny enough to keep us all laughing.

Bridget and a Brazilian man went next. Just as their verbal banter was reaching its peak, the Brazilian sang, "I've forgotten the words!" This alone would have been amusing, but the American's ability to continue improvising in Portuguese brought us to hilarity. Other pairings were not quite as successful as these. In two cases, the partners were told to stop playing and just sit in front of Mestre Valmir who guided them through the song, encouraging them to improvise as much as possible.

When the exercise was over, he asked us why this was difficult. Like so many of his questions, this was rhetorical. He said the primary challenges are breathing, thinking about multiple things at once, and the language. He said we must stop speaking our own languages among ourselves at capoeira (in the dressing rooms, before class, etc.) because it interferes with us learning Portuguese and being able to improvise verses, which he sees as intimately connected to playing capoeira. Ironically, in most pairings, the foreigners did just as well if not better than the Brazilians. Nonetheless, we all agreed that our Portuguese would develop faster if we refrained from speaking our own native language or even a second language that was still more comfortable than Portuguese. However, the lure of speaking freely with other members of our speech community proved just too strong for most of us, myself included.

Looking at the broad manifestation of the apprenticeship pilgrimage phenomenon, most capoeira pilgrims are not fluent in Portuguese. Sometimes this is because students have not yet reached the point in their own training where they see this as being important. Kassie, who trained with a *Capoeira Regional* group in Los Angeles, said that only four members of her group spoke Portuguese because the others are beginners and have not yet had the opportunity to learn; however, this did not prevent them from attending an international event held in Brazil during July of 2008. The situation seemed to be similar at another academy in Bahia whose *mestre* travels to Europe regularly and has made many connections there. Many Europeans e-mail him when they want to come to Brazil, and he helps facilitate their entrance into the local capoeira group. A woman from California told me that people from the United States like her appreciate his punctuality, which can never be taken for granted in Brazil. This *mestre* understands foreigners' expectations and needs and works hard to make sure that they have an enjoyable and safe stay in Brazil. The majority of foreigners that this woman, who speaks English, Spanish, and Portuguese fluently, encountered at this academy did not speak Portuguese; less than one half of them spoke it at all, and less than one half of those spoke it well. This was also the case at a third academy where I occasionally observed *rodas*. In fact, it tended to be a general trend among capoeira pilgrims outside of the academy where I trained unless they had another reason for speaking Portuguese such as their family heritage, working abroad in Brazil or another Portuguese-speaking country, or postgraduate study that required language training.

Based on these observations, I conclude that *capoeiristas* in the FICA system are somewhat unusual in their degree of fluency. In 2007, when several members of the Estrela do Norte group attended the FICA women's conference in Atlanta, we were struck by how many of the FICA students spoke Portuguese and how comfortable they were interacting with the instructors who did not speak English. Not only do non-Brazilian FICA students make the effort to learn Portuguese, they learn to speak it well. This was one of my first impressions of FICA Bahia.

When I attended my first *roda* there, I was amazed that almost all of the English-speaking foreigners continued to speak Portuguese to me even after they found out I was American, even in the privacy of the dressing room. In time, however, I came to hear more and more English being spoken, especially when we socialized outside of the academy. Interacting with other Americans and many of the Europeans felt more comfortable in English, but Portuguese continued to be the *lingua franca* at the academy because it facilitated conversations with Brazilians and with foreigners who had no other languages in common. Speaking Portuguese is thus a marker of one's dedication, a sign of respect for the *mestres* and other Brazilian *capoeiristas* who are monolingual, and a pragmatic tool necessary in an environment that attracts students from such a diverse set of countries.

Although this is not uniformly the case in the FICA system, some capoeira academies mandate that students study Portuguese in conjunction with their physical and musical training. For example, all the foreign students of Abadá are required to study Portuguese because the founding *mestre,* Mestre Camisa, believes certain aspects of capoeira's philosophy are destroyed by translation (Costa 2007). Even though Mestre Cobra Mansa told me that he would like more of his students to study Portuguese, he resists any such mandates because he believes each group should be given the autonomy to develop in accord with their local culture. However, FICA students worldwide are still remarkable in their mastery of the language, particularly when contrasted to some of the other groups in Bahia that also receive pilgrims, but must make more accommodations for them like providing a translator.

There are several possible explanations for the prevalence of Portuguese speakers among the non-Brazilian FICA groups. For one, language acquisition and its importance is frequently referenced on the FICA archives web site. For example, a historical look at capoeira during the 1920s and 1930s was recently published by a former member of FICA Bahia as the result of her master's thesis. The thesis is written in Portuguese. A review of this book was posted in English on the FICA archives site, and members of the group were encouraged to read it in its entirety. There was even a note saying not to be intimidated by reading it in Portuguese because the author writes in a very accessible style. This web site also features workshop announcements, cultural and historical facts, current events, photos, and lyrics to capoeira songs. Sometimes translations are given, but in several cases, the person posting the lyrics encourages English-speaking *capoeiristas* to invest the time in translating the lyrics for themselves because it would be a worthwhile exercise for their development as a *capoeirista*. Another possible explanation for this phenomenon is the regularity with which teachers from FICA travel around the world. In any given month, a Brazilian instructor from the FICA franchise is likely giving classes abroad. Each teacher may speak a smattering of other languages, but it is far simpler if everyone communicates in Portuguese.

It is also possible that being able to speak Portuguese is more important at FICA Bahia than in other academies because of the *mestres'* focus on communal reflection after each class. Classes at FICA Bahia typically conclude with students sitting in a circle and discussing the class. Students are given an opportunity to ask questions about the movements or how to apply them in the context of the *roda*. These chats often take a philosophical turn. In response to a question about how to learn a particular movement or to improve its execution, the teacher might say that students have to respect their own bodies, their own unique histories, and the time it takes to become a master of anything. Though efforts were often made to include them using translation or gestures, those foreigners without a sufficient grasp of the language were sidelined during these conversations.

Learning Portuguese, as the majority of pilgrims that I interviewed had done, is conducive to gaining acceptance in the local academy, understanding the nuance behind the form, and appreciating the songs sung during the *roda*. However, some accommodations are available for those who have been unsuccessful in their attempts to learn Portuguese or uninterested in trying to do so. Some Brazilian capoeira teachers have learned English or another common language such as French or Spanish because they believe this will help them teach pilgrims/tourists in Brazil and will also be useful if they are ever given the opportunity to travel and teach capoeira abroad. This is the tactic adopted by *capoeiristas* like Brittni, a woman from the United States who was not a pilgrim, but fell in love with capoeira while living abroad in South America. Her bilingual Spanish–English upbringing made for an easy transition into speaking fluent Portuguese, at which time she began undertaking translation projects.

To help her capoeira friends preparing to teach abroad, or those who specialize in teaching capoeira to tourists, Brittni created a bilingual Portuguese–English teaching manual. This small booklet included useful phrases such as, "one more time," "don't stop," and "where does it hurt?" Through a stroke of good fortune, Brittni was able to find a publisher who printed the booklets free of charge. Another way for academies to help foreigners study capoeira at their facilities when they do not speak Portuguese is to draw upon a local network of friends who speak English, French, Spanish, Russian, and so on, whenever they need translators. This is the strategy used by the Associação de Mestre Bimba, which has extensive contacts within the capoeira community who have traveled internationally. Translators can be of great assistance during the limited confines of class, but without being able to communicate freely in Portuguese, pilgrims will find it difficult to engage in *troca de informação* with local players and other members of the community.

*Troca de informação* is perhaps the strongest argument for why foreigners should learn Portuguese. Without speaking Portuguese, it is very difficult to engage in information exchange with local *capoeiristas,* particularly the *mestres.* Because of their age, they are even less likely to have been exposed to formal foreign language education than younger participants. Capoeira pilgrims often went home without gaining some of the precious knowledge they sought just because they did not know how to ask. Without linguistic preparation, pilgrims find themselves isolated and lonely, as relatively little English is spoken by residents of this part of Brazil. Those who do learn Portuguese find their opportunities to interact with locals greatly expanded.

Although some aspects of learning capoeira can be negotiated with body language, speaking Portuguese has many benefits for a non-Brazilian *capoeirista*. Benefits include a more nuanced understanding of the performance form itself, a deeper understanding of the songs associated with capoeira, and most importantly, being able to communicate with *mestres* and Brazilian *capoeiristas* and entering into that all-important *troca de informação*. Capoeira pilgrims are sometimes surprised at first by how important speaking Portuguese is, and it is an admittedly daunting task. However, those who acquire even rudimentary skills see a large payoff. This is particularly evident among non-Brazilian FICA *capoeiristas*. There are unique demands of participating in this group. For example, taking part in philosophical discussions or hosting Brazilian teachers regularly make it easy to see why the group places so much importance on speaking Portuguese.

## Giving Back to the Local Community

Volunteer work is another way in which pilgrims can show that they have a humble attitude and are willing to dedicate themselves to service. However, most pilgrims do not avail themselves of these opportunities, either because of time constraints or safety issues. Others simply think this is extraneous to the mission of becoming a better *capoeirista*. Such a perspective could indicate that an individual has the first kind of dedication discussed above, dedication to his or her own training, but not the second kind which is more highly valued by the community.

Local *capoeirisitas,* particularly those who are Afro-Brazilian,[1] value volunteerism as part of their development significantly more than do foreign pilgrims. However, they do not deny foreigners legitimacy nor do they prevent them from assuming increasingly central roles in the academy if they fail to serve in this way. What is notable with respect to a pilgrim's progression in the field, however, is that those who do serve tend to find themselves interacting with their *mestres* more. This increases their opportunities for legitimate peripheral participation, which is described in the next chapter as a pedagogical approach that gradually brings students into the center of a community of practice by virtue of their participation in events and activities that are not available to those *capoeiristas* who treat training as a strictly economic exchange (Lave and Wenger 1991).

While most *capoeiristas* who volunteer their time in Brazil do so through informal opportunities arranged by their academies, some do so through more structured opportunities. For example, I met several young women that were interested in various aspects of Afro-Brazilian culture who were volunteers with Cross

Cultural Solutions. This is an organization that seeks to achieve their humanitarian goals by putting people from more privileged situations into contexts where individual acts of kindness and compassion can effect change at the local level (Cross Cultural Solutions). These individuals are short-term volunteers who work on one of many projects, including a nursery for children with HIV. As part of the voluntourism package they purchase from the organization, these individuals are housed together in one of the more upscale areas of the city, are given regular Portuguese lessons, and are exposed to other cultural practices such as capoeira. This is a private lesson for the Cross Cultural Solutions volunteers, thus their interaction with Brazilian *capoeiristas* is minimal unless they choose to seek out additional training opportunities on their own. For some, visiting Brazil on an organized voluntourism trip exposes them to aspects of Brazilian culture, like capoeira, that they will later pursue more seriously. This was the case for Kassie, who began her forays in Brazil through a voluntourism organization but later came back on her own as a capoeira pilgrim.

Kassie has both Portuguese and Brazilian family members, so she has had considerable exposure to the language and is now completely fluent. She began working with HIV patients in Salvador in 2003. During this trip she met a few *capoeiristas* who were also volunteering at Cross Cultural Solutions, but she was not yet a *capoeirista* herself. She has made four or five trips specifically for volunteer work, and her trip in 2008 was the first one dedicated specifically to training capoeira. Despite her intense involvement in volunteer work, she took a neutral stance regarding its importance to capoeira. While not essential to one's development as a *capoeirista,* she did say:

> A lot of *capoeiristas* that I know, if they had the chance they would love to come down and give back to this country that has given them so much, especially knowing the history of capoeira, it comes from areas that do need a lot of help.

Other visitors to Salvador, however, find themselves accidental volunteers. These are *capoeiristas* whose primary motivation for traveling to Bahia was training capoeira. Oftentimes, a Bahian capoeira group has at least a loose relationship with a local charitable group. It is through these more informal organizations that foreigners often find themselves contributing to the local community.

When asked about the importance of volunteer work, most interview subjects immediately assumed I was talking about physical education classes in *favelas* or poor neighborhoods. Repeated over and over again was the sentiment that foreigners should give back to the culture that has given them so much on a personal level. When discussing volunteer work, Brazilians and foreigners alike focused on poor, Afro-Brazilian children whose life circumstances are likely to lead to drug abuse and often drug trafficking. Foreigners liked the idea of teaching them capoeira because it would give them a feeling of self-worth and expose them to a healthier way of life. Brazilians echoed these sentiments but added that because training in an academy has become so expensive, these children cannot afford to learn about their own heritage and therefore should be the recipients of free classes. Participating in capoeira was believed by my consultants to uplift these children whose lives are made more difficult by their extreme economic deprivation, often living in crowded homes without running water or electicity. Pilgrims also believe that practicing capoeira liberates empoverished children from other negative influences like drugs and gang membership, regardless of whether or not this is actually true.

Teaching capoeira to disadvantaged youth is a good fit for foreigners whose facility with the language may be spotty at best. In my own experience of visiting the Pierre Verger foundation, a cultural space that had been established to serve underprivileged children, the kids saw the three foreigners in our group as a novelty. They seemed to enjoy watching us play capoeira, sometimes laughing at us despite the fact that we were more advanced than most of them, and just spending time with adults who were interested in them. Granted, our few visits did not amount to much more than a novel diversion, and the ethics of voluntourism should certainly be debated, as the tourist often benefits more from these interactions than does the local community. Nonetheless, this is an avenue of action that capoeira pilgrims see as being accessible to them. One pilgrim/volunteer thought that going into a dangerous slum without knowing the language could be a very intimidating prospect, but interacting with children within the framework of a well-known ritual such as capoeira was very natural for him. Of course the danger is real, and in many places, it is not advisable for a foreigner to go into a *favela* unaccompanied; in 2008 at least one famous academy had stopped allowing foreigners to volunteer at their project because of this.

Some individuals find ways to contribute to the capoeira community in a personalized way that does not involve movement instruction. Some of these projects have a great impact on the people involved. Recall, for example, the work that Brittni did to help her friends learn some instructional phrases in English. In addition to having numerous copies of the booklet printed, she also gave a class in which teachers had the opportunity to practice these phrases. A few native speakers of English, including Kassie and myself, were in attendance, and we were paired up with local instructors to give them targeted feedback on pronunciation and word usage. The workshop started with a panel presentation by a group of *mestres* and instructors who had spent time abroad teaching capoeira. They discussed some of the challenges that they had experienced, especially dealing with the shockingly cold weather in the United States and Europe. Most of all, however, they discussed how alienating it was to be in a place where they could not be self-sufficient because of their inability to communicate in the local language. Being unable to speak the local language also inhibited their ability to conduct business.

With this endorsement from the leaders of the capoeira community, Brittni had no trouble assembling a packed house of eager instructors who wanted to learn some basic English phrases.

Volunteerism is more common among the foreigners who stay in Brazil for more than a few weeks. One woman in my study felt that fifteen days was not a sufficient amount of time for her to become directly involved in volunteer work, but seeing some of this work in action made her think about how she could start reaching out to American children through capoeira. Among those I interviewed who said they had not been involved in any volunteer work in Brazil, most felt that they were remiss in not doing so. Their reasoning was that the culture had given them so much on a personal level that they should find a way to give back. Regardless of whether their remorse was genuine or not, it does suggest that they are at least aware of the community disapproval of foreigners who only take from Brazil without giving something back.

Sometimes, however, the local population may be cynical about the tourists who try to do good in their community. One of the employees of a local Internet café that I regularly frequented was born and raised in a nearby *favela*. He said that he sees lots of foreigners who come to Bahia with great intentions, but they do not really accomplish much. A white *capoeirista* who has moved from the United States to Salvador to be with his Brazilian wife was also cynical with respect to the efficacy of foreigners' charitable contributions. He doubts that foreigners can really do much good without being taken advantage of in Brazil. He also said that while foreigners visiting Brazil is not charity per se, they do support capoeira financially and in terms of respect. He thinks this type of tourism has opened the eyes of a lot of Brazilians who have an inferiority complex about anything Brazilian. In this sense, tourism has become a twenty-first century version of the folklore movement in the early twentieth century that valorized African contributions to Brazilian society. And while the commodification of black bodies for the purposes of tourism marketing should be questioned, it does, at least, index the international interest in Afro-Brazilian traditions.

Mestre Janja's reaction to foreigners who try to do volunteer work in Brazil was even more intriguing than these previous two examples since she has received a great deal of attention locally and internationally for her work with women and children in capoeira. As mentioned in chapter 5, she uses her position as a platform for teaching children about serious issues like violence against women. The children in her group, many of whom are from low-income families, have assumed impressive leadership roles within the academy. At least one child in Janja's group has been trusted with a key to the academy. Several children arrive before class to clean and prepare the training space. Interestingly, of everyone I interviewed, Janja was the most hesitant to endorse foreigners' volunteer projects. She understands the foreigners' desire to visit Bahia because it is a fount of knowledge, but she also has to walk a line between making foreigners feel welcome and maintaining strict traditions. The only thing she really dislikes is foreigners' interest in working with children, often treating them like guinea pigs, because she believes foreigners' short-lived efforts might introduce instability into the kids' lives. Similarly, anthropologist Margaret Wilson (2007), who helped start the Bahia Street nonprofit organization supporting girls' education, has remarked upon the brash attitudes of entitlement displayed by many foreign volunteers. These individuals go to Bahia Street, often without an appointment, expecting that any "help" they can offer will be appreciated. In reality, however, their presence is often a distraction from the carefully planned lessons the local staff has prepared.

Overall, this type of engagement with the local community seems to be hit or miss with many of the *capoeiristas* who make pilgrimages to Salvador. For Mestre Cobra Mansa, founder of FICA, volunteerism is very important. For foreigners, this is one of the ways they can show that they are not just tourists but a part of the community. In actual practice, however, volunteerism may be something that the pilgrim has briefly considered during his or her preparations to travel. Acting on this impulse is a different matter entirely.

## Romantic Relationships in the Academy

In a chapter on how a pilgrim's attitude, and manifestations of that attitude like speaking Portuguese or undertaking volunteer work, helps him or her become integrated into the local community, it may seem odd to include a section on romantic relationships. However, becoming romantically involved with a local *capoeirista* is similarly an optional behavior that deepens one's involvement with the social field. While I am not so callous as to suggest that pilgrims regularly seek out local partners to date with the hopes of becoming more integrated into the academy where they are studying, dating someone from the academy does open up a wealth of new opportunities for interacting with local *capoeiristas*. While not intending to be crass, I mention that this too provides evidence that a pilgrim is *aberto* and willing to engage in an exchange with local residents. Obviously not all pilgrims engage in this type of interaction with the local community. However, it can be a significant route to belonging for those who do, which can help facilitate their legitimacy.

While all of the components of a pilgrim's attitude discussed above contribute to his or her integration into the local academy, some barriers remain that can often be mediated by a sexual or romantic relationship. Over coffee one day, Amity told me about one of her friends from back home who had also made a capoeira pilgrimage and spent some time training in a poor area of Rio de Janeiro. This woman, Amity explained, had a very hard time being seen as part of the group, but the reasons for her isolation were different for males and females. The female *capoeiristas* in the group were hesitant to accept her because they felt like she was getting all of the attention from the males, which they apparently resented. The men in the group kept making sexual advances toward her until she became attached to one man, at which point his competitors relented. Once she began seriously dating this guy, however, she was treated as a regular member of the group.

In some situations, when a charismatic foreigner dates a local who is also well liked in the group, their union instigates a period of increased cultural exchange. One of the American women who was training intensively at the academy where I conducted my research had also spent time training there a few years ago. She said that the level of sociability had been much higher then than it was in 2008. At that time, she said, the students did much more together as a group. In 2008, however, we went through waves of sociability and small cliques occasionally formed and dissolved as the pilgrim population shifted. During her previous stay in Brazil, this woman had been dating a Brazilian member of the group. The couple served as a bridge to connect the two groups, locals and foreigners, and they would frequently go out together for beer or juice after class. During my visit, it was rumored that the "high level guys," meaning the instructors and their close friends, went out together after the weekly *rodas,* but no foreigners went with them unless they were females being sought out romantically. This did not cause resentment per se, but some individuals wondered why they did not want to come out with us to our regular lunch spot.

During my time at FICA Bahia, there was one visible foreign–local relationship. It was kept under wraps for about two months, though they eventually gave up the pretense after arriving at class together one too many times. The American woman, a college student who was a bit younger than the majority of the pilgrims training at the academy, was concerned that people at the academy would judge her or treat her differently because of this relationship. She was afraid the Americans at the academy would think that their relationship was developing too quickly. While she was very happy with this romantic relationship, she could also see that it constrained platonic relationships with other people at the academy because her time was somewhat monopolized. She also avoided attending group social events because she would have to confront the implications of the relationship. However, she was also able to see that the established Brazilian members and leaders of the group accepted her more quickly than other foreigners because of this relationship. Specifically, it opened up opportunities for her to interact with the instructors while she was hanging out with her boyfriend. Generally, other foreigners were not present at these informal gatherings, giving her unparalleled access to this corner of the community. This kind of relationship might be termed "associative access" (Jonathan Marion, telephone conversation with the author, personal communication 2014). Rather than having to slowly work her way in from the periphery, she was able to claim a more "centrally situated belonging" (Jonathan Marion, telephone conversation with the author, 2014) by virtue of her relationship with someone who was already part of the inner circle.

There were also times when foreign–local romances endangered women. Foreign women's difficulty with the language and naïveté about local culture was sometimes exploited by local *capoeiristas* who saw them as sexual conquests. Though some women abstained from drugs and alcohol because it would be counterproductive for their training, the licentious behavior associated with tourism (excessive drinking, drug use, etc.) was not uncommon among capoeira pilgrims and could put women in perilous positions. I was told of one young woman whose romantic relationship afforded her entrance into a circle of young Brazilian men who were also *capoeiristas*. When she terminated the relationship, she assumed that she would still be friends with these other men. The men, however, saw this as an opportunity to hook up with a foreign woman. On one occasion after drinking she was lured to an hourly motel under false pretenses and on another night was groped and followed home. I myself was put in an awkward, and potentially threatening, position when a group of *capoeiristas* shared a taxi after a party at a friend's home. When we got to my apartment complex, one of the Brazilian men who was affiliated with our academy tried to get out with me. He said that he had defended my honor, as an engaged woman, when another man was talking about me at the party and had been punched in the mouth for his efforts. My fiancé not withstanding, he thought this meant I should let him come home with me for the evening.

While some of the sexually forward behavior in capoeira academies is merely about conquest, which props up a man's reputation in a machismo-oriented society, and may be brushed off as just having fun, there are sometimes deeper motivations, especially for male *capoeiristas* who dream of going abroad to open their own academy. Many male *capoeiristas* are given their first opportunities to teach abroad through foreign women who provide the necessary capital and documents necessary to leave Brazil. These women then become instrumental in establishing and running their boyfriend's/husband's academy because they have more access to the language and laws of that country (Taylor 2007: 209).

Barely clad men doing flips in the surf is a common sight in Bahia, especially in the neighborhood of Barra where I lived because its beachside location attracts a lot of tourism. These men show off their bodies and their flashy moves in hopes of catching female tourists' attention. In the short term, they see women as marks for sex tourism, but in the long run, they see these women as tickets out of Brazil. While sex tourism is often thought to be a male-dominated phenomenon in which wealthy, Western males seek out poor people of color to fulfill their sexual fantasies, this is more akin to romance tourism in which women seek out local partners albeit with the added twist of local men seeking out these relationships because of the possibility it may afford for their long-term career advancement. It is these men whose legitimacy as *capoeiristas* is most often called into question, primarily by Brazilians, but oftentimes by foreigners as well.

In some cases, the Brazilian *capoeiristas* do actually succeed in securing a foreign wife. A 23-year-old street performer of capoeira was quoted in a local Salvador newspaper. His Spanish girlfriend gave him a plane ticket, so he could fly there and marry her. He explained to the reporter that he has to be married to a citizen in order to live and work in Spain. He also said that he would trade his future life in Spain for a grant to finish his studies in nursing, a marriage to a woman of his choosing, and work where he could help lots of people (Araujo 2006). Unfortunately, his life circumstances would not permit this, and he felt marriage to this Spanish woman was a better option. Reading this story, I wondered if she was aware of how her fiancé felt about their upcoming union. Some partners do enter into these relationships knowing that the *capoeirista* is just looking for a visa. Amity, for example, told me that she had dated a Brazilian *capoeirista* in London who was involved in one of these marriages of convenience. He described it as a business transaction and had no qualms about having both a wife and a girlfriend.

One of the foreign women I interviewed said she used to look at these relationships with disdain because they were so similar to sex tourism, but eventually stopped judging them because she realized that both parties are getting something out of the exchange. Local *capoeiristas,* mostly male, entice foreign women to take them to Europe or America where they can start their own academies. Given the global demand for capoeira instruction from an actual Brazilian, this is a good strategy. A foreign woman who dates a local *capoeirista* may be learning dance or capoeira from him and getting an inside look at the culture at the same time that he is getting money from her or possibly even an invitation to travel abroad. Of course, not all unions are so Machiavellian. Some are based on true emotions and wind up being very successful. What I wish to highlight here is that either side of the foreign–local equation may use romantic/sexual relationships to achieve a larger goal related to their advancement within the world of capoeira.

## Conclusion

Although individuals who fit the traditional image of a *capoeirista* by being black, Brazilian, and/or male may have an easier time to become integrated into the Brazilian capoeira scene, it is not impossible for individuals who lack these qualities to become accepted. They just have to find other ways to prove their willingness to become part of the group, which is primarily done by displaying an appropriate attitude. This includes being open, humble, and dedicated. Concrete manifestations of this attitude include helping out with menial tasks at the academy, learning how to speak Portuguese, and giving back to the local community. Even engaging in romantic relationships with local *capoeiristas* can be seen as evidence of one's openness, though it is certainly not a required element of advancement within the field.

These actions will matter most to the other members of one's group. In a city of nearly three million people, pilgrims will not have the opportunity to demonstrate their openness, good humor, dazzling linguistic abilities, good-hearted volunteerism, and so on to even half of the local capoeira community. In the social field at large, *capoeiristas* must demonstrate their mastery of form, visible in performance. By the end of chapter 7, it will become clear how both the traditional claims to authenticity discussed in chapter 5 and the charismatic factors addressed in this chapter increase the odds that a *capoeirista* will learn to successfully execute the form of capoeira and move toward the center of the social field where they too might one day have a hand in shaping the rules of the game.

## Notes

1.  Though my sample size was not large enough to make claims about statistical significance, this was a clear pattern in my data. Afro-Brazilians were the only group in my study that consistently rated volunteerism as an important quality for *capoeiristas*. Although further research would be needed to justify any definitive conclusions, it is possible that this is linked to their positions in a social system that generally conflates race and class. Greater awareness of the challenges faced by Afro-Brazilians might predispose one to be more active in contributing to efforts designed to benefit less privileged communities.

## Works Cited

Araujo, Ana Carolina. 2006. "Capoeira Tipo Exportação." *Correio da Bahia,* 3 August.

Costa, Flavio. 2007. "Jeito de Corpo." *Correiro da Bahia,* 27 August.

Downey, Greg. 2005. *Learning Capoeira: Lessons in Cunning from an Afro-Brazilian Art.* Oxford: Oxford University Press.

Lave, Jean, and Etienne Wenger. 1991. *Situated Learning: Legitimate Peripheral Participation.* New York: Cambridge University Press.

Lewis, J Lowell. 1992. *Ring of Liberation: Deceptive Discourse in Brazilian Capoeira.* Chicago: University of Chicago Press.

Peterson, Richard A. 2005. "In Search of Authenticity." *Journal of Management Studies* 42 (5): 1083–98.

Portela, Maira. 2008. "Lingua da Capoeira." *Correio da Bahia,* 5 May.

Sheridan, Sam. 2007. *A Fighter's Heart: One Man's Journey through the World of Fighting.* New York: Grove Press.

Stephens, Neil, and Sara Delamont. 2013. "Mora Yemanja? Axe in Diasporic Capoeira Regional." In *The Diaspora of Brazilian Religions,* edited by Cristina Rocha and Manuel A Vasquez, 271–88. Leiden: Brill.

Taylor, Gerard. 2007. *Capoeira: The Jogo de Angola from Luanda to Cyberspace.* Vol. 2. Berkeley, CA: North Atlantic Books.

Timbers, Caroline C. 2000. "Building an International Quilombo: Meaning, Marginality, and Community in Capoeira Angola and Its Practice in the United States," MA thesis. Georgetown University.

Titunik, Regina F. 2005. "Democracy, Domination, and Legitimacy." In *Max Weber's "Economy and Society": A Critical Companion,* edited by Charles Camic, Philip S Gorski, and David M Trubek, 143-163. Stanford: Stanford University Press.

Wilson, Margaret. 2007. *Dance Lest We All Fall Down: A Journey of Friendship, Poverty, Power and Peace.* Nashville, TN: Cold Tree Press.

Yamazaki, Kazuko. 2001. "Nihon Buyo: Classical Dance of Modern Japan," PhD dissertation. Indiana University.

# Chapter 7

# Does Form Really Matter?

At the end of one particularly grueling class in which we had been told to play with our partners for about fifteen minutes but were only allowed to use a handful of movements, Mestre Cobra Mansa told us that his job is to teach us the alphabet, but it is up to us to put them into words and phrases. This activity had been designed to help us develop creativity even when working with a restricted set of "letters," to use his metaphor. Tyrell, Ellis, and I approached him as he left the dressing room. Where are the limits on innovation in capoeira, I wanted to know. He told us that with the building blocks we are given in class, there is no limit to our innovation. Feeling feisty, I argued that at some point, without any limits, our games would devolve into free fights. "No," he said. "With the 'letters' I teach you, you can make all sorts of words, but it is still language, not mathematics." In retrospect I can understand that he was trying to tell us something about the incorruptibility of the basic formal units that have been passed down from teacher to student across generations. At the time, however, I was not satisfied. We temporarily agreed that within capoeira, we are all speaking the same language but with our own *sotaques* (accents). It seemed like an appropriate metaphor given the international nature of our group.

We three students then continued our conversation at a nearby café. Ellis agreed with Mestre Cobra Mansa that the creativity of capoeira has no limit, but I kept arguing my point. "What about *Capoeira Regional*? Where is the line between being creative and bastardizing capoeira?"[1] "You can do anything in the *roda,* and it is still going to be capoeira," Tyrell said. "Even a Judo throw would be capoeira if it occurred within the bounds of the *roda*." I wondered if he was right. Does the context of a performance matter more than the formal elements used to construct it? Which matters more, the way a movement is performed or the logic that motivated that movement? Furthermore, how does one learn the proper form if even their most esteemed *mestres* cannot or will not articulate it explicitly? These were the thorny questions related to form that I would have to answer.

## Introduction

It is challenging to identify the boundaries of proper form in capoeira because its practitioners value both tradition and innovation. However, I have found that the form can be understood in terms of several dichotomies. In the beginning, the student will learn basic movements that can be assembled in a number of different ways. These are the building blocks of all *capoeiristas'* repertoires; however, more experienced players eventually develop a unique style that goes beyond technique and enters the realm of artistry. This demands attention to both beauty and efficacy. Efficacy is not, however, the same as aggressiveness, and this is another lesson that is best learned through experience.

Breaches of form are sometimes, but not always, censured by the individual in charge of the *roda*. This can happen subtly, through song, or more overtly. In other cases, there is no need for a verbal correction because a poorly executed move will generally bring about its own punishment. There are some situations, however, that are even more ambiguous. Some breaches of form are not only allowed, but actually encouraged if they exemplify the principle of *malícia,* trickery through deceit.

This chapter explores these sometimes-contradictory mandates of form and explains how students learn these norms. As it turns out, the real purpose of classes is not to perfectly transmit a corpus of knowledge from one body to another, but to cultivate a particular aesthetic sensibility in students. These lessons are not easy, and while it is *possible* for anyone to learn them, it is decidedly easier for the students who have the most access to the *mestre's* knowledge and insights.

## Reconciling Tradition and Innovation

My original hypothesis was that mastering the form of capoeira would result in an all-access pass to the backstage areas of this culture, but this was a naïve assumption. In her work on how status is achieved in capoeira, D'Aquino (1983) also rather narrowly defined the mechanism of advancement as having to do with one's performance in the *roda*, with the exception of some *mestres* who are awarded high standing in the capoeira community and Brazilian society at large thanks to their visibility and handling of public relations. In today's globalized capoeira field, however, the situation is more complex. While it *is* necessary to master the formal requirements of capoeira, this is not the end of one's journey. Being seen as a competent performer demands balancing innovation with tradition. Tradition and innovation may seem antithetical to one another, but they can be reconciled. Performances must conform to the norms of the genre, but within those bounds, originality confirms that a performer's style is genuine and not copied (see Peterson

1997: 209). Timbers discusses Americans' desires to adhere to the Brazilian standard as closely as possible without becoming mindless mimics. She says:

> [Americans] do not want to make capoeira anew, they want to conform "their" capoeira as closely as possible to the capoeira played in Brazil (not necessarily to copy it, but to match its levels of creativity and expressionism). Mestres function as the most legitimate (and oftentimes, the only) sources of information on capoeira, and thus, their actions, ideas and knowledge are closely imitated and absorbed so that Americans can be "true" capoeiristas. (Timbers 2000: 69)

This statement conveys foreign *capoeiristas'* commitment to living up to Brazilian standards in their own practice of capoeira.[2] Foreign *capoeiristas* want to be considered legitimate performers, and to that aim, they model their performances after Brazilian capoeira and their Brazilian *mestres'* teachings, but they do not necessarily want to copy it. Rather, they want to stay within the idiom while simultaneously developing their own unique style and expression.

Within *Capoeira Angola,* students are urged to be creative with the movements they have in their repertoire. Six of the most basic movements in a *capoeirista's* arsenal are *rabo de arraia, tesouro* (scissors), *au* (cartwheel), *rolê, negativa,* and *bananeira.* Learning these movements and how to implement them comprises literacy for *capoeiristas,* though there are infinite variations and flourishes that can be added to these basics. There are certain sets of movements that the beginner will learn together, for example *rabo de arraia* and *negativa,* which form basic adjacency pairs, a term I am adapting from linguistics to indicate that within capoeira there are certain attack and defense moves that are seen as logical complements to one another. Capoeira scholar Edward Powe has made an attempt at listing the common adjacency pairs within *Capoeira Angola* (see Powe 2002). For example, a *tesouro* should be answered with either another *tesouro* under the first player's outspread legs or with an *au* that launches the second player over the first player's body.

While Powe's work may be an interesting and useful primer, the potential for new combinations is endless, making any such attempt at cataloguing movements inherently incomplete. A player who only used these combinations would soon be ridiculed for a lack of creativity or "feeling"; the mockery would be even worse if it were discovered that the student had learned these movements from a book (or, heaven forbid, a DVD or YouTube). For while *capoeiristas* tend to be voracious consumers of literature written about their art, they are critical of those who do not have the lived experience of training with a *mestre* or other instructor in person. In a face-to-face learning environment, the *capoeirista* becomes disciplined to the aesthetic expectations of the genre and learns that there are no predetermined moves. Performance in the *roda* is judged largely by an individual's creativity in answering his or her opponent's attacks (Essien 2008: 14).

Individual creativity may introduce incremental change into a form, but adherence to tradition normally prevents major changes that would disrupt the genre. Capoeira changes as a result of the inherent instability of performance in general. Each iteration of an adjacency pair opens up the possibility that something will be changed as a result of intentional innovation or unintentional error. Thus, changes to a form may take place almost without participants' awareness, particularly in a form like capoeira that lacks notation. Hahn points out that despite the invention of Laban's notation system, dance has largely remained an art form that is "passed from body to body" (2007: 6), which makes it similar in many ways to oral tradition. This is equally true of capoeira, for which there are very few written scores.

In the late 1990s, Juca Ferreira, Brazilian cultural minister, expressed his concerns about the viability of traditional capoeira and was assured by members of GCAP, the group popularly credited with reviving *Capoeira Angola* in the 1980s, that there was no cause for worry because the innovations that do not adhere to tradition die on the vine (Ferreira 1997). What is interesting in this comment is that the group admits that change will happen, but at the same time, they fervently believe in the basic incorruptibility of their tradition. Similarly, a Russian woman who was training at FICA said there was nothing to worry about at our academy because if a group adheres to the rituals and traditions passed down from the previous generations of *capoeiristas* and uses these to shape their overall practice, then individual movements within capoeira games are of little consequence. Nonetheless, all but two of my interview subjects said that proper form was important or very important for *capoeiristas*.[3] Because none of them were able to articulate what proper form meant, however, I turned my attention to the actual class sessions during which students practiced capoeira technique and looked for evidence that they were developing an idiosyncratic way of executing these techniques.

## Developing Both Technique and Style

Despite his skill as a teacher, there were some things that Mestre Valmir confessed could not be taught. Mestre Valmir says *"tem que ter sentimento, e isso, infeliz-mente, não pode ensinar"* (you have to have feeling, and this, unfortunately, you can't teach). Nor can one learn it from a DVD, though the market continues to be flooded with these instructional guides. The distinction Mestre Valmir was making here is between technique versus style/artistry, which he called *sentimento*. Technique as a conservative force relies upon a codified vocabulary and style as an innovative force necessitates a metaphorical vocabulary to describe performances (Royce 2004: 23). Technique is shared by members of the performance community, but style is an individual hallmark (Royce 2004: 24). While these definitions can be used to discuss performance in a broad sense, they may not be valued equally in every genre (Royce 2004: 34).

Within *Capoeira Angola,* it is common to praise *capoeiristas* for their artistry, but very uncommon to praise someone for technical mastery alone. In fact, technical virtuosity without artistry might be a source of ridicule. A technically brilliant performance of *Capoeira Angola* without any of the stylistic elements so valued by the community would be considered overly mechanical or "robot capoeira," which is a common phrase used to disparage those who mimic their teachers' movements too closely. However, it is useful to think about the concept of artistry as a level of accomplishment that happens after one has gained legitimacy by mastering the form.

While arguing that *sentimento* cannot be taught, Valmir occasionally tried to create opportunities for us through which we might begin to understand the principle. One day he noted our lack of *sentimento* and said we should pretend we were doing the movement with our eyes closed, just listening to the music. Developing *sentimento* was often linked to musicality, but in a tangential way as even the instructors had a hard time articulating exactly what *sentimento* encompassed. *Mandinga* (magic) is related to the concept of *sentimento. Mandinga* technically refers to the magic associated with *Candomblé,* which is sometimes used by *capoeiristas* to close the body's vulnerabilities. Mythical feats like Besouro, a legendary *capoeirista* from Santo Amaro, being able to fly are attributed to *mandinga.* This tradition is not well understood by most pilgrims, and if such rites still exist, they are conducted in secret. In practical discourse, saying that one has *mandinga* references his or her sneaky way of moving. In terms of its aesthetics, a player with lots of *mandinga* will be comfortable using quick and broken, yet fluid movements that initiate from a posture both relaxed enough to convey a carefree or cocky attitude *and* tensely coiled like a spring. Mestre Valmir told students that the purpose of *mandinga* is both to decorate our game and to confound our opponent.

In the end, performance theorists often struggle to define what it is that makes certain performances transcendent and leaves others, while technically perfect, still lacking. Hahn calls this "presence," though she writes "[she is] not certain it is possible to definitively provide a formula for the transmission of presence" (2007: 163). For *capoeiristas,* the element that transforms a performance from being technically superb (or virtuosic to use the paradigm established in Royce 2004) to artistic is *mandinga,* the embodied attitude of using magic and wits to circumvent oppression. Like Hahn, I am not sure that this can be taught directly nor articulated. The closest Mestre Valmir got to actually articulating the answer to this question was by saying *"objetividade e beleza são as chaves"*—to roughly translate: having an objective (efficacy) *and* making a beautiful game are the keys.

I am frequently asked whether capoeira is a dance or a fight. The popular narrative of *Capoeira Angola* holds that African slaves had to disguise capoeira as a dance, so it retains this dancelike playfulness, but it is also a fight, a martial art to be executed with intent. This dual sensibility is precisely what instructors at FICA Bahia sought to teach their students. As the title of this section claims, having an objective and doing movements beautifully are the keys to success in capoeira and to understanding what is meant by the capoeira aesthetic.

Mestre Cobra Mansa says that there are three things *capoeiristas* have to remember when they train: (1) to do the movement correctly; (2) to do it beautifully; and (3) to do it efficiently. Following this formula, it is necessary but not sufficient to do the movements with proper technique. In addition to mastering the technique, *capoeiristas* must strike a balance between aesthetic considerations and efficiently achieving their martial objective. Adding the aesthetic flourishes provides great rewards in terms of establishing a recognizable, idiosyncratic hallmark and in terms of audience appreciation. However, it also introduces vulnerability into the game as the *capoeirista* opens him- or herself to attacks.[4] Therefore, it is this third element, efficiency, which proves trickiest for *capoeiristas* as they seek to strike a balance between *beleza* (beauty) and *objetividade* (achieving an objective).

*Capoeiristas* must be attuned to both technical and stylistic considerations. Some conventions have a strictly technical basis like *Angoleiros* kicking to the torso and not the head like in *Capoeira Regional* because it protects them from leg sweeps. Kicking too high leaves a player's support leg vulnerable to being attacked. Sometimes, technical corrections to a *capoeiristas'* form were made because of the latent violence inherent in the art. For example, Mestre Valmir insisted that *negativas* (low, lateral dodges) be done low to the ground when students evaded a spinning kick because "not everyone is your friend," and some people might actually kick their opponent and cause that person harm if he or she is not close enough to the floor.

Other decisions in the *roda* are made based on their stylistic merits. For example, circular kicks are considered more elegant and interesting than straight kicks that interrupt the flow of the game. Sometimes the dueling considerations of efficacy and aesthetics come into conflict with one another. While it is technically incorrect to do a flatfooted pirouette in front of an opponent because it leaves a player extremely vulnerable to leg sweeps, as I found out the hard way, some *mestres* and advanced players will do precisely this because it is an aesthetically pleasing way of underscoring their technical superiority and ability to flout convention.

Within the *roda*, *capoeiristas* are expected to be creative in the assembly of their movements and development of the game. After class one day, a student asked what was the proper way to respond to a certain attack. Mestre Valmir supplied him with a number of options, saying that some people might respond with a kick that flicks outward from the knee (like kicking a soccer ball), but that shows a lack of creativity. He says that people who choose that option want capoeira to be clear-cut, and they do not want to tax their brains with creativity and invention. In capoeira, there are a multitude of options available, and it takes creativity and mental labor to decide what is best. Capoeira cannot be reduced to a set of rules and formulae. As Mestre Valmir points out, students have lots of options, and even though he teaches movements in a sequence, "in a *roda* it is not necessary to follow these steps ABCDE. You can go ACD or ABE." Training is almost exclusively done in preparation for playing in *rodas,* so developing an understanding of how movements should be assembled with respect to actual game situations is a vital part of a *capoeirista*'s development. There is a significant difference between being able to *do* the movements versus being able to *use* the movements.

Capoeira is not just a dance; it is a latent weapon held in reserve until it is needed. *Capoeiristas* are supposed to execute strikes with proper technique so they could potentially bring down an adversary, but in day-to-day exchanges, players are expected to blunt them by withholding their full force. Many of the movements used in play can be modified to injure an opponent if necessary. Students at FICA were taught both variations but were expected to use the safe alternative in the academy. For example, if a player is in a handstand and is charged by his or her opponent, the player can lower one foot and tap the opponent's back with the top of his or her shoe (where the shoelaces are) in warning. However, if the opponent is not deterred by this counterattack, it is permissible for the player to lower his or her foot with more force, using the point of the tennis shoe, which would be painful. Some elements of technique came up more frequently than others. For example, one important lesson was creating the right amount of distance between players. Students were also frequently drilled on striking the correct portion of the body and making contact with the correct part of the foot so that they would convey intent, but not injure their adversary.

Mestre Valmir and Aloan were fond of telling us that the key to executing most movements in capoeira is "*não é força, é jeito*" (used in this context, his statement translates as "it is not force, it is technique"). Unsurprisingly, many of the movements in capoeira are extremely difficult to execute, and students spend hours training to achieve them. When the entire class struggled, Mestre Valmir would ask us what our difficulties were. Almost universally, people said that they did not have sufficient strength to perform the movements. Valmir responded by saying that it is not force, but *jeito* (technique) that is required to perform the movements. Generally, this made me want to scream, as I was nearly certain that I *was* indeed lacking the strength to do a back walkover with my head on the ground as a pivot point. Nonetheless, they had a good point. Students need to understand the physical mechanics of the movement in order to perform them with ease rather than trying to use brute force to compensate for sloppy technique. In this case, technique is not an arbitrary standard to which *capoeiristas* are held but a necessary route to mastery, without which no amount of strength will help.

Instructors likened capoeira movements to pedestrian movements as a way to emphasize their naturalness. Students were playfully mocked for not being able to walk in a handstand. We were supposed to "just stand up," and walking on our hands was supposed to be as simple as walking upright. When walking upright, we breathe and talk as a matter of course; walking upside down should be no different. In the move that caused me so much frustration, trying to flip over backward while keeping my head on the ground, students commonly made the mistake of trying to kick off with their knees locked, using both feet. When students did this, Aloan would stand upright and try jumping into the air with his knees similarly locked and his feet together. Obviously, this was not very successful. His point was to show that the same mechanics we use in our everyday lives apply to capoeira.

Loosening the body is a key part of developing the capoeira aesthetic, but there are technical reasons for this in addition to stylistic ones. On the technical side, performing movements like the *ginga* too mechanically sets players up for *rasteiras* (leg sweeps). Being light on one's feet and moving unpredictably through the *ginga*, on the other hand, allows players to respond to their opponent's attacks. What is more, this "elastic resiliency" allows *Angoleiros* to catch their opponents off guard (Brough 2006. Brough cites elastic movement as a key feature of African American dances and notes its use in *Capoeira Angola*, under the guise of *malícia*, as a quality that allows the *capoeirista* to confound the opponent with quickly shifting movements that are nonetheless rooted in the ground.

Because *malícia* is so highly valued in capoeira, exercises in class often taught students how to use their bodies to misdirect and trick their opponents. Students were often corrected if their feints were not believable. We were expected to execute these tricks with the objective of making our opponent secure in our intentions and then exploiting that security. The player's acute awareness of the tension between being both rooted in the ground and capable of quickly shifting directions is what allows her to avoid leg sweeps and other disequilibrating attacks. This resiliency also enables players to disguise where their weight is actually rooted; this makes surprise attacks their best weapon (Brough 2006).

Technical corrections almost always have both aesthetic and practical functions, but balancing the two competing demands is not always easy. As mentioned, the *ginga* should be done with a broken aesthetic; however, this is not to disregard alignment entirely. Maintaining alignment of the spine, but not too stiffly, looks nice and centers the body's weight between the feet. This allows players to respond more quickly to attacks. Keeping the body's weight distributed between both feet during the *ginga* while simultaneously maintaining a relaxed torso provides the neutral stance that is necessary to respond to the often unpredictable attacks in *Capoeira Angola*.

Striking this balance was difficult for me, and Mestre Valmir often got frustrated with my body, which is habituated to stand straight with everything in alignment from my long-ago dance training. He would frequently take me by the shoulders and shake me until things fell out of alignment. As he shook me one day, he shouted *"mais sentimento moça"* (more feeling girl!). I recognized that conveying sentiment was somehow related to my rigid posture, a trace of the *habitus* that had been instilled in me through years of dance training and my middle-class upbringing, but I did not know how to "fix" it.[5] Assunção addresses the interrelation of class and physical comportment directly:

> This raises the issue of to what extent capoeira, or specific substyles, are still part of a specifically black or lower class "habitus," and to what extent it can be transposed into other ethnic, class, and gender contexts. In other words, can white middle class females move like black lower class males? (Assunção 2005: 207)

Eventually, Mestre Valmir more or less gave up breaking my posture, and it became a running joke. What I failed to see at the time was that proper form in capoeira includes both executing movements with correct technique *and* embodying the playful, deceitful attitude that was the default posture for the original *capoeiristas* who had to live by their wits.

In capoeira, there is always more than one way to respond to an opponent's movements. When choosing between equally effective options, *capoeiristas* should choose the more elegant, the more unique movements. When escaping an attack, a player should exit elegantly and with subtlety, and then give a counterattack quickly and suavely. Relying too much on *rabo de arraia* and *negativa* (the most basic adjacency pair that novices learn) is like having just rice and beans for every meal: it may be filling, but it gets boring quickly. Learning more movements and thinking of creative ways to apply what we know makes things more interesting and enjoyable. The more talented *capoeiristas* always maintain this dual sense of efficacy and style. Take for example, the words of this American *capoeirista* living and teaching in Oakland, California:

> If I were to stand there waiting for my partner to do something so I could then pounce, it would be considered bad form and ugly—in capoeira you should always be moving and striving for "*o jogo bonito*" or "the beautiful game." (Essien 2008: 17)

In this case, a strategic maneuver like waiting to pounce may be effective but is nonetheless improper form because of its inelegance. In his book, this teacher then goes on to talk about what happens when one player lies in wait for the other so he or she can pounce. This strategy limits the game and creates a situation in which aggression is likely to arise (Essien 2008: 17).

## Distinguishing Between Aggression and Efficacy

Prior to my first training session with the FICA Austin group as an undergraduate, my academic mentor assured me that most of the violence in capoeira was symbolic and that people feigned their kicks rather than actually making contact. Looking back, I wonder if he really believed that or if he knew it was the only way to get me to go. Initially, I found his advice to be accurate. I did not feel as though the group's style was particularly aggressive until Mestre Jurandir came to give us a workshop in 2003.

At this workshop, the president of the University of Texas capoeira club remarked upon the aggressiveness of these movements and asked why we were learning them. Mestre Jurandir replied by saying that the entire world is capoeira and not everyone is going to be friendly; therefore, we should have a set of offensive moves too. He was not encouraging us to be aggressive all the time, but to calibrate our game in response to the attitude of our opponent. Until this moment, everyone I had encountered within capoeira had highlighted the cooperative, ludic aspects of the martial art, and I then began to wonder when I might see this latent aggression emerge. As I gained exposure to more schools of capoeira, I began to feel that FICA had a more aggressive style than did other groups; however, in time, I learned to distinguish between aggression and efficacy.

As mentioned previously, lineage greatly affects the type of games played at particular academies. For example, games at Mestre Joao Pequeno's academy tend to be collaborative in nature. Players work together to create a beautiful and intricate game that, while still strategic, highlights cooperative interaction. The FICA style, on the other hand, involves more intent to show technical and creative superiority. This style, which descends from Mestre João Grande through Mestre Moraes, is distinctive. Play involves setting traps for one's opponent. It also involves a large number of kicks to the chest and perhaps more time spent upright than other *Capoeira Angola* groups. They frequently transform the *rabo de arraia* into a *martelo,* a hammer kick that is brought around by the hip and snaps out from the knee. *Rasteiras,* disequilibrating leg sweeps, figure prominently in this type of play. I initially interpreted these moves, particularly the kicks and *rasteiras,* as being aggressive.

When we were in the dressing room after class one day, I told Bridget that I was having trouble understanding the etiquette of the game and what moves were considered off-limits.

"Cheap shots are generally looked down upon."
"That's my problem. I don't know what's considered a cheap shot."
"Don't worry, in time you'll figure these things out."
"Sure, but people generally don't tell you when you're breaking form."

I was at a loss for understanding how I could sort through the etiquette of capoeira if there was no direct instruction, even though in reality I was learning etiquette through my everyday interactions in class. Bridget illustrated her point with an example, saying that giving a lot of *chapas* (straight kicks) is considered cheap.

Her justification for this position was both aesthetic and technical in nature. For one thing, the *chapa* is an inelegant attack and is not very creative. Furthermore, a straight kick interrupts the flow of the game, which is why circular movements are generally preferred. Mestre Valmir said that it is easy to lose composure and do a *chuta* (the flick-kick similar to shooting a soccer ball) in the *roda,* but practicing the more complex movements beautifully in class, trying them again and again until they work, makes it easier to do them in the *roda.*

I also worried that knocking my opponent off of his or her feet was rude. *Capoeira Angola* may be more dancelike than *Capoeira Regional,* but its martial utility has not been lost. Players at FICA, local and foreign alike, delighted in knocking one another off balance. During class one day, "Velho" (a middle-aged man so nicknamed because he always told me to go easy on him because he was "old" even though he was far more talented than I was) told me he would coach me as we played. He went into a handstand and told me I should slide my feet under his as he descended back to the ground. This would, presumably, cause him to fall on his face. I looked at this sweet man with horror and said "But wouldn't that be impolite?" He gave me a very funny look, paused, and conceded that it would be impolite to do it to him, because he is so old, but in general this is not considered rude. When I told Bridget that I did not like *rasteiras* because they seemed mean-spirited, she laughed at me and said, "they're fun." I asked Bridget to tell me if I accidentally did something rude. Her response was "well, it's capoeira," telling me that anything goes in the service of trickery and deceit. It is all part of the game.

Despite her self-assuredness, Bridget too sometimes found it hard to identify the line Mestre Valmir was trying to draw for us between *objetividade* (having an objective/goal) and *agressividade* (aggressiveness). The barrier between intent and just plain rudeness was often paper-thin. Mestre Valmir demonstrated a combination in which one person gives a *rabo de arraia* while the other enters with a sharp kick to the stomach or ribs. The first player responds to this by terminating their *rabo de arraia* early and countering with a backward headbutt. Mestre Valmir asked if anyone in the class thought this movement was violent. Several people did, but Valmir maintained that this was not aggression but simply a response to the opponent's opening movement.

Toward the end of my time in Bahia, I gave up trying to glean the difference between *objetividade* and *agressividade* from Mestre Valmir's sometimes-opaque speech. We were working on our *rasteiras.* As he came by to monitor our progress, I threw up my hands and said I still did not understand this difference. He had a solution for that. "Do a *rabo de arraia,*" he instructed. I did and quickly found myself crashing to the ground, struggling to catch my breath. "That was *objetividade.*" "Oh really?" I thought, "it felt like aggression to me." His demonstration did not help me understand, it only gave me a sore backside. After discussing it with him some more and getting a firsthand demonstration of *agressividade* for comparison, I came to understand that the difference is not in the movement itself but in the execution of it.

*Objetividade* requires *jeito,* or proper technique. As Valmir says, if you are going to do something it should be *bom feito* (done well). *Agressividade,* on the other hand, is a question of attitude; within the academy, students were expected to perform movements with a smile to show their partner that they harbor no ill will. To try and teach me about *objetividade,* Valmir launched a kick at my face but stopped it mere inches from my nose. The movement was accurately aimed and executed with both proper form and a friendly expression. The kick was also terminated before causing injury. Had he been aiming for a softer spot on my body, he could have made contact without injuring me, so it still would have been considered *objetividade* rather than *agressividade.* By way of contrast, *agressividade* is sloppy or brutish and often betrays a negative emotional state like frustration rather than playfulness. When another foreigner tried to take me down with a brutish and aggressive *rasteira,* using far more force than should have been required if it were well-timed and properly executed, my tennis shoe squeaked loudly, poetically underscoring its inelegance.

Sometimes overt aggression in *rodas* at FICA was curtailed by the presiding *capoeirista.* During a game between an Italian man and a man from Martinique, things became quite heated. It did not seem unfriendly, just intense. The man from Martinique typically played in this manner, quite possibly because of his prior training in *ladja,* a Martinican martial form. Aloan, who was in charge of the *roda,* started singing "*Idea,*" a song that instructs players to play a pretty game, one that the spectators would like to learn. This should have calmed the guys down, but they did not seem to respond to it in any way. Aloan started another song, but instead of singing the normal lyrics, he substituted them with impromptu comments like "you'd better stop playing like this or I'm going to end your game."

## Breaches of Form

It is the responsibility of the *capoeirista* playing the *gunga* to monitor games and censure breaches of etiquette or extreme violations of formal expectations. Many breaches are overlooked, but some demand curtailment. For example, during *one roda,* a handicapped Brazilian man was playing with Jorge, an experienced *treinel* in the group, and grabbed his ankle. This was clearly not permissible, and Aloan immediately called them back to the foot of the *berimbau* to scold him. Even for someone like this man with severely limited physical capabilities, there were some clearly demarcated boundaries that could not be breached.

In other cases, there is no need for *mestres* to correct breaches of form because these novelties are ineffective and quickly censured when the innovator is "caught" by an opponent, kicked or knocked to the floor. Amity said she often sees people try to create their own movements, get kicked, and then wonder why that happened. She exhibited no sympathy for them because they broke form. Oftentimes, movements done with improper form are inherently ineffective, and a knowledge-able opponent will simply reject them, refusing to react because there is no threat. So while capoeira encourages innovation in the assemblage of movements, in many ways it remains very technical.

Sometimes errors in form are pointed out to the player and to the spectators by taking advantage of an opening or weakness created by the breach. For example, in one variation of the *chamada,* the players touch their right palms together in the air while moving together. The left hand should be positioned in such a way that is it available to deflect kicks from the abdomen. At a GCAP *roda,* a French woman failed to block her midsection, and her Brazilian opponent delivered a sharp flick-kick to her stomach, pointing out her mistake. The kick itself was not the most elegant, but it was effective in terms of pointing out her error.

Metacommunicative gestures like these are the primary means by which improper form is censured. A French pilgrim played with a young Brazilian man who had been part of the group for several years. It was an aesthetically unpleas-ing game, and the pilgrim was clearly outmatched. In her frustration, she began grabbing at the man as if she wanted to grapple. Aloan called the pair back to the *berimbau,* shook his head disapprovingly, and pantomimed flicking dirt off his shoulders. He was showing her and the rest of us that excessive use of the hands is not only considered impolite because it soiled her partner's clothes, but that she was breaking form, and this would not be tolerated.

Watching Mestre Valmir's facial expressions as he watched the action in the *roda* was incredibly useful for learning how to evaluate games. He commonly made eye contact with other people in the *roda* when he wanted to underscore something about the present game. Again, it bears noting that those closer to Valmir were more often the recipients of these informative gazes. When players got tired and sloppy, Valmir would furrow his brow and act confused as if he could not possibly figure out why the person in question was acting that way. During one of my games, tired and flustered, I blocked an oncoming kick with my hands instead of dodging it in an appropriate and aesthetically pleasing way. Valmir turned to his younger son and made a slapping motion with his hands, pointing out that I had reacted incorrectly by using my hands.

Breaches of form can be divided into several categories. First, there are the mistakes that novices make because of their lack of knowledge. These mistakes are generally well tolerated if the group recognizes that the player is a beginner. A second type of breach is playing sloppily, which happens frequently when a *capoeirista* has a sufficient amount of knowledge but becomes frustrated, careless, or tired. These mistakes are often commented upon, verbally or through metacom-municative gestures, exploited physically with a takedown, or explicitly corrected. Metacommunicative gestures in this context might be eye rolling, head shaking, or smirking. The third type of breach is violating the aesthetics of capoeira, which is far more difficult to articulate, but experienced players are attuned to what "looks" or "feels" right and wrong in the *roda*. Breaches of this nature are rarely addressed directly but may be a subject of discussion after the *roda* and certainly contribute to a player's reputation within the immediate scene and the social field at large.

No movement, as Mestre Valmir often says, is "100% *seguro*" (safe). Cobbling their games together with an eye toward style as well as functionality means that *capoeiristas* are almost always vulnerable. Though it might be considered a breach of good manners, there is really nothing to stop an adversary from charging at him or her with a malevolent kick when that person is precariously balanced upside down. When a player launches her body forward into a headstand, she can be fairly confident that her opponent will not swipe her arms out from underneath her because that would violate both capoeira etiquette and form. Grabbing a player's arms is discouraged. The unspoken pledge to stay within the confines of the form gives players confidence that they will not be abused in the *roda,* but as *capoeiristas* are often reminded, not everyone is a friend, and players need to be prepared for the latent violence of capoeira to come to the surface.

There are occasions when it is okay to ignore or blatantly violate the dictates of form. Veneration of aging *mestres* clearly trumps form. Though younger *capoeiristas* are eager to have the privilege of playing with older *mestres,* they are normally deferential, sparing the *mestre* the loss of face associated with being dominated in the *roda* (D'Aquino 1983). An older *mestre* played at Mestre Joao Pequeno's *roda* frequently during 2008. He still shone with *malandragem* (cunning) and *malícia,* but the decades had not been kind to his dexterity. Still, he played with young hotshots who could have taken him down easily. The old *mestre* and a young Brazilian began to awkwardly walk back and forth in the *chamada.* The old *mestre* was clearly not using correct technique, but the younger man neither corrected him nor took advantage of his vulnerability as he had earlier with a young woman who had not yet achieved fluency in the form.

Still other breaches of form are permissible if they are made in the spirit of *malícia.* Lewis (1992) has drawn a connection between *malícia* and Scott's concept of "weapons of the weak" in so far that *malícia* can be used to get the best out of a situation without having to engage in a direct confrontation with someone who is structurally more advantaged. As my friend Tyrell was trying to impress upon me during our conversation at the café, some actions generally fall outside the scope of capoeira but may be considered appropriate depending upon the situation. I repeatedly heard a story about an old *capoeirista* who used to carry pepper in his pocket to throw into his adversary's eyes if he began to lose ground. A cheap shot for sure, but this kind of Machiavellian behavior is also part of the *capoeirista* mentality. Because early *capoeiristas* were often living at the margins of legality and had the reputation for being ne'er-do-wells, they had to be crafty in order to survive. While it is certainly true that some practitioners of capoeira still live in a precarious hand-to-mouth state, the majority of individuals training at the academy where I studied led relatively stable lives, and some students were well-respected professionals. Nonetheless, the trickster figure continues to reign supreme in capoeira lore and is embodied in performances through this strategic violation of form.

*Malícia* is one of the hallmarks of capoeira. The literal translation of this word is malice, but it is a poor approximation of what the word actually connotes. A better gloss is deceitful trickery. For example, during one *roda,* my opponent's jaw suddenly dropped, his eyes widened, and he leaned forward and pointed to something just over my shoulder. By the time I realized there was nothing to see, his forked fingers had already stopped mere inches from my eyes. I had become one of the three stooges.

The slave culture in which capoeira was born necessitated living by one's wits. In the capoeira game, what often seems like a dirty trick is tempered by playfulness. This is the essence of *malícia.* Players try to get into their adversary's head, and it becomes an emotional game as much as a physical contest. To the inexperienced, it feels like being the butt of a joke, and many then let frustration get the better of them. Among the initiated, *malíciaa* must be met with good humor.

Most capoeira pilgrims that passed through the doors of FICA Bahia were able to maintain their good humor in the face of *malícia.* However, in the few cases where this mechanism broke down, metacommunicative gestures were employed to reinforce the playfulness of capoeira. In one *roda,* two female pilgrims, one Spanish and one French, were completely bested by Mestre Valmir, but they welcomed the abuse and kept smiling. Playing capoeira with Mestre Valmir was a bit like walking on ice; every time we played, I fully expected to fall, but was still surprised when I found myself lying on my backside, staring at the ceiling.

Until someone completely masters capoeira, which seems unlikely at best, there will always be someone to outdo him or her in the *roda,* and showing frustration only intensifies his or her domination. On one occasion the *roda* was halted because a visitor from Germany lost her good humor. She had been playing with Mestre Valmir's younger son, and the game became a bit too intense for her. Her face became red, and her eyes filled with tears. Mestre Valmir called the pair to the foot of the *berimbau* and told her to relax. When he felt confident that she could continue, he slowed the pace and his son started to smile more and wink at her. These simple metacommunicative gestures signified to her that this was indeed play and helped her remain in control of her emotions.

Because capoeira teeters on the edge between fight and play, these metacommunicative gestures are very important and are even incorporated into teaching sessions. Teachers at FICA Bahia consistently emphasized the importance of maintaining a friendly or happy facial expression while playing capoeira. During class one evening, students practiced kicks in pairs. Aloan stopped them after a few minutes of practice and told them that if they executed the movement with a sour look on their face it would appear aggressive, but if done with a smile, then their kicks would seem playful. Students continued practicing with a smile on their faces, and the entire mood of the room lifted. During the wrap-up discussion, Aloan fell back on a common theme in capoeira, the parallel between the small *roda,* which refers to the capoeira game itself, and the big *roda,* which refers to life. He said that in both capoeira and in life, having a pleasant expression makes people appear more open and inviting.

Negotiating between the poles of tradition and innovation and between beauty and efficacy requires finesse and nuanced understanding of the rules of the game. Within capoeira, explicit instruction is a necessary but insufficient tool in learning how to walk this tightrope. Mastery comes about by gradually assuming the *habitus,* or embodied dispositions, of a *capoeirista.* Often this is facilitated by entering into a more intimate teacher–student relationship than is normally afforded by the mass classes dominated by economies of scale. More time with the *mestre,* or simply getting more attention from him during class, puts the student in a better position to learn the aesthetic guidelines and contextually dependent etiquette that characterizes appropriate play. Whether or not one will be able to do this, however, depends on how successfully a pilgrim marshalls his or her available cultural capital.

## How Most People Learn (Mass Classes)

When I began my fieldwork in Brazil, I assumed that I would learn the most about the aesthetic values of *capoeiristas* during their performances at *rodas.* A few months into my study, however, I began reflecting on how my evaluation of performances had transformed as a result of the small changes happening to my body during daily practice sessions. What occurred to me during this moment of reflexivity was the importance of training for the cultivation of an aesthetic sensibility in all embodied disciplines. In many Japanese forms:

> It is believed that regular practice of prescribed dance poses and movements reinforces artistic skills in the habitual body, and as movements become embodied, an experience of freedom and realization may occur. From a highly disciplined and structured pedagogical foundation it is thought that the skills of an artist can flow "naturally" or effortlessly from the well-trained body. (Hahn 2007: 43)

Even though performance in capoeira is very different from *Nihon Buyo* because of the emphasis on improvisation in the former and precise execution of choreography in the latter, both require a well-trained body in order to achieve fluency in performance. Training is the time during which the body is prepared, and it is the central site of a performer's education. Thus, daily class sessions became my primary focus of inquiry. My study of form shifted from product to process, from the performance in its ritual context to the development of a *capoeirista*'s sensibilities.

Capoeira instruction has changed dramatically over the years. In a previous era, interested students would approach an older *capoeirista* and learn directly from them or just hang out in the vicinity of *capoeiristas* and try to study their moves (see Lewis 1992). Prior to the 1930s, "organized or group lessons were unheard of and a capoeirista had to believe that an individual was trustworthy as well as worthy before he would take him on" (D'Aquino 1983: 86). However, *capoeiristas'* need to clean up their image in the first half of the twentieth century moved instruction into the safe confines of academies. In addition to this, the recent growth in demand for capoeira instruction has turned some of these small academies into virtual capoeira factories. This transition has had a profound effect on capoeira (see Downey 2005: 39–40). As Nestor Capoeira writes:

> In the traditional Capoeira Angola teaching method (which is not used by capoeira Angola teachers and mestres any more), the learning was loose, few, intuitive, organic, and this resulted in players with very different styles although they were all Capoeira Angola. Today all capoeira pupils of a certain Capoeira Angola academy play in a similar way. (Capoeira 2006: 64)

New methods have standardized many players' style, which is antithetical to the ethos of *Capoeira Angola.*

Standardization threatens the creativity and individuality that has always been a hallmark of *Capoeira Angola.* Reflecting on his own intensive participant-observation fieldwork among Mestre Moraes's group GCAP, Downey says that his teachers were highly critical of robot capoeira or mimicking teachers' movements too closely. Flawless copying was not seen as a mark of skill, rather "too-faithful repetition was considered dreadfully boring, counterproductive for learning, and anathema to a cunning game" (Downey 2005: 28). Mass classes that encourage mimicking are almost unavoidable with the present level of demand for instruction, but these classes are not necessarily effective ways of transmitting the aesthetic principles of *Capoeira Angola.*

One danger of practicing a movement too mechanically is that students stop thinking about the movements, their adversary's potential reactions, and their options for counterattacking. Despite the fact that students in most large classes learn by mimicking their instructors, failure to develop an individualized style is considered detrimental for a *capoeirista.* Each player's game is informed by his or her own consciousness, and a *capoeirista* should not try to match what his or her opponent is doing but follow his or her own guide. Likewise, *capoeiristas* must learn which movements work best for their own bodies. This awareness is particularly important in a martial art like capoeira where opponents are selected at random and not by weight class or sex.

In many ways, trainings sessions are more about habituating students to a certain aesthetic sensibility than fixing specific movements in their repertoires. During class, students' bodies are disciplined into a new comportment, a new way of moving that in time becomes second nature. Students are chided for doing movements "too mechanically." Not only does this violate the expectation that *capoeiristas* should have an idiosyncratic style, but moving this way actually makes it more difficult to flow between movements. While the body should be "broken" in its alignment, flow between movements should never be choppy. Even if there were five different movements included in a series, they should flow together like one single movement.

Classes at FICA Bahia invariably started with *ginga,* done in a free form and individualized manner. Developing an individualized, yet aesthetically interesting and unpredictable *ginga* is key to being a better *capoeirista*. In classes, students are constantly told to "*salta*" their *ginga,* meaning that they need to loosen their bodies and be freer in this movement. By these standards, a good *ginga* is off-centered. The torso sways from side to side with each step. And while it is important to maintain muscular control over the abdominals in this movement, the torso is never aligned vertically nor pulled inward like that of a ballet dancer. The shoulders remain relaxed and slightly slumped forward, allowing the arms to swing freely. The *capoeirista* normally remains slightly tilted forward from the hips, though this is variable, and rather than keeping the legs extended and locked, there should be enough tension in the quadriceps to allow the *capoeirista* to launch his or her body in any direction at a moment's notice. The *ginga* can be as strategic as it is functional; a relaxed *ginga* can misdirect an opponent or lull him or her into a false sense of security.

I often noted that the students in the back of the class, myself included, were struggling to copy the form of our teacher's movements precisely whereas the students in the front, those with enough confidence to claim such a prominent position, were creating their own riffs on the basic movement that had been demonstrated. Giving students the freedom to invent their own style of *ginga* makes FICA's variant of capoeira look more like a dance than what is seen at some academies that follow a more rigid pedagogy. It also leads to more improvisation during the *roda* because students are not overly reliant on the same sequences that are taught in class. Mestre Valmir is consciously aware of this and tells his students that his classes permit them lots of freedom to think and move in the way they think best. As Mestre Pastinha reportedly once said, "*cada um é cada um*" (each one is each one), and FICA's pedagogy supports this mantra.

Sometimes students were given complete freedom with their movements in order to develop creativity and an individual style. In other cases, students were heavily restricted in their choice of movements. For example, the instructor might choose three or four movements and tell students these were the only permissible options. Though it might seem counterintuitive, this strategy also developed creativity in students. This exercise makes students think about how they can apply standard moves in creative ways to achieve their objectives. The mental dimension of capoeira is very important for adepts, and skilled *capoeiristas* constantly reflect upon their own games and the games of others, pondering the different ways they could react in a certain situation. Students were encouraged to develop reflexivity and think about what they could have done better in their games.

Every aspect of training at FICA Bahia was explicitly oriented toward performance in an actual *roda,* and movement for movement's sake was criticized. Most movements, particularly the more complicated sequences, were explained with reference to how they would articulate with an opponent's moves. When students learned a new movement, Mestre Valmir expected them to think of one or two instances in which the move could be applied in their games. The more advanced students in the group tended to modify the movements they were taught, experimenting with the different ways in which they could be applied. Valmir stressed the maturity necessary for students to advance to this stage.

Mestre Valmir created a comfortable environment during class, and students felt safe experimenting with new ways of movement. After letting students try out a new movement for a while, he would turn down the music and give general corrections to the group. Often Mestre Valmir would model a new sequence for students and let them try it on their own. After a few minutes, he would ask them if they knew what they were doing, meaning had they completed the visualization necessary to understand how this sequence would articulate with an opponent in an actual game situation. The attack move that students had just practiced can be thought of as a "question," and Valmir was asking them to provide hypothetical "answers" or solutions to the problem. This pedagogical technique is similar to what educators call "problem-based learning," and I have argued elsewhere (Griffith 2014) that this constitutes a signature pedagogy within capoeira, facilitating the transfer of training sequences into actual game scenarios.

Most of the instruction was conducted from the front of the room, and students were expected to practice the movement on their own while the teacher circulated and made some individual and group corrections. These corrections were normally verbal, but on occasion, the teachers would actually manipulate a student's body to make sure he or she completed it correctly. For example, the teacher might position the student's body so that it becomes impossible, or nearly so, for him or her to turn in the wrong direction when completing a *rabo de arraia* or other rotational strike. Downey (2008) refers to this as scaffolding imitation, enhancing the training sequence with additional structures that make it easier for the novice to imitate the *mestre's* movement.

Most classes at FICA Bahia ended with at least a few minutes of free improvisation time. Students paired off and played together. Mestre Valmir always reminded students to be conscientious in their movements. He did not expect students to perform all of the movements they had learned in class but to find space within their game to execute a few well-chosen movements with intent and proper form. Mestre Valmir said it is better to do one movement with intent than to do ten or eleven movements without it. Preference was clearly given to the development of an aesthetically pleasing yet effective game over a high intensity one that used interesting, but poorly executed, movements.

Mestre Valmir taught each sequence using a low level of support. He would either explain a sequence verbally or give a rough demonstration of it, generally expecting students to figure out the directionality and the exact body placement of the sequence for themselves. If students failed to visualize the entire sequence he was trying to teach, Mestre Valmir would work with them and enact the opponent's movements as a way of scaffolding (see Downey 2008). In other situations, the sequences taught in class were intentionally left unfinished, and students were asked to supply an appropriate ending. After showing the beginning movements, the instructor would ask students what attacks could be initiated from that position. Students would supply answers, and the teacher would say why that was or was not a wise choice. Often, the teacher would choose a student to use as a demonstration partner to dramatize the different options for the rest of the class. Mestre Valmir's flexibility as a teacher allowed him to recognize a weakness in his students' games and create inventive training exercises on the spot to address that issue. For example, when he thought we were relying too much on sight in reacting to our opponents, he turned off the lights and scattered candles around the room so all we could see were vague outlines of our partner's body. This taught students to use senses other than sight to gauge where their opponent's body was in relation to their own.

## How the Most Legitimate Pilgrims Learn

In spite of the creative pedagogies the teachers at FICA Bahia used, a student could learn these lessons faster and more thoroughly if he or she had special access to the teacher outside of regular class times. As I described in the previous section, this individual attention is not possible in very large classes, especially if pilgrims are merely paying for a session or two rather than developing an ongoing relationship with one particular teacher and their fellow students in that academy. Lave and Wenger use the phrase "legitimate peripheral participation" (LPP) as a way of discussing socially embedded learning that takes place as novices learn from masters and move from peripheral to more central roles within a given field. They coined this phrase because they felt that the term apprenticeship had become overused and near meaningless by the late 1980s (Lave and Wenger 1991: 29). Their perspective refutes traditional understandings of learners as passive receivers of knowledge and proposes a "comprehensive understanding involving the whole person" who has agency and who both constitutes and is constituted by her social world (Lave and Wenger 1991: 33).

Studies of apprenticeship have typically assumed that it leads novices to reproduce the behaviors and skills of their masters, but Lave and Wenger's theory of
legitimate peripheral participation challenges this assumption (1991: 65). They
suggest that this kind of relationship provides the potential for newcomers to
create their own idiosyncratic interpretations of the general skill set required
of masters. This is central to understanding how *capoeiristas* not only develop a
performance style that bears a strong resemblance to that of others' within their
lineage, especially their *mestre,* but also develop idiosyncratic and identifiable traits
of their own. Previous authors have generally treated the apprentice's quest as an
individual one; apprentices learn the skills they need to function as a master of a
craft. Lave and Wenger, on the other hand, see that "a deeper sense of the value
of participation to the community and the learner lies in *becoming* part of the
community" (1991: 111). The entire community, rather than one teacher and one
student, are part of the legitimate peripheral participation process. The novice's
centripetal movement (Lave and Wenger 1991: 100) necessitates a greater commitment to the community, but it is rewarded with a greater sense of belonging.

Masters remain in the most powerful roles independent of what their social
status may be outside of the field in question. Although in theory, anyone can
develop the *habitus* needed to excel in a performance genre like dance (see
Thornton 1996) or martial arts, in actual practice, not everyone has the same
likelihood of becoming a capoeira *mestre.* A doctor or a dockworker could be
equally suited to becoming a capoeira master if he or she meets its requirements.
Yet this provides a good example of the circularity of cultural capital. Those with
the most capital ascend to the top of the hierarchy and are then in a privileged
position where they can shape the field, theoretically guaranteeing their continued
success in the field. Capoeira *mestres* and *contramestres* have reached their present
station by acquiring the right credentials and now find themselves in the position
to shape the field as they police the boundaries of legitimacy for the next generation of *capoeiristas.*

The *mestres'* powerful position within the capoeira social field may seem too
entrenched to change, but Lave and Wenger's model of legitimate peripheral participation provides for this. The dialectic between apprentices and the social field
in which they learn allows them to shape one another and rewrite their respective
trajectories (Hanks 1991: 16). Lave and Wenger move theories of learning outside
the confines of individual minds and situate learning as an emergent process that
results from participation within complex social structures (Hanks 1991: 15).
Such a view distributes the responsibilities and results of learning across many
participants instead of localizing it within one individual (Hanks 1991: 15). In
some instances of apprenticeship, learned content is of less importance than the
process of becoming, but "even in cases where a fixed doctrine is transmitted, the
ability of a community to reproduce itself through the training process derives not
from the doctrine, but from the maintenance of certain modes of coparticipation

in which it is embedded" (Hanks 1991: 16). In other words, it is the learning of form, not form itself, which gives continuity to an artistic genre. The picture that emerges from this theory is one of relationships and exchanges versus strict divisions and policed boundaries.

Understanding how legitimate peripheral participation facilitates a novice's integration into a community of practice necessitates an understanding of reproduction within that field, how roles are assumed over time, and how actors relate to one another (Lave and Wenger 1991: 56). A social field is composed of many more actors than just the master and student. For example, *rodas* provide informal learning opportunities for students where they learn by peripheral participation as players, musicians, singers, *and* by observing their fellow students. In a *roda,* the *mestre* does serve as a model for novices, but so do their peers. Sometimes learning from one's peers is just as important as learning from the *mestre.*

Classes provide many opportunities for peer-to-peer learning. In classes at FICA Bahia, certain people were consistently selected to help the teacher demonstrate new movements to the rest of the class. The other students in the class modeled their movements after these examples but did not copy them with perfect fidelity. Indeed it would have been difficult to do so for, as we were frequently reminded, everybody and every body is unique. The teacher's selection of a demonstration partner was never random. The students providing demonstrations had to understand the movements, have enough skill to execute the movements, and be able to present a clear model with proper technique for other students to follow. Daisuke, Bridget, Tyrell, and a few others were consistently used as demonstration partners. They were also called upon to lead class when other teachers were unavailable. This was a visible sign of their legitimacy; not only had they been making centripetal progress from the periphery to the center of the social field, at least within the context of our academy, but they were also serving as models to junior students.

Intimate study with a master not only facilitates learning, but also legitimizes the apprentice. Lave and Wenger argue "the form that the legitimacy of participation takes is a defining characteristic of ways of belonging, and is therefore not only a crucial condition for learning, but a constitutive element of its content" (1991: 35). The very fact that someone is included in a master–apprentice relationship verifies his or her legitimacy. This is a much different situation than someone who lurks at the margins of a community without authorization by an insider/master. A martial artist in another discipline explained this legitimacy to me as the difference between merely taking class and actually *being* someone's student. At the academy where I trained, virtually anyone could take classes if he or she could afford the fees; however, not everyone developed the same kind of relationship with the *mestre* and other teachers. Daisuke, Bridget, and Tyrell had, without a doubt, become Mestre Valmir's students.

Facilitating apprentices' access to resources for learning is actually more important than direct instruction (Lave and Wenger 1991: 92). Masters will often control the flow of information that novices receive (Lave and Wenger 1991: 92), making sure that they are pushed into the proximal zone of development (Vygotsky 1978). The novice should neither be overwhelmed by the amount and complexity of the tasks they are being asked to complete nor should they be allowed to stagnate from lack of challenge. Capoeira *mestres* meet students at their level, creating learning opportunities that are appropriate for that student's current ability.

This customization of challenge was often evident in the *roda*. Mestre Valmir always taught his students something about capoeira through their interactions in the *roda*. A student who habitually left herself open to being taken down with a leg sweep would be given repeated *rasteiras* until she learned to protect herself better. Other students might be taught that they were exposing their torso too much during handstands. A quick headbutt to the stomach was an effective form of feedback. Whereas I initially felt like I was being picked on when this happened, my fellow students told me that I should look forward to these moments. I was being selected for a learning opportunity that not everyone would receive. And while the teachers did make an effort to spread this honor around, it was not possible for them to play with all students during every *roda*. Those who were able to play with the teachers most often learned the most from their participation in the *roda*. Delamont and Stephens explain that "playing the teacher tests the physical and mental agility of the students, and that test is itself a reward for their commitment" (2013: 56). The teacher does not play with each student, and this attention therefore constitutes a special learning opportunity not available to everyone.

## Conclusion

As I hope to have made clear in this chapter, the aesthetic values of capoeira are not taught directly. Similarly, within *Nihon Buyo,* Hahn writes, "[students] gain an understanding of such a sensibility through practice and embodiment of the tradition—through observing dance in the studio and at performances, and through discussions during lessons" (2007: 51). The case is the same for capoeira. Oblique ways of learning about aesthetic values add up over time to give performers an embodied sense of what is right and wrong in a given form without having to refer to a set of static rules.

The *capoeiristas* I interviewed overwhelmingly agreed that adherence to proper form is an important part of their practice, yet very few were able to articulate what this means. Some thought it meant verbatim copying of the capoeira ancestors while others felt anything motivated by the *capoerista*'s worldview could be considered capoeira. The one point on which they agreed was the importance of tradition, yet individual innovation is also highly prized.

Capoeira emphasizes both adherence to tradition and innovation. While this may seem to be a contradiction, these two opposing tendencies are reconciled in performance. *Capoeiristas* must adhere to tradition closely enough to be credible performers of the genre, yet must also display enough individuality to demonstrate their understanding of capoeira versus mere mimicking. This is achieved by adhering to an overriding aesthetic that is traditional while also developing an idiosyncratic style that is vetted through both technical and social repercussions.

*Capoeiristas* may acquire this aesthetic sensibility through legitimate peripheral participation or apprenticeship within a community of practice, though not all pilgrims achieve this status. Students who remain on the margins of mass classes will largely learn to mimic their teachers and perform robot capoeira. Those in a legitimate peripheral participation role, on the other hand, learn the underlying stylistic principles of capoeira. This allows them to simultaneously innovate and honor tradition.

Through formal learning opportunities, like classes, and informal opportunities like attending and participating in *rodas,* successful *capoeiristas* come to understand what is expected of them in terms of form. This is an embodied sensibility that they may or may not be able to put into words. In time, they understand that key elements of capoeira form, like balancing correct execution with beauty, will allow them to achieve their objectives. Furthermore, they learn to distinguish between being aggressive or brutish and achieving a conscious objective within the game. In the end, a mature player who has begun moving toward the center of this community of practice begins to play with the form itself, breaching norms to which novices are held in order to underscore dramatic points of the game. Acceptance of these innovations is the ultimate test of legitimacy.

## Notes

1. *Capoeira Regional* is often criticized by *Angoleiros* as a bastardization because it incorporated moves from Asian fighting styles like jujitsu and from *batuque,* an African combat game that was supposedly common in Bahia through the early 1900s.
2. This sentiment also echoes the definition of authenticity offered by Peterson (1997) in his study of country music.
3. Significantly, the two respondents who did not think that proper form was important both fall outside of the norm in that they are not affiliated with a particular capoeira group. One regularly moves between playing *Capoeira Angola* and *Capoeira Regional.* The other is something of a "free agent" with no ties to a specific group or style. This suggests that within traditional master–apprentice relationships, adhering to proper form is seen as being important, but those individuals who do not choose to affiliate with a particular group are either unaware of this convention or deliberately choose to ignore it.
4. An informant who trained *Capoeira Regional* with the Filhos de Bimba academy in Pelourinho told me that *capoeiristas* in their academy are not allowed to do *floreiros* (flourishes) until they have achieved the rank of graduate because they are so risky.

5. See Wacquant 2004 for an excellent exploration of how the body's *habitus* is transformed through martial training.

## Works Cited

Assunção, Matthias Röhrig. 2005. *Capoeira: The History of an Afro-Brazilian Martial Art, Sport in the Global Society*. London: Routledge.

Brough, Edward Luna. 2006. "Jogo de Mandinga (Game of Sorcery): A Preliminary Investigation of History, Tradition, and Bodily Practice in Capoeira Angola," MA thesis. Ohio State University.

Capoeira, Nestor. 2006. *A Street-Smart Song: Capoeira Philosophy and Inner Life*. Berkeley, CA: North Atlantic Books.

D'Aquino, Iria. 1983. "Capoeira: Strategies for Status, Power and Identity," PhD dissertation. University of Illinois.

Delamont, Sara, and Neil Stephens. 2013. "Each More Agile than the Other: Mental and Physical Enculturation in Capoeira Regional." In *Fighting Scholars: Habitus and Ethnographies of Martial Arts and Combat Sports*, edited by Raul Sanchez Garcia and Dale C Spencer, 49–62. London: Anthem Press.

Downey, Greg. 2005. *Learning Capoeira: Lessons in Cunning from an Afro-Brazilian Art*. Oxford: Oxford University Press.

Downey, Greg. 2008. "Scaffolding Imitation in Capoeira: Physical Education and Enculturation in an Afro-Brazilian Art." *American Anthropologist* 110 (2): 204–13.

Essien, Aniefre. 2008. *Capoeira Beyond Brazil: From a Slave Tradition to an International Way of Life*. Berkeley, CA: North Atlantic Books.

Ferreira, Juca. 1997. "Experiência de Cidadania." *A Tarde*.

Griffith, Lauren Miller. 2014. "Signature Pedagogies in the Afro-Brazilian Martial Art Capoeira: Why Problem Based Learning Produces Better Performers." *Theatre Annual* 67: 1–22.

Hahn, Tomie. 2007. *Sensational Knowledge: Embodying Culture through Japanese Dance*. Middletown, CT: Wesleyan University Press.

Hanks, William F. 1991. "Forward." In *Situated Learning: Legitimate Peripheral Participation*, edited by Jean Lave and Etienne Wenger, 13-24. New York: Cambridge University Press.

Lave, Jean, and Etienne Wenger. 1991. *Situated Learning: Legitimate Peripheral Participation*. New York: Cambridge University Press.

Lewis, J Lowell. 1992. *Ring of Liberation: Deceptive Discourse in Brazilian Capoeira*. Chicago: University of Chicago Press.

Peterson, Richard A. 1997. *Creating Country Music: Fabricating Authenticity*. Chicago: The University of Chicago Press.

Powe, Edward L. 2002. *Danced Martial Arts of the Americas, Black Martial Arts*. Vol. 3. Madison, WI: Aiki Publications.

Royce, Anya Peterson. 2004. *Anthropology of the Performing Arts: Artistry, Virtuosity, and Interpretation in a Cross-Cultural Perspective*. Walnut Creek, CA: AltaMira Press.

Thornton, Sarah. 1996. *Club Cultures: Music, Media and Subcultural Capital*. Middletown, CT: Wesleyan University Press.

Timbers, Caroline C. 2000. "Building an International Quilombo: Meaning, Marginality, and Community in Capoeira Angola and Its Practice in the United States," MA thesis. Georgetown University.

Vygotsky, LS. 1978. *Mind and Society: The Development of Higher Psychological Processes.* Cambridge, MA: Harvard University Press.

Wacquant, Loïc. 2004. *Body and Soul: Notebooks of an Apprentice Boxer.* Oxford: Oxford University Press.

# Chapter 8

# Will I Ever Be Good Enough?

At the beginning of my fieldwork, I attended a *roda* at the famous capoeira fort with my companions from Indiana. I played with a fairly cocky Asian American male named Kidlat. I thought I had performed fairly well, but it was clear that our styles were very different. After the *roda* ended, Kidlat, my friends, and a few other foreigners went out for drinks together. On the way, Kidlat made fun of a movement that I had used quite a bit. He scoffed when I told him that I had been playing for several years and asked us how many advanced players we had in our group back home. Camille took offense at his question. She was upset by the very notion that *capoeiristas* could be divided into skill level, arguing that capoeira is much more about spiritual sustenance than it is about skill. Even after we had left the bar, Camille continued to obsess over what this man had said. Camille had found capoeira during a very challenging period of her life, and it had helped her overcome these struggles, for her it was insulting to reduce the depth of her experiences to something as crass as skill.

## Introduction

In support of Camille's position that skill is unimportant in capoeira, one might remember that *Capoeira Angola* does not use a belt system to denote rank like *Capoeira Regional* or many Asian martial arts systems. At the same time, however, competition, either against oneself or against an adversary in the *roda* is a prevalent theme in the capoeira community. FICA in particular has a reputation for being very skilled, and this reputation attracts many foreigners to its weekly *rodas*. As I explain in this chapter, there is a noticeable difference in how locals and pilgrims feel about physical skill.

While the pilgrims are often single-mindedly focused on improving their own level of proficiency in a relatively short amount of time, the Brazilian teachers with whom I worked were more focused on the process of becoming a *capoeirista* rather than the final outcome. This led to a climate of tolerance for those who were not spectacularly skilled. However, proficiency in music was demanded by the *mestres*. Whereas physical skill was seen as an individual achievement that was bound to take time, knowing how to play the instruments and sing the songs was seen as a sign that one respected the ritual significance of capoeira.

## The (Un)Importance of Physical Skill

Despite lacking a gradation system, the skill level at FICA Bahia and throughout the FICA franchise is considered to be very high. Many groups, like those who descend from Mestre João Pequeno, rely upon basic moves like *rabo de arraia* and *negativa* as mainstays of their games. This does not necessarily mark them as less skilled; it is just a stylistic difference. FICA players tend to use many different kicks, leg-sweeping techniques, and movements that show off their strength such as descending from a handstand into a headstand. Jerome referred to the FICA group as "a hard family," meaning that throughout the franchise, the standard of excellence is quite high. I talked to one of Mestre Iuri's Brazilian friends about my first experience playing in a FICA *roda* and told him I was embarrassed, but he told me not to be because they play at such a high level, perhaps the best in the city. Nearly every week during my time in Bahia, the FICA *roda* hosted Brazilian players from throughout the city who had come to play with us, which is an indicator of its reputation.

Among the regular members of FICA, skill was appreciated, and novices nurtured. The situation at a nearby academy was similar where foreigners are introduced at the end of every class, and a point is made of clapping for each one regardless of their skill level. In that school, Brittni claims, "as long as you are training, it doesn't matter if you're not good." Respect was extended to all *capoeiristas* who participated in the group's activities. This does not necessarily mean, however, that skill is irrelevant to a pilgrim's experience in Brazil.

Personally, I was far more comfortable playing in *rodas* during my 2008 fieldwork than I had been on my previous visit. This was in large part because my own skill level had increased over the two-year period. So while skill may not be essential for acceptance into the Bahian capoeira community, having a certain level of competency made me far more comfortable and gave me more confidence to interact with other members of the community. Confidence is central to projecting the right kind of attitude necessary for acceptance. However, my skill level was still lower than many of the players, both local and foreign, at FICA.

Wondering how people at FICA felt about the skill level of their fellow students, I was keenly attuned to other students' facial expressions during class, especially during mock *rodas* and music class when I was able to do as much observation as participation. Mestre Cobra Mansa led music class one day in August. The class was composed mainly of foreigners. He went around the circle and instructed students to play a few iterations of a *berimbau* rhythm individually so he could hear them and make corrections. Two foreign students in particular struggled with this. Kidlat, who had gotten into the debate with Camille over the importance of skill, laughed, rolled his eyes, leaned in toward me, and whispered, "they're even worse than you." I do not think this was meant to be hurtful. After all, I am fully aware of my limitations on the *berimbau*. Nonetheless, it stung a bit and made me wonder if all of the students were similarly critical of their peers.

I found the frequency of this kind of judgmental behavior among some of the foreigners to be unsettling, especially because it contrasted so wildly with Mestre Cobra Mansa's position. He was encouraging to everyone and said, "even if you don't have patience for yourself, I have patience for you." During classes, Mestre Valmir reminded us that training was the time to try new movements, not only to perfect our skills, but to build our confidence so we would be comfortable trying our new skill set in the *roda*. The same was true for practicing new rhythms and songs in music class. He would occasionally laugh when students appeared excessively uptight and remind us that this was just training, not a test.

Both Mestre Valmir and Mestre Cobra Mansa were explicit about the development of capoeira skills as a progression over time. After class one evening, Mestre Cobra Mansa talked about the four stages of development in capoeira (see also Almeida 1986). He said that at first, novice *capoeiristas* are playing in darkness and cannot see the kicks that are coming. They are at the mercy of their opponent. In the next stage, *capoeiristas* enter the light and now have the ability to see the kicks, but do not yet have sufficient skill and experience to avoid them. They continue to get kicked around a lot. Then they enter the water phase, during which things flow together and the objective is simply to swim to the other side without drowning. Finally comes the crystal ball stage, in which one can predict the movements of his or her adversary. This stage is a result of personal experience.

After one class session during which I had really struggled, Mestre Valmir addressed us as we sat in a circle reflecting on the experience. He said that everyone was equal. We all have the same parts and organs, and "*graças a Deus*" (thanks to God) none of us are physically deficient. The primary difference among us is our minds. Mestre Valmir said we have to respect the *mestre* of our *mestre*. I thought this was going to be his segue into discussing the importance of lineage, but in reality, the *mestre* of our *mestre* is *tempo* (time).

History is never entirely behind us because it is inscribed on our bodies. The individual paths that people take through life are continually replayed in the present, thus "history, memory, and perception are central elements that contribute to the instabilities of lived experience" (Stoller 2009: 75). This is what Mestre Valmir was trying to teach us by stressing the different paths each individual body had taken, the difference this would make in our game, and that we were better off for this idiosyncrasy. He said that it takes a lifetime to build up the sensibility of a *capoeirista*.

Aloan said that when he first started playing capoeira, there were a lot of movements that he did not want to try. Then he saw other people who had started capoeira at more or less the same time as him who were developing faster than he was. Little by little, he started tackling these moves. His point was that it takes time and dedication for our skills to develop. He urged us to do any movement to the maximum of our ability because only then would it become habitual enough for us to use in the *roda*. To my utter joy, he pointed out that some people, like "Lorena," were finally succeeding with movements they had never been able to do before, and this growth is good.

Sometimes a beginner might think they are getting beat up in the *roda*, but a good teacher does these things to instruct, not to injure the new student. Despite my initial concerns after the first time we played together in the *roda*, in time I came to see that Mestre Valmir was very conscious of his students' stages of development. While the teachers push their students hard and underscore their shortcomings with physical commentary, they also play to each student's level. This was largely absent among the foreigners who, for the most part, played near maximum capacity regardless of their opponent's skill or experience.

When Mestre Valmir played with a student, there was clear pedagogical intent in his movements, and he was able to knock them down without putting them in unnecessary peril. However, when other members of FICA started to play too rough with someone at a lower skill level, he was attentive and ready to stop the game before someone got (too) hurt. The reverse was also true. During one *roda*, I knelt nervously at the foot of the *berimbau* next to Jorge. Sensing my trepidation, he patted my hand and smiled assuring me that I would not be too terribly abused. When I unexpectedly landed a kick on him, Mestre Valmir called us back to the *berimbau*, gave me a wink, and whispered just loud enough for me to hear, "now you can give her a hard game."

On rare occasions people who were far below the requisite skill level came to play in FICA *rodas*, either because they were complete novices or in one case because of physical and mental handicap. Generally speaking, the leaders of the academy were indulgent of these individuals. Mestre Valmir even called out to one of these novices during a game, practically begging him to dodge the oncoming kicks. And whenever the handicapped man that I introduced in the previous chapter came to play, whoever was in charge of the *roda* would initiate the song "*Bate Palmas Pra Ele,*" which means clap your hands for him. He was physically unable to completely straighten his legs and even walking was challenging for him, so his participation in the *roda* was very limited. When they played with him, Aloan or Jorge would often manipulate the game so as to put this individual in a position from which he could do whatever movements he was capable of and would then praise him for whatever he could manage. Foreigners, on average, were less kind.

Many capoeira pilgrims tended to be more concerned with their own performance than with creating a supportive and inclusive atmosphere for all players. One female pilgrim played the handicapped man in her very first *roda* at FICA Bahia. As they began to play, she gave him a strange look that conveyed her annoyance, but as his handicap dawned on her, she became slightly more indulgent. Later, she and another foreigner were discussing the handicapped man's presence at the *roda*. While they could somewhat appreciate the generosity of allowing him to participate, they both were slightly irritated because it detracted from their own games. Bridget once said to me that she did not mind if people played hard with her, but not if they were going to flail about in the *roda*. Contrary to what I expected, a foreigner was actually expressing dissatisfaction about the skill of Brazilians and their gall to play her. I had anticipated the reverse situation.

During a game between Bridget and a novice Brazilian man, she was doing an *au com cabeca no chão* (cartwheel with head on the ground) when he attacked. Though not prohibited, the etiquette of attacking someone in an inverted position during a friendly game like this is debatable. This exchange happened too fast for the spectators to understand exactly what had happened, but Bridget quickly got up from the floor with a bitter look on her face. She quickly hid this look and joked with him that she would get him next time. Considering that he was a complete novice and she very experienced, she should have had the composure and grace to deal with any breaches of etiquette he may have made. Instead, she was quite irritated and continued to talk about the incident after the *roda*. Rather than being an isolated incident, I see this as being representative of the general attitude of many foreigners toward skill. Mestre Valmir and Mestre Cobra Mansa both stressed the processual nature of capoeira and the necessity of respecting ourselves and each other at every stage; in contrast, many of the foreigners at FICA Bahia were progress oriented and had limited patience for people below their skill level.

Pilgrims may select *rodas* to attend based on the level of competition it offers. There are many different *rodas* that *capoeiristas* can choose from on Fridays, Saturdays, and Sundays in Bahia. One particularly dedicated American *capoeirista* who trains intensively and is incredibly skilled said that he dislikes the Nzinga *roda*. Others among us favored it because of its playful energy and reputation for being inclusive of women and children. In this pilgrim's opinion, however, there are really only two kids there worth playing. Likewise, he rarely goes to the *rodas* at Mestre Joao Pequeno's school. While skilled, the style of that academy is slower and less intense than what is found in other *rodas*. He prefers *rodas* that can offer more in the way of competition.

At some academies, there is a clear progression within each *roda*. The games at the beginning are slower and easier, but as the evening progresses, the games get faster and are played at a higher level. At one particular academy, foreigners tended to play more frequently toward the beginning of the *roda* than at the end. While I was observing at this academy, I only saw two foreigners play at the end of the evening. This may lead to the impression that foreigners are being marginal-ized, as a number of visitors at that academy told me, but it is equally likely that the majority of foreigners there do not have the skill level necessary to play in the faster, more intense games toward the end of the *roda*.

At other academies, *rodas* can be hard and intimidating from beginning to end. I casually mentioned one day that I still found the *rodas* at FICA Bahia to be rather intense. Tyrell laughed, but ultimately agreed. He attributed this to the presence of so many foreigners who are in Bahia for a short time and so desperately want to improve that they really "go at it" in the *roda*, trying to prove themselves by constantly attacking their opponent. This violates the normal expectation that players will take turns attacking and defending, but makes sense when one consid-ers that these pilgrims are trying to attain maximum benefits from their relatively short stay in Bahia.

In the end, skill level cannot be discounted as an important part of capoeira, especially when a *capoeirista* is playing in a *roda* outside of his or her own academy. As I explained in chapter 6, at the level of the academy, a *capoeirista*'s peers will evaluate him or her based on a propensity for being open, engaging in *troca de informação*, and showing dedication to the group. However, when playing with someone from another group who does not know anything about the individual's attitude, one's performance in the *roda* takes on additional significance. Yet even within this context, most local *capoeiristas* are less concerned about a player's skill, meaning level of advancement, than they are about the individual's adherence to formal features of the game like understanding the difference between *agressividade* and *objetividade,* conveying *sentimento,* and using metacommentary to highlight one's knowledge of form even in the face of physical shortcomings. Capoeira pilgrims, on the other hand, may view this differently because of their specific goal to improve as much as possible in the limited amount of time available to them and are often disappointed when they have to play with someone who is less skilled than themselves.

## The Clear Importance of Musical Skill

Stressing the holistic nature of a true *capoeirista*'s development, D'Aquino argues that someone who is only interested in the mechanics, the physical aspects of the art, "will never become *capoeiristas*" (1983: 92). Therefore, my original assumption that physical skill would be a primary route to legitimacy was somewhat off the mark. For Mestre Cobra Mansa, founder of FICA, musical skill is equally if not more important than physical skill. Even a *capoeirista* from the infamous Mercado Modelo, widely disparaged for hosting inauthentic tourist-oriented capoeira shows, stressed to me the importance of learning to play the instruments and sing the songs, not just throwing my legs around.

Music adds nuance to the game as the "songs draw to awareness latent traits in the game" (Downey 2005: 85). Performing music correctly is also essential to the preservation of capoeira ritual. Speaking of GCAP, the group from which FICA descends, Downey says that "overwhelmingly, when critics complained that traditions were being forgotten, their anxieties concentrated on singing, instrumental rhythms, the relation of music to play, and rituals like the chamada" (Downey 2005: 116). Much like learning Portuguese, learning to play the instruments correctly is a way of showing one's dedication to maintaining the traditions of capoeira, and it is likewise an important step on the road to legitimacy.

Being able to maintain and/or manufacture the instruments was another highly valued trait. FICA instructors constantly stressed the importance of owning our own instruments, so we could develop a relationship with them and practice with them continually. Perhaps one of the ways in which I felt most distanced from the "real" *capoeiristas* was in my inability to string a *berimbau*. Many *capoeiristas* brought their *berimbaus* to class in disassembled form and strung the wire just before class. I resorted to stringing mine in the privacy of my own apartment where I could cheat and whine as the wire bit into my soft academic hands. When the wire on my *berimbau* snapped after music class one evening, I turned to a Japanese student for help. I said that I was timid about working with the instruments because I did not really know how to do any of it, and no one had taught me. He said he understood because he used to feel the same way but came to realize that being a complete *capoeirista* necessitated this versatility.

There were two sets of *berimbaus* owned by FICA Bahia. The *berimbau* regulates the *roda* (Almeida 1986: 75) and therefore commands respect. Some hold it as quasi-sacred. One set of *berimbaus* could be used by anyone during music class. The other set was reserved for *rodas* and for use by the instructor(s) during music class. It was not uncommon to run out of *berimbaus* during music class as demand normally outnumbered supply. During one class, Tyrell was given explicit permission to use a *berimbau* from the *roda*/teacher set. A little while later during class, he passed it off to Bridget and took the drum. That these two individuals were allowed to use a *berimbau* from the special set indexed their legitimacy.

Of all the instruments, the *gunga* (largest and deepest sounding *berimbau*) was the most prestigious. Whoever controls the *gunga* holds responsibility for the entire *roda*. As the popular capoeira song below suggests, playing the *berimbau* comes with responsibility and will not be given away lightly:

*Esse gunga é meu, não dou pra ninguem*
This *gunga* is mine, I don't give it to anyone

My one and only experience with the *gunga* came during the first week of my 2008 trip. I had attended a kids' *roda* at the Pierre Verger Foundation along with Mestre Iuri, Jerome, and Camille. Toward the end, Nuno, a middle-aged man who trained at FICA and also periodically volunteered with this group, urged me to take the *gunga* so he could take a photograph of me. In comparison to most of the children there, I was certainly qualified to take the *gunga*; however, there were five or six adults present who would have had a better claim on it. Furthermore, this is not an instrument I normally feel comfortable playing outside of our own group because it connotes authority. In retrospect, this exchange feels significant because Nuno was staging a photo opportunity for me in which I appeared to have authority and legitimacy within this capoeira community. It was *not,* however, an indication of my actual legitimacy.

During training *rodas* at FICA, it was common for a foreigner, normally one of the Japanese men, to play the *gunga*. In formal Saturday morning *rodas,* however, this was far less common. In these situations, the *gunga* was almost always played by Mestre Valmir, one of his two sons, or Jorge. In some cases, the *gunga* would be offered to a special visitor like another *mestre* or *contramestre*.

The upper echelon of players at FICA Bahia is almost exclusively male, and only on one occasion did I see a female Brazilian play the *gunga*. When she was done playing it, she passed it to Tyrell. This was my first time to see a foreigner take the *gunga* in a *roda* at FICA Bahia, though that is not to say that it never happens. As he accepted the *gunga,* Mestre Valmir gave them both a hard look as if they had broken protocol, but did not make any move to take the *berimbau* away from Tyrell. Two games later, however, Jorge took the *gunga* from Tyrell. That he was allowed to take the *gunga* at all was an indication that he had achieved some degree of legitimacy within the group, but the fact that he was only allowed to play it for a short period of time was an indication that he had not yet fully moved to the center of the social field.

At FICA, the only time I was handed a *berimbau* aside from during music class was during Aloan's birthday *roda* in class. This was an informal and impromptu *roda* in which he wanted to play everyone in the class for approximately one minute, which meant that people were changing positions on the orchestra with high frequency. One of the women in class had to leave a few minutes early, so she called me over and passed me the medium sized *berimbau,* which I was allowed to keep until the end of the *roda*. While I never would have been allowed to play the *berimba*u during a regular *roda,* apparently I had enough skill to remain in this role during an informal *roda*. The same could not be said of everyone, including a Brazilian student who was removed from the *berimbau* during a similar *roda*.

As Nestor Capoeira put it, "You may be ... rich, but if you grab a *berimbau* in a respectable *roda* without knowing how to play it well, it won't be ten seconds before someone takes the instrument off your hands and shoves you quite impolitely aside" (2006: 142–43). Mestre Valmir did not hesitate to relieve students of their role either playing an instrument or leading a song if it was not up to his standards. During an in-class *roda,* Mestre Valmir removed a middle-aged Brazilian man from the *berimbau*. He reminded students that music class is on Tuesdays and Thursdays and that is the time to learn a new instrument.

Although I could not say exactly why, the music class was attended almost exclusively by foreigners. On any given evening, there might be one or two Brazilians attending alongside five to ten foreigners. The music class was taught at a high level. No instruction was given on how to play the various instruments; rather, class consisted of the teacher leading students in complex variations on the *berimbau*, having them lead songs, and having them improvise verses in Portuguese to choruses of his choosing. After about four months of training with the group, Aloan pointed out to everyone that I should be able to sing a *ladainha*. Public shaming was intended to push me to learn this new skill but also signaled my standing within the group and his expectations of me as a student. Interestingly, however, this kind of public shaming regarding what one should or should not be able to do after a certain period of time was never utilized during the movement classes.

## Conclusion

While physical skill is not totally irrelevant for one's advancement within the social field, I found that the Brazilian teachers under whom I studied were more concerned with the continual process of becoming a *capoeirista* than whether or not one could perform a particular movement. This contrasted with the attitudes displayed by many of the pilgrims, particularly those who seemed to think that their own cultural capital was depleted by having to play with less skilled students. Foreign *capoeiristas* with a high degree of skill were sometimes visibly annoyed with having to play a lower level player. Sometimes they would just try to avoid being paired with the less advanced player. When they did have to work with the less skilled partner, their distaste would sometimes manifest in a rolling of the eyes, shortness of temper, and complaints made to other foreigners after the class. In part, this is because they learn more when playing with a more advanced *capoeirista*. Whereas the Brazilian students and teachers will be continually immersed in this cradle of capoeira, the pilgrims have one foot out the door already and know that they have only a certain amount of time to prove themselves and learn as much as they can before heading back home.

It is likely that some pilgrims resent playing with less advanced *capoeiristas* because that game becomes a lost opportunity to display their cultural capital (see Urquía 2004). According to this logic, partnering with a highly skilled individual can raise an individual's status whereas partnering with a novice can deplete that individual's status (Urquía 2004). Assuming that non-Brazilian *capoeiristas* are in the most tenuous position within this social field, it makes sense that they would be most aware of the potential for status depletion and would avoid and possibly resent playing with beginners. By way of contrast, "those rich in social capital don't need to show off, and they receive praise even when they simply clown around" (Urquía 2004: 107), which helps explain why Brazilian players at

FICA would be more willing to play with beginners at their level, rarely showing frustration or resentment at naïveté.

In contrast to these divergent attitudes toward physical skill, however, there is a greater deal of consensus within the field regarding the importance of musical skill. Being able to sing the songs and understand the improvised lyrics allows *capoeiristas* to participate more fully in the nuanced interactions of the *roda*. Being able to play the instruments correctly indicates one's dedication to upholding the traditions of capoeira. Despite all of the energy that is put into physical training, being offered the *gunga* during a *roda* is one of the key markers of an individual's legitimacy within the capoeira community and quite possibly a defining moment in one's pilgrimage.

## Works Cited

Almeida, Bira. 1986. *Capoeira, a Brazilian Art Form: History, Philosophy and Practice.* Berkeley, CA: North Atlantic Books.

Capoeira, Nestor. 2006. *A Street-Smart Song: Capoeira Philosophy and Inner Life.* Berkeley, CA: North Atlantic Books.

D'Aquino, Iria. 1983. "Capoeira: Strategies for Status, Power and Identity," PhD dissertation. University of Illinois.

Downey, Greg. 2005. *Learning Capoeira: Lessons in Cunning from an Afro-Brazilian Art.* Oxford: Oxford University Press.

Stoller, Paul. 2009. *The Power of the Between: An Anthropological Odyssey.* Chicago: The University of Chicago Press.

Urquía, Norman. 2004. "'Doin' It Right': Contested Authenticity in London's Salsa Scene." In *Music Scenes: Local, Translocal, and Virtual,* edited by Andy Bennett and Richard A Peterson, 96-112. Nashville, TN: Vanderbilt University Press.

# Chapter 9

# Conclusion and Future Directions

At FICA Bahia, both locals and visitors found it important for pilgrims to get some sort of closure before departing. In some cases, visitors took the initiative themselves and organized a group outing for juice, beer, or caipirinhas after class. During one session, a visitor announced that she was going home and thanked Mestre Valmir for all his wisdom. "Aren't you going to invite people out tonight?" he asked. Occasionally, when we were inundated with foreign visitors, especially during July and August, Mestre Valmir made a point of asking at our Saturday morning *rodas* if anyone was planning to leave. If so, they had the honor of getting to play with him. Generally speaking, the better integrated an individual became, the longer and more public their send-off would be.

A *despedida* is a ritualized farewell that involves playing capoeira with all comers, an honor that can last an hour or more or until the honoree drops from exhaustion. However, most of the pilgrims' *despedidas* are relatively short. However, Daisuke, one of the Japanese students who had become extremely well integrated into the FICA Bahia family, had the honor of receiving two long *despedidas,* which testified to his legitimacy within the group. Daisuke decided to return home to Japan in October, but before he left he received two *despedidas*. Not all pilgrims receive a *despedida,* so Daisuke's experience was indeed remarkable.

Daisuke's first *despedida* was during a regular weekly *roda*. As Mestre Valmir knelt beside him and sang a song in his honor, tears rolled down Daisuke's cheeks, a visible indication of how meaningful this experience was for him. The second *despedida* took place during class. After working Daisuke to the point of absolute exhaustion, Aloan said a few words. He spoke about the importance of contributing to the group and said that Daisuke was one of those people that could always be counted upon to help out and come early when work needed to be done.

Aloan said the doors of FICA Bahia will always be open to Daisuke, and Daisuke thanked everyone for giving him the chance to grow. FICA Bahia had become Daisuke's family, and several weeks after his departure, the group even sent him a Christmas card signed by virtually everyone in the group with notes written in Portuguese. During my fieldwork, I did not encounter any other foreigner who was held in such esteem.

My own *despedida* was a little less dramatic, but touching nonetheless. That Mestre Valmir would dedicate part of our class time to publicly recognizing the completion of my study with him, and, incidentally, the completion of my fieldwork, made me feel that I had indeed accomplished what I set out to do. Three days before Christmas, I attended my last class at FICA Bahia. There was only a small group: three pilgrims and five Brazilians. Most of the pilgrims had already gone home for the holiday, and of the three that remained, one did not celebrate Christmas and another had more or less permanently relocated to Brazil and thus was already at home. After an hour of regular class, I played each of the students in attendance for a total of thirty minutes. However, it was clear that this *roda,* even if it was my *despedida,* was still a pedagogical tool. Through the entire half hour, Mestre Valmir periodically stopped our play and made corrections. As the clock neared two, I dodged an attack, sprung into a handstand, and was promptly felled by my opponent's leg sweep. How fitting, I thought, to end this adventure in the same way it had begun.

## Returning Home

Pilgrimage to Bahia is a highly valued part of a *capoeirista*'s development and, depending on the group one belongs to, may even be a nonnegotiable milestone in his or her progression. In some groups, visiting Bahia is a prerequisite for graduation (Assunção 2005: 205). FICA, for example, only awards titles in Brazil, meaning that a pilgrimage becomes a de facto requirement for foreigners who want to accept a title. In her study of Canadian *capoeiristas,* Joseph (2008) shares the view of one individual who feels that every "real" *capoeirista* has to go to Brazil at least once to imbibe the culture associated with capoeira. For him, just adopting the corporeality is not enough. For those who are not required to visit Brazil, pilgrimage still contributes to their charismatic cultural capital because it exemplifies their dedication.

For many pilgrims, being a *capoeirista* gave them a sense of belonging when they arrived in Brazil. Other pilgrims view their pilgrimage as a way to pay homage to an amazing cultural history that, while it may not be their own, touches people across the world. Individuals with this perspective may profess a deep affinity for capoeira, but be reluctant to assert ownership over the tradition. Camille once said to me, "I've seen other younger *capoeiristas* from other cultures who ... come here and kind of presume that they're going to learn it all. And I think that keeping in mind that we are all on a very long journey ... I think that's very important to remember. I think as Americans we live in an individualistic society and to come here with your money and your whiteness and your bag of capoeira skills and [think] that you're going to somehow become a *capoeirista* like a native Brazilian is very presumptuous and kind of rude."

While the majority of pilgrims I worked with did not explicitly discuss issues of privilege and oppression as did Camille, their relationship to the local community is strikingly different from that of the general tourist population in Bahia. At the same time that I was working with capoeira pilgrims at FICA, sociologist Danielle Hedegard was working with a more generalized group of tourists who attended classes periodically at a different capoeira academy within the city. The majority of tourists who attended classes at the academy where she was based were "light skin-toned, twenty-something, female, and heterosexual" (Hedegard 2013: 6). This academy did not cater to pilgrims; rather, the tourists who attended classes there were naively attempting to build their own social status by consuming the racialized Other (Hedegard 2013: 6).

These tourists' fascination with blackness and their association of blackness with authenticity is particularly pronounced. For example, the women would be particularly disappointed if the black male students would leave the training space and would sometimes lament not being able to work with Brazilians that day even if they had been training under the supervision of a lighter skinned Brazilian man (Hedegard 2013: 6). While these comments may seem incomprehensible, it bears remembering that these students were novices. Therefore, they were largely unfamiliar with the formal demands of capoeira, and this increases the likelihood of them relying on stereotypical markers of authenticity like skin color that are readily apparent to the untrained eye.

Many of the pilgrims that I worked with proudly acknowledged the African heritage of capoeira, as is to be expected within the *Capoeira Angola* tradition; however, they did not fetishize the blackness of local players in the same way that Hedegard's population did. What really mattered to the pilgrims at FICA Bahia was the opportunity to play, learn from, and enter into communion with local *capoeiristas* as equals. As I prepared for this field research, I wondered what would happen when foreigners and locals collided in Brazilian *rodas*. One party has economic capital, the other has cultural capital, and the terms of exchange are negotiated during physical encounters. I found that for the most part, foreigners and local *capoeiristas* coexist peacefully in the physical manifestation of this imagined community. Tensions tend to arise, however, when existential authenticity comes into conflict with the granting of legitimacy. Foreigners for whom being a *capoeirista* is central to their existential authenticity believe wholeheartedly that capoeira belongs to them as much as it does to Brazilians. They often feel entitled to legitimacy and may resent others whose less competent performances highlight the tenuous position that foreigners in general hold within the social field. This may explain why some foreigners at FICA acted condescendingly toward other foreigners who were unskilled. This fervent belief in the fit between themselves and the practice of capoeira motivates pilgrims to prove their legitimacy, the ultimate test of which is ascendency through the social field, rooted symbolically and physically in Brazil.

Although "authenticity" features prominently in *capoeiristas'* discourse, it is a value judgment, which is subjective and hard to define. This creates much of the confusion in academia over this term and the temptation to disregard the concept entirely. Approaching a contested performance or genre such as capoeira from the position of legitimacy and authority within an economy of authenticity, on the other hand, better equips us to say why particular notions of authenticity become dominant and how one goes about claiming that status. As I have argued here, once capoeira becomes important enough to a non-Brazilian's sense of self, he or she may make a pilgrimage to train with a Brazilian *mestre*. Once there, the pilgrim will use a combination of his or her traditional forms of legitimacy like race, nationality, and gender, as well as charismatic forms of capital, like attitude and dedication, to develop a close relationship with the teacher. It is from that privileged position that the pilgrim will be most able to understand the fine line between tradition and innovation and between aggression and efficacy.

What is not yet clear, however, is whether or not non-Brazilians will be able to follow the centripetal path of legitimate peripheral participation all the way into the core of the community. In chapter 7 I argued that technique is a conservative force, and beginners have few opportunities to innovate. Indeed, novice *capoeiristas* who attempt technical innovations may be seen as having made a mistake rather than an innovation (Downey 2005). Artistry, on the other hand, is precisely about choosing among the various internal and external resources available to the performer (Royce 2004: 65). As such, this level of expression is only available to those individuals who have gained legitimacy within the social field because they have moved beyond needing to prove that they understand the form and can begin to play with the form. It is this status to which my consultants are referring when they say that someone must know the rules before he or she can break them. Players must show that they understand the rules before their deviations will be authorized. Whether or not non-Brazilians will be granted such a privileged position within the capoeira community that their innovations become accepted and even adopted widely by others is something that will be answered in time. For now, it is evident that foreigners are gaining greater degrees of legitimacy and responsibility for reproducing this cultural tradition even while some older *mestres* and some capoeira purists decry their participation as appropriation.

Whether a pilgrim visits Bahia hoping to improve her skill level, make connections with the local community, better understand the culture that gave rise to the art she loves so much, or gain the respect of other members in the community, these trips are not to be taken lightly. As one of my consultants told me after she made it back to the United States, "I can't really explain why, but before I left, as I was in the cab almost to the airport, I was really upset and almost cried, but I couldn't tell why." Passing from the main thoroughfare to the airport through a dense thicket of bamboo, the liminal phase of a pilgrim's trip comes to an end, and she begins the process of reincorporation into the world she had temporarily left behind.

What happens when these pilgrims return to their group is another matter that needs additional study. My own return felt pretty triumphant. Although I downplay the importance of skill for a pilgrim's acceptance into a Brazilian academy, I had certainly become a better *capoeirista* by virtue of my intensive training. I was suddenly permitted by my teacher to try moves that I had not done before while others were admonished for doing so. I also noticed some students modeling their own movements after my own, suggesting that there might be benefits to the entire group when one individual makes a pilgrimage. According to Joseph, whose sample of *capoeiristas* in Canada included a high percentage of individuals who had made a pilgrimage to Brazil, the stories that these returnees share with the group become part of local lore and allow the nontravelers to also imagine that they have had this experience (2008: 201). In other words, the narratives that pilgrims bring back to their home group can become collective property, bolstering the group's legitimacy rather than just that of the individual.

## The Pilgrim's Footprint

Thus far, I have primarily discussed this phenomenon from the point of view of the non-Brazilian capoeira pilgrims. With any form of tourism, however, there are transformative effects for both the host and the guest, and the changes for the host are often more lasting. The FICA family has been incredibly gracious in their acceptance of my research, and FICA Bahia is consistently hospitable to foreign visitors. Not all groups are as willing to embrace the internationalization of capoeira and sometimes resent the intrusion of so many gringos in their community. These individuals charge capoeira pilgrims with appropriation. This position has a basis in history because outsiders who fail to credit or compensate their cultural teachers have too often plundered Afro-Brazilian culture for their own gain.

Pilgrims with a sense of social responsibility are sensitive to fears about appropriation and prioritize engaging with the local community as equitably as possible. Developing this awareness was one aim of the Sixth International Encounter, sponsored by Capoeira Mangangá. Mestre Tonho Matéria had this to say about foreigners' engagement with the community:

> The goal is that these foreigners manage to enter into the communities not just to play capoeira, but to learn its origin, its history. It is also an idea of managing to bring the gringo here, to know the city, at the same time, to give a bit of contribution here, transferring what they learned with mestres in those countries. (Dantas 2007, translation mine)

According to this position, foreigners have a responsibility to share their own knowledge with the rest of the capoeira community. In other words, making this exchange equitable requires capoeira pilgrims to give back to the local community in some way.

*Troca de informação* is a commonly cited benefit of foreigners' pilgrimages. The central issue of this book is how pilgrims acquire a deeper relationship with masters and how this relationship is transferred into legitimacy. However, the pilgrimage phenomenon can also benefit the local community. Local *capoeiristas* are able to learn about other cultures and ways of being in the world without leaving home. This is particularly significant for *capoeiristas* who do not have the time or financial resources to travel abroad. In fact, locals may stay in contact with capoeira pilgrims for several years after their initial meeting, using social media to facilitate ongoing communication. Foreign interest in capoeira has also given Bahians pride in this aspect of their culture, which is a significant benefit of tourism for marginalized populations (see Cole 2007).

However, despite the lip service paid to *troca de informação,* the integration between locals and foreigners is far from seamless. Social divisions remained between Brazilians and foreign *capoeiristas* at FICA Bahia. For example, the Saturday before Christmas everyone from FICA was invited to a barbeque on the beach in place of our regular *roda*. Mestre Valmir said that "capoeira, capoeira, capoeira all the time is cool, but there is another side too." The objective of this *confraternização* (social event) was having fun together as a group, and we were encouraged to bring our loved ones too. This outing was indeed a lot of fun, but foreigners and Brazilians did tend to stay segregated at the party. Several of us went to a concert together later that night, and though we acknowledged each other's presence, the Brazilians and foreigners interacted very little.

Several people at FICA noticed this disconnect between discourse and actual practice. At one point, Tyrell and a local *capoeirista* who had only started training a few months before I started my study conspired together to start planning more intercultural social gatherings. This conversation followed a going away party that Bridget and her housemate hosted for a Brazilian *capoeirista,* which was one of five major gatherings that brought local and foreign *capoeiristas* together outside of the academy. Two of these were organized by Mestre Cobra Mansa's son Marcelo, two by Bridget, and one by Mestre Valmir. Each event strengthened the bonds between all members of the group, yet on a day-to-day basis, *capoeiristas* gravitated toward other members of their own nationality or speech community. When other foreigners were unavailable, pilgrims tended to feel isolated and alone. Pilgrims anticipated the arrival of other foreign *capoeiristas* because a spike in social activities normally followed, which made them feel more connected to the greater capoeira community. There was a special bond, if not quite *communitas,* that infused relationships between pilgrims, a sense of shared immersion in this sometimes-strange experience. Locals were often impressed by this solidarity, and frequently referred to the peaceful interactions of Israelis and Palestinians or Americans and Iraqis within the context of the *roda*.

Pilgrims were not always content with their interactions in Bahia, sometimes feeling that FICA Bahia had less of a community spirit than their group at home. According to Cary, an American who has made multiple pilgrimages to Brazil and taught capoeira in Ireland, capoeira in Brazil is "not quite as much of a community thing as it is in the United States." This is surprising to most pilgrims who imagine the Brazilian capoeira community as being very close-knit. However, just because pilgrims like Cary do not *see* the community spirit operating in the Brazilian capoeira scene does not necessarily mean that it is not there. It is possible that an unseen barrier prevents pilgrims from experiencing this sense of community.

I never felt intentionally sidelined from any of the activities at FICA Bahia, but foreigners were naturally limited in some ways. We did not have the same history as the Brazilians who had been in the group for long periods of time. We did not know Mestre Valmir nearly as well as some of the long-term members, especially because he travelled so much during the span of my research. After Saturday morning *rodas,* many of the foreigners and a few of the locals would go to lunch together, but the majority of the Brazilian members of the group went to other places without us. Furthermore, none of us were completely fluent in Portuguese, making intercultural conversations laborious. The games between local members of the group were often richer, if not more skillful, because of long-term relationships that provided them with more material for the physical dialogue in the *roda*. Though we felt very welcomed at FICA Bahia, many of the foreigners continued to ask me how the *mestres* really felt about the presence of so many non-Brazilians in their group. Such questions index the insecurity and discomfort that may come with being an outsider.

Though *troca de informação* was the most frequent response when I asked local Brazilians how they thought capoeira tourism benefited them, they also referenced financial benefits. Street performers of capoeira rely almost exclusively on contributions from tourists, though their revenue is extremely low. Local business owners and entrepreneurs have seized upon this phenomenon, and shops in the Pelourinho district cater to capoeira tourists' needs. There are shops selling capoeira clothes, instruments, and trinkets. Tourism agencies specialize in taking foreigners to cultural attractions like *Candomblé* ceremonies and are beginning to take tourists to capoeira classes as well.

For local academies, admitting pilgrims can be quite profitable. Most reputable academies do not charge *capoeiristas* for participating in their *rodas*. However, notable exceptions include Mestre Curio's academy and the Associação Brasileiro de Capoeira Angola. Classes, however, are another matter, and local groups gain significant benefits from foreigners attending lessons at their academy. Because academies often charge higher prices for foreigners than they do for Brazilians, this income can be significant.

Mestre Cobra Mansa is among those who believe it is appropriate to charge a different price for foreigners versus Brazilians. Part of his rationale for this decision was to combat certain foreigners' assumption that they can go to a place and appropriate local knowledge and culture without reciprocation. In addition to talking to people and trying to change their mentality, he created the differential pricing system for events in Brazil to show foreigners their level of responsibility vis-à-vis the Brazilian capoeira community. He was criticized at first for charging foreigners a higher price than locals, but he claims that people now understand that if locals had to pay the same price as foreigners, no locals could afford to participate. Then it would become an event entirely for foreigners, and they would lose the opportunity to interact with local *capoeiristas*. This pricing system is intended to help foreigners better understand their privileged economic status in contrast to most Brazilian *capoeiristas*. In theory, this understanding should lead to social awareness; in actuality, many foreigners resent paying the gringo price. They feel it is a form of reverse discrimination or a sign of their own naïveté in this foreign culture because they have not managed to get the same deal as the locals do.

Other groups benefit from capoeira tourism as a way to expand their own franchise. When Bridget first met a senior student at FICA Bahia, who later went on to travel abroad, she commented on his outgoing personality and willingness to spend time with foreigners:

> I thought that was really smart of him. And I'm sure he didn't do it on purpose, I'm sure it was just he was interested in other people, and sort of that Brazilian friendliness. He was very outgoing, but to really cultivate those relationships because if you're going to be a capoeira person and you want to make a living off of it, it's all about knowing people ...You can see the *mestres,* you can see the *mestres* when people from different countries come to the *roda.* When a girl from France came to one *roda,* the *mestre* was so nice to her. I was like, "Wow, he wants to go to France."

*Mestres* and other locals who want to make a career out of capoeira are attuned to the potential benefits available to them through networking. However, because most pilgrims are sensitive to being seen as suckers, locals must be skillful and subtle in developing these relationships so that they never seem too strategic. When foreigners come to Brazil, they open up a dialogue with local teachers, paving the way for future opportunities. Brazilian teachers may be invited to a capoeira pilgrim's home in order to host a workshop. Sometimes they are even invited to start a new group. Some capoeira pilgrims visit Bahia with the explicit purpose of recruiting a new teacher.

In other cases, local *capoeiristas* may exploit tourists to further their own individual agendas. In touristic centers like the Pelourinho or Mercado Modelo, Brazilian *capoeiristas* often solicit tourists hoping to start a romantic relationship with them in hopes of gaining entrance to another country where they could migrate and open a capoeira school.[1] This practice is common and potentially lucrative but is looked down upon by many certified capoeira teachers. Because such teachers rarely have certification, this type of expansion contributes to Brazilians' skepticism about the legitimacy of foreign students.

## The Future of Capoeira

Capoeira in Brazil recently entered a new period. On 15 July 2008, the Instituto do Patrimônio Histórico e Artístico Nacional (Institute of National Historic and Artistic Patrimony—IPHAN) announced that capoeira would become Brazil's fourteenth documented cultural practice with the title "immaterial cultural patrimony."[2] The municipal plaza erupted into a giant *roda* as *capoeiristas* from all over the city came out to celebrate the news (Lemle 2008). The pronouncement makes some big promises to *capoeiristas* by committing the government's efforts to the preservation of this representative Afro-Brazilian practice (Carmezim 2008). For one, it promises to reverse the discriminatory practice of requiring capoeira instructors in schools and universities to hold a diploma in physical education (see chapter 1. As Nestor Capoeira (2008) points out, capoeira has already spread well beyond the borders of Brazil so its existence is not threatened, but older *mestres* in Brazil do find it difficult to pass on their knowledge because of this requirement. Remembering that the traditional knowledge bearers are Afro-Brazilians who came of age in the early to mid 1900s and came from humble backgrounds, very few of them had access to higher education.[3] The proclamation also promises to protect the *biriba* wood from which traditional *berimbaus* are made.

This proclamation elicited strong, but mixed, reactions from the capoeira community. Most *capoeiristas* seemed to think that this action by the government was overdue, particularly because of the international popularity of capoeira. Mestre Paulinho Sabia, who has taught for thirty-two years pointed out the necessity of carving out a place of respect for capoeira in Brazilian society, saying that while capoeira is highly valorized as a profession in Europe, it continues to be *"clandestino"* (clandestine) in Brazil (M Ribeiro 2008). The spread of capoeira to other countries, aside from spreading capoeira as part of Brazilian culture, valorizes *mestres* as part of the Brazilian cultural patrimony (Lima 2007). On the other hand, the word *tombar,* which indicates the process of patrimonialization, also means to crystalize or freeze, suggesting a symbolic violence that robs the art of its inherent dynamism for the sake of official exploitation (Collier 2006). This raises questions about the true intent of making a dynamic art like capoeira part of the nation's cultural patrimony.

While everyone from legendary *mestres* to novices that casually train capoeira with friends on the beach were absorbed in this news, their discourse centered on some unexpected topics. Local buzz focused on two major themes: (1) that foreign interest in capoeira was a motivating factor for the pronouncement, whether one looks at it as legitimizing capoeira in the eyes of middle-class Brazilians or as a threatening appropriation of Brazil's intellectual property; and (2) that the pronouncement is a way for the Brazilian government to make reparations for the years of persecution and marginalization of capoeira. The second theme dialogues with the myth of racial democracy, valorizing Afro-Brazilian culture in a superficial way while simultaneously divesting capoeira of its blackness by naming it as the patrimony of all Brazilians. Not only does this give Brazil another national symbol, but it also paves the way for increased commercialism.

In many ways, it seems that Brazil is caught between dueling desires, to sell their traditional culture as uniquely Brazilian while also proving that they are equal to the rest of the world in terms of progress and modernization. Informal interviews and archival research suggest that this pronouncement of capoeira as part of Brazil's cultural patrimony may have more to do with global pressures and commodification of culture than respecting Afro-Brazilians' intellectual property. The local newspapers conveyed many *mestres'* sentiment that the *tombamento* (elevation of capoeira to official cultural patrimony) would finally grant *capoeiristas* the same level of respect in Brazil that they are afforded abroad. Mestre Russo, who attended the official events surrounding the pronouncement, credits foreigners' recognition of capoeira as the impetus for the government pledging their support for capoeira (Lemle 2008). While the pronouncement does valorize capoeira, it also points to the ironies of global culture. At the same time that foreign *capoeiristas* are trying to claim their own legitimacy among Brazilian *capoeiristas,* foreign interest valorizes capoeira in the eyes of the Brazilian government and population at large.

In the discourse that circulated immediately after the pronouncement, there was also an undercurrent of fear that foreigners were taking ownership of Brazilians' cultural heritage. Mestre Boa Gente was quoted as saying that "already abroad there are people who are very interested in appropriating an asset that is ours" (Carmezim 2008). On the other hand, it was argued that the recognition would guarantee Salvador's cherished position at the center of the capoeira cosmology and would allow Brazilian *capoeiristas* to regulate diffusion of this tradition (P Ribeiro 2008). For his part, Mestre Curio remained skeptical that the pronouncement would change anything for *capoeiristas,* charging that the government wants to benefit financially from the global popularity of capoeira while denying the capoeira *mestres* respect (P Ribeiro 2008). Fear of losing their art to foreign interests is a powerful catalyst, but it appears that foreign interest in capoeira generally, whether benign or exploitive, provided the impetus for the Brazilian government to protect their cultural heritage.

In conjunction with this new development, the Ministry of Culture partnered with Petrobras and the Gregório de Mattos Foundation to offer grants in support of capoeira-related research initiatives. By way of introducing their new initiative, they ask "how could Bahia define what is *capoeira*, if *capoeira* defines what it is to be Bahia?" (Ministry of Culture 2007). Studying this physical form does tell us a great deal about the people and worldview that created it; their interactions with foreigners in the context of globalization tells us even more about who they are today and what capoeira will become in the future.

On 26 November 2014, UNESCO announced that capoeira had been added to their list of Intangible Cultural Heritage of Humanity. UNESCO's recognition is intended to call attention to the importance of these cultural practices, of which there are more than 300, and safeguard them into the future (BBC 2014). This has been welcomed by many *capoeiristas* as an overdue recognition of the significance of this art, and by Brazilians in particular as recognition of their contribution to world culture. At the same time, however, it bears asking from what does capoeira need to be protected?

Having survived the horrors of slavery, official prohibition during the early days of Brazil's independence, and persistent stigmatization in the early part of the twentieth century, capoeira would seem to be among the most resilient of all art forms. The global demand for capoeira instruction would seem to prove beyond a doubt that capoeira will continue to be practiced for quite some time. Yet globalization brings about its own threats. At the global level, it remains to be seen what affect the IPHAN and UNESCO pronouncements will have on the future of capoeira. It is my personal hope that this recognition will enhance Brazilian teachers' abilities to make a living from capoeira and maintain control over their culture's representation. It is equally possible, however, that these pronouncements, particularly the most recent one, will embolden foreign *capoeiristas* in their appropriation of the art.

While I am in complete support of those foreigners who sincerely submit themselves to the study of capoeira and Brazilian culture, I have also encountered a great deal of presumptuousness and arrogance on the part of a small minority of foreigners who expect to benefit from their engagement with the Brazilian capoeira community without reciprocating. Apprenticeship pilgrimage is about more than just journeying to a place that is personally meaningful or acquiring skills that are unavailable at home; it is about proving to the local community that one is a legitimate tradition bearer. Ultimately, a performer will be judged on his or her ability to execute form properly, but failure to demonstrate one's dedication, humility, and openness will block a pilgrim's access to the learning opportunities that would allow him or her to master the form. That, in the end, may be the most valuable safeguard available to the local capoeira community.

## Notes

1. In every case I have seen, male *capoeiristas* are soliciting female tourists. However, this is not to suggest that the reverse situation does not occur. Further research is needed on the connection between sex tourism and capoeira networks.
2. In many places, this is referred to as intangible cultural patrimony.
3. Although coming from humble backgrounds, both Mestre João Pequeno and Mestre João Grande, the two best-known inheritors of Pastinhas's legacy, have both received honorary doctorates for their work with capoeira.

## Works Cited

Assunção, Matthias Röhrig. 2005. *Capoeira: The History of an Afro-Brazilian Martial Art, Sport in the Global Society.* London: Routledge.

BBC. 2014. "Brazil's Capoeira Gains UN Cultural Heritage Status." Retrieved 9 December 2014 from http://www.bbc.com/news/world-latin-america-30219941.

Capoeira, Nestor. 2008. "A Capoeira na Globalização." *A Revista de História da Biblioteca Nacional.*

Carmezim, Vitor. 2008. "Ê Camara, a Capoeira é Patrimonio Cultural!" *A Tarde.*

Cole, Stroma. 2007. "Beyond Authenticity and Commodification." *Annals of Tourism Research* 34 (4): 943–60.

Collier, John. 2006. "'But What If I Should Need to Defecate in Your Neighborhood, Madame?': Empire, Redemption, and the 'Tradition of the Oppressed' in a Brazilian World Heritage Site." *Cultural Anthropology* 23 (2): 279–328.

Dantas, Laura. 2007. "Cultura da Capoeira Valorizada em Eventos com Arte e Educação." *A Tarde,* 3 September.

Downey, Greg. 2005. *Learning Capoeira: Lessons in Cunning from an Afro-Brazilian Art.* Oxford: Oxford University Press.

Hedegard, Danielle. 2013. "Blackness and Experience in Omnivorous Cultural Consumption: Evidence from the Tourism of Capoeira in Salvador, Brazil." *Poetics* 41: 1–26.

Joseph, Janelle Beatrice. 2008. "'Going to Brazil': Transnational and Corporeal Movements of a Canadian-Brazilian Martial Arts Community." *Global Networks* 8 (2): 194–213.

Lemle, Marina. 2008. "Maestria Reconhecida." *Revista de História da Biblioteca Nacional.*

Lima, Aurelino. 2007. "Almas em Movimento." *A Tarde,* 20 August.

Ministry of Culture. 2007. "Capoeira Viva." Retrieved 12 August from www.capoeiraviva.org.

Ribeiro, Marcelle. 2008. "Capoeira, Tombada, Pode Ser Apreciada No Rio." *O Globo Online,* 18 July.

Ribeiro, Perla. 2008. "Capoeira Se Torna Patrimonio Cultural." *Correiro da Bahia.*

Royce, Anya Peterson. 2004. *Anthropology of the Performing Arts: Artistry, Virtuosity, and Interpretation in a Cross-Cultural Perspective.* Walnut Creek, CA: AltaMira Press.

# Glossary

*aberto*: Open, both literal and figurative

*agôgô* : A double-sided cowbell that is also used in religious ceremonies in Brazil and Western Africa

*agressividade*: Aggressiveness

*Angoleiro*: Someone who plays *Capoeira Angola*; may be used to describe a male or female, though the latter is technically grammatically incorrect

*atabaque*: A drum that is also used in *Candomblé* religious ceremonies as well as in Western African religious traditions; a semi-sacred instrument in capoeira

*au*: Cartwheel; can be done with the legs tucked close to the torso or extended into the air

*bananeira*: Literally "banana tree"; used in capoeira to refer to a handstand, either stationary or walking

*baqueta*: The stick used to play any of the percussive capoeira instruments, particularly the *berimbau*

*batuque*: A martial dance/game practiced by African and Afro-Brazilian men; widely considered to be a precursor of capoeira

*beleza*: Beauty

*berimbau*: The most sacred instrument used in capoeira; it consists of a wire stretched over a curved stick of *biriba* wood with a hollowed-out gourd serving as the resonating chamber; sound is produced by holding a washer, coin, or rock against the wire and striking it with a wooden stick while holding a basket rattle over one's striking hand

*bloco afro*: Carnival performance groups that use Afro-Brazilian percussive rhythms to celebrate a message of black pride

*brasilidade*: Brazilianness

*brincar*: To play, connotes the carefree playfulness of a child

*Candomblé*: An Afro-Brazilian religion that uses drumming and dance to induce spirit possession

*capoeira*: An Afro-Brazilian martial art that combines elements of dance, song, music, and theater into a playful mock battle

*Capoeira Angola*: The style of capoeira advocated by Mestre Pastinha, which claims to be more traditional and closer to the African roots; play is slower, more controlled, and relies on trickery through deceit

*Capoeira Contemporânea* A hybrid style of capoeira that includes elements of both Capoeira Regional and Capoeira Angola

*Capoeira Regional* : The style of capoeira codified by Mestre Bimba; it is faster, more acrobatic, and uses belts as an external marker of a student's progress

*capoeirista*: Someone who plays capoeira

*chamada*: A ritualized interlude in play, predominantly used in the *Capoeira Angola* style, where one player calls the other to perform this aside before returning to general play; this is one of the most potentially dangerous moments in the game

*chapa*: A straight kick that can be executed from a standing or crouched position, backward or forward

*chorridos*: Choruses, sung throughout the *roda* and employing a call and response structure

*chula:* A formulaic call-and-response song that is often sung just prior to the beginning of a capoeira game

*chuta*: A slap kick similar to kicking a soccer ball, not considered to be proper capoeira technique

*clandestino*: Clandestine

*confraternização:* Social event

*contramestre*: One step below *mestre*

*despedida* : Sendoff/fairwell

*estrangeiro/a*: Foreigner

*eventos:* Literally "events": refers to workshops at which one or more instructors will teach as special guests

*favela*: Slum, generally built on the hillsides surrounding Brazilian cities

*fechado*: Closed, both literal and figurative

*floreiros:* Literally "flourishes": decorative embellishments to one's game that often leave a player open to attack, but nonetheless serve to underscore his or her skill level

*ginga*: Literally "to swing"; it is the moving base to which *capoeiristas* return during play

*gunga*: The deepest sounding *berimbau* with the largest gourd; controls the *roda*

*jeito*: Manner or way of doing something, often used to describe technique in capoeira

*jogar*: To play, used when referring to sports or games

*jujitsu*: A Japanese martial art descended from Judo, which became popular in Brazil and was transformed into a distinctly Brazilian form by the Gracie brothers

*ladainha*: Litany that is sung to begin the capoeira ritual

*malandragem*: Cunning, related to the term *malandro*

*malandro*: A term traditionally used to describe vagrants that live by their wits, but reinterpreted as a positive term within the capoeira worldview

*malícia* : Trickery through deceit; a highly prized quality in a *capoeirista*

*maluco*: Crazy

*mandinga*: Literally "magic"; refers to the historical use of *Candomblé* to close the *capoeirista*'s body and protect it from an adversary's attack; today, may be used without religious connotations and refers to a sneaky way of moving; the aesthetic manifestation of *malícia*

*medio*: The *berimbau* producing a middle pitch, responsible for keeping the rhythm

*mestizos*: People of mixed ethnic or racial heritage

*mestre*: A master of capoeira; generally this title is given after 25 years or more of practice, though recent developments are challenging this notion

*negativa*: A defensive move achieved by stretching one leg out to the side while extending the torso in the opposite direction, supporting the weight of the body on both arms, the elbow of one tucked into the torso near the kidney

*objetividade*: Having an objective, acting with purpose

*orixás*: Deities in the Afro-Brazilian religion *Candomblé*

*pandeiro*: Tambourine

*pardo*: Someone of mixed ethnic or racial heritage (used interchangeably with mestizo)

*Pelourinho*: The historic district in Salvador that has been revived under the direction of UNESCO

*Povo:* Literally "people": more often used to indicate 'folk,' or non-elite

*rabo de arraia* : Literally "stingray tail"; a typical capoeira move that involves sweeping one leg in a circle approximately 16–24 inches from the ground while supporting the body on the other leg and both arms

*rasteira*: Leg sweep intended to unbalance or knock down an opponent

*reco-reco*: An instrument made of bamboo with ridges carved into it, across which a stick is passed to make a grating sound

*roda*: Literally means wheel, but is the terminology used to describe both the circle in which capoeira participants sit/stand and the central activity of the capoeira ritual

*rolê*: Literally "roll"; the many variations on the basic move can be used to evade oncoming attacks or simply to move around the circle while staying close to the ground

*salta*: Jump or loosen

*seguro*: Safe

*sentimento*: Feeling

*tempo:* Time

*tesouro*: An attack move in which one player positions his or her legs in a scissor-like position along the floor while the hips are held low to the ground; the weight of the torso is supported on both hands; the player slides across the floor in this position with the intent to trip his or her opponent

*tocar*: To play an instrument or touch something/someone

*tombar:* This verb is used to indicate the process of patrimonialization, in which a cultural art is objectified and codified for preservation

*treinel*: An authorized teacher in capoeira; one step below *contramestre*

*troca de informação*: Information exchange

*vadiagaem* : The act of loafing

*viola* : The highest pitch *berimbau,* responsible for most of the variations

# Index

ource UK Ltd.
UK
4190821
K00014B/1397